Racism and migrant labour

RACISM AND
MIGRANT LABOUR

Robert Miles

Routledge & Kegan Paul
London, Boston, Melbourne and Henley

First published in 1982
by Routledge & Kegan Paul Ltd
39 Store Street, London WC 1E 7DD,
9 Park Street, Boston, Mass. 02108, USA,
296 Beaconsfield Parade, Middle Park,
Melbourne, 3206, Australia, and
Broadway House, Newtown Road,
Henley-on-Thames, Oxon RG9 1EN
Printed in Great Britain by
The Thetford Press Ltd, Norfolk
© Robert Miles 1982

Library of Congress Cataloging in Publication Data

Miles, Robert, 1950-
Racism and migrant labour.
Bibliography: p.
Includes index.
1. Race relations. 2. Ethnicity. 3. Occupations
and race. 4. Europe - Race relations. 5. Migrant labour -
Europe. I. Title
HT1521.M496 1982   305.8   82-10224

ISBN 0-7100-9212-1

CONTENTS

FIGURES

ACKNOWLEDGMENTS

The writing of this book allows me to record an acknowledgment
to those who taught me in the past and to those with whom I
worked at the SSRC Research Unit on Ethnic Relations at the
University of Bristol between 1973 and 1978. Amongst the latter,
Taro Brah, Mary Fuller, Verity Kahn, Delroy Loudon and Sandra
Wallman require special mention. A particular note of gratitude
must also go to Michael Banton and Theo Nichols (both of the
Department of Sociology at the University of Bristol) from whom I
have also learnt a great deal over the years, despite the fact that
I maintain a number of different disagreements with each of them.
  It must be said that my students at the University of Glasgow
bear some responsibility for this book: its origin lies in my
attempt to explain to them, without the benefit of a written text,
the limitations of the sociology of 'race relations'. But of more
importance to its final appearance have been the efforts of Annie
Phizacklea, with whom I worked for five years and with whom I
share a friendship and many arguments, and Kate Lyon, who
taught me patiently at the University of Bath and who remains
a friend: both have read and criticised previous, complete drafts
of the book. Rohit Barot, a friend a previous colleague at the
University of Bristol, also read a complete draft at a late stage
and provided me with useful criticisms. To all three, very many
thanks. At a crucial stage, Derek Sayer provided considered
criticism and encouragement: thanks to him too. In addition, I
am grateful to Barbara Littlewood, Jim McGoldrick and John
McInnes for willingly providing me with answers to various quer-
ies over the past two years and to Kate Kelly who advised me
on the presentation of the diagrams. I also owe a great debt to
Philippa Brewster of Routledge & Kegan Paul who must be the
ideal editor, always ready to give encouragement and to offer
sensitive criticism when they are required.
  Finally, I must mention those who have helped with those many
and varied demands that writing creates. Pru Larsen has been
ready to help with secretarial tasks and to instil a sense of calm
when Departmental responsibilities have led to a feeling of crisis.
And last, but not least, thanks to Veronica who did most of the
typing at great speed and bore most of the personal consequences
of my selfish commitment to the written word and academic argument.

Robert Miles
University of Glasgow

INTRODUCTION

This book is offered as an explicitly critical text. It aims to provide a critique of the development of the sociology of 'race relations' which has a dual institutional reality in the form of courses on 'race relations' in colleges and universities and of books which claim to provide a perspective on 'race relations'. This academic institutionalisation of 'race relations' mirrors the construction of 'race relations' as a political issue in Britain in the past twenty years. The origin of this 'problem' is said to lie with the arrival in Britain of people from the New Commonwealth in the 1950s and 1960s. The fact that these migrants were physically distinctive from the majority of the indigenous population is referred to in order to conceptualise as 'race relations' the social interaction between the migrants (and their children) and the indigenous population, especially when conflict arises between them. Successive governments since the mid-1960s have claimed repeatedly their intention of working for 'good race relations', an intention which has been politically institutionalised in the form of the Race Relations Board and, since the latter's abolition, the Commission for Racial Equality (CRE). Governments have maintained that 'good race relations' will arise from the elimination of racial discrimination and from the development of a mutual awareness and 'tolerance' on the part of both 'indigenous' and 'immigrant' populations (as well as from 'strict' immigration control). It is the task of the CRE to ensure that these two things happen.

That there has been conflict between 'indigenous' and 'immigrant' populations has ensured the sociology of 'race relations' a slot on any self-respecting sociology of modern Britain course. After all, sociologists are reputed to be all liberals/ Marxists to a person and 'race relations' is where the action is if one wishes to be 'relevant' and 'up-to-date' as well as to fly a flag of moral concern and outrage from an academic mast. As a result of such concerns, the sociologist of 'race relations' is able to enter the political arena, claiming that 'race relations' are 'bad/deteriorating/worse', in order to claim for some alternative policy a greater likelihood of success. Such sociologists, and the sociology that they generate, have become obsessed with 'race relations' policy.

Such an obsession has another source, which also encourages the academic institutionalisation of 'race relations'. The politically defined aim of encouraging mutual understanding has as one corollary the aim of ensuring that those members of the

1

'indigenous' population who are likely to deal with 'immigrants' as part of their institutionally defined work role should know something about their 'background' in order that they may offer a more efficient service which does not discriminate on 'racial' grounds. Thus, factory managers and teachers and social workers and housing visitors, etc., who perform their work duties in 'multi-racial' areas are deemed to require knowledge about the numbers of 'immigrants', their cultural background, the pattern of racial discrimination, the nature of Sikhism, etc. The result is more courses on 'race relations': even the police are deemed to require a lecture on 'race relations' during their pre-service basic training. Thus, state institutions and private capital require a sociology of 'race relations' which will ensure that certain categories of their employees can successfully 'deal with' immigrants.

The 'determination' of the academic by the political is not complete or one-way. If one attempted to understand the real world by reference solely to academic initiative and development, one could be forgiven for believing that 'race relations' in Britain have disappeared, to be replaced by 'ethnic relations' and/or 'community relations'. This change in terminology arises from academic recognition that what distinguishes the 'immigrant' from the 'indigenous' population is not so much physical appearance but culture. Thus the notion of 'coloured immigrants' is replaced by the apparently more sophisticated notions of 'Asians' and 'West Indians' as distinct cultural collectivities, which are as different from each other as from the 'indigenous' population. These cultural collectivities are defined as 'ethnic' groups or communities, and suddenly the aim of political policy is to improve 'ethnic' or 'community' relations. Within academic discourse, this change in terminology has given rise to a flurry of argument about the criteria which distinguish 'race relations' from 'ethnic relations'.

A textbook written for the sociology of 'race relations' in Britain would, therefore, have a predictable form. It would describe the New Commonwealth immigration to Britain, emphasising the respective 'push' and 'pull' factors to explain the immigration, and the social and cultural characteristics of the 'immigrants'. It would detail the social and political reaction to the immigration, paying special attention to the development of immigration control and to policies aiming to improve 'race relations' by making racial discrimination illegal. Finally, it would describe and comment on the 'immigrants'' political reaction to racism and racial discrimination, no doubt concluding that 'race relations' can hardly be expected to improve unless the government 'does more'. This is not such a book, although the text that follows does refer to some of these issues and debates, but for a very different reason. Rather, it is my intention to argue that the sociology of 'race relations' has been constituted as a phony and misleading field or focus of study.

Reduced to its essentials, the argument of this text falls into two parts. First, it will be claimed that the concepts of 'race' and 'race relations' have no analytical value. This will probably be the most difficult to establish because 'everyone' acknowledges that Britain has a 'race relations problem'. My argument will, therefore, be interpreted by some to mean that I am denying the existence of the obvious. Let it, therefore, be said at the outset that I acknowledge first, the existence in Britain of migrants from the New Commonwealth; second, a pattern of extensive racial discrimination which is both individual and institutionalised; and third, an ideology of racism. These are real phenomena which lie behind an important dimension of economic, political and ideological conflict in Britain. However, events in the 'real world' are selected, appropriated, and analysed by reference to a set of concepts. Concepts serve to filter action and belief into categories which are then deemed to stand in some sort of 'causal' relationship to each other. This process is not restricted to academic discourse but is, as Gramsci so cogently observed, evident in the everyday world of 'common sense': in this sense, everyone is a philosopher or intellectual. Hence, I acknowledge that the world of everyday/political discourse identifies a 'race/race relations situation/problem'. What I wish to question is the way in which common sense discourse has come to structure and determine academic discourse so that it too admits to the existence of 'races' and 'relations between races', with the consequence that a distinct and separate field of study is deemed to exist, i.e. the sociology of 'race relations'. In other words, I shall argue that the notions of 'race' and 'race relations' have no descriptive or explanatory utility and should not, therefore, be carried into academic discourse from the everyday world. Indeed, I could go further and argue that their continued academic utilisation serves to legitimate their continued utilisation in the everyday world.

This is an argument which has political implications in a context where successive governments have introduced and supported racist immigration controls and where there exists at least one political party which aims to preserve the British 'race' by, amongst other things, the compulsory and enforced 'repatriation' of all 'black people' in Britain. This should not be interpreted to mean that sociologists who utilise the concepts of 'race' and 'race relations' are racists (although the work of some social scientists does warrant the attribution of that label), for that is to extend the logic of my argument beyond its target. Rather, I would argue that continued utilisation of that terminology ultimately hinders any attempt to counter racist arguments, whether they be in the world of academic or everyday discourse. This claim applies not least to Marxist arguments which continue to utilise 'race' as an analytical concept. One's surprise at this follows from the expectation that it would be within Marxist discourse that one

would find the clearest 'break' with the world of everyday discourse.

The second strand to the argument of this text is that the
sociology of 'race relations' has, by its obsession with 'race',
systematically distorted our understanding and analysis of
the situation of migrants in Britain. There are two dimensions
of this distortion which receive special attention below. The
first relates to the fact that the sociology of 'race relations'
always begins its analysis of 'black people' in Britain as an
excluded social category. That is to say, its analytical starting
point is racism and racial discrimination, with the result that
the analysis presupposes that what is most important to their
situation in Britain is their reaction to racism and discrimination.
Put in other words, the analysis begins with 'black people' as
objects of racism and discrimination who only become subjects
in their reaction to these ideological and practical constraints.
It will be argued that, by posing black workers as active subjects primarily or only in reaction to such constraints, attention is drawn away from more fundamental factors which locate
them as active subjects on other economic and social dimensions.
These factors can be conveniently summarised at this point in
the claim that the sociology of 'race relations' fails to attribute
sufficient analytical significance to the position of 'black people'
in class relations. This should not be interpreted to mean that
the analytical problem is to be posed as the relationship between
class and 'race'. As has already been suggested, for this
writer, 'race' has no analytical utility (and hence its appearance in quotation marks) and so it will be argued that this
interpretation poses a false dichotomy. What will be argued is
that the analytical problem is to locate the place and impact of
what I shall term the process of racial categorisation on class
relations. This process is an ideological process and has its
own determinate effects on political and production relations
and, hence, the constitution of and struggles between classes.
Consequently, I shall be wanting to argue that the ideology
of racism, which is a constitutive element of the process of
racial categorisation, has, qua ideology, a relative autonomy:
the articulation and reproduction of racism by people occupying positions in class relations have both a material basis and
material effects.

The second dimension of the suggested systematic distortion
concerns the specificity that the sociology of 'race relations'
attributes to the 'immigration' of 'black' people to Britain.
There are a number of objections to such a concentration which
will be explored in more detail below. Historical analysis shows
that 'black' people have entered and left Britain since the mid-
sixteenth century in a variety of situations and circumstances.
Moreover, as some writers have emphasised, the history of
immigration to Britain shows that the vast majority of 'immigrants' to Britain have been 'white'. Those who have studied
these immigrations in detail have reported that they, in common

with the immigration of the former, have prompted a hostile reaction from the indigenous population, suggesting that an analysis of immigration should not focus exclusively on 'colour'. Despite their comparative focus, such studies tend to ignore or treat as tendential the material basis of population movements. One of the main arguments of this text is that the focus of analysis should not be 'black immigration' but labour migration. Such a concept allows us to consider the most recent instance of 'immigration' in the wider context of the vast spatial movements of population required by the development of capitalism as both a national and an international phenomenon. So, instead of emphasising and concentrating on 'blackness', this analysis will conclude by arguing that the focus should be upon the place of migrant labour in capitalist relations of production and thence upon the place of racialised migrant labour in political and ideological relations. It is in and through those relations that, in the case of Britain since 1945, migrant labour has become the focus for the articulation and reproduction of racism.

In developing these arguments, it will be necessary to summarise much of the standard literature which passes for the sociology of 'race relations'. This should allow the reader to appreciate the way in which this alternative theorisation differs. Accordingly, in Part I, the analysis begins with the notion of 'race' and proceeds to establish the analytical importance of the concept of racism. In the process, there is an extended critique of attempts to establish the sociology of 'race relations' as a theoretically defined entity and of the more recent emergence of 'ethnic relations' studies. Thereafter, in Part II, a case will be made for beginning with an analysis of the political economy of migrant labour. This, however, is not to be understood as economic determinism. The argument of Part II will be concerned to reject those common claims that racism is to be defined and analysed simply as functional to capitalism and will identify some of the political and ideological determinants of racism and some of the determinate effects of racism upon political and economic relations in British capitalism.

As a footnote to this project, the reader should consider its intention in relation to some recent writing which has been concerned with what is to count as the object of an analysis of the oppression of women (e.g. Cowie, 1978; Adams, 1979) and the way in which that object relates to the predominant, extant strands of theory (e.g. Barrett, 1980). One of the interesting contributions to this debate has pointed to the ahistorical and atemporal nature of the category 'woman' and has argued for the importance of analysing the social construction of gender identity, stressing that this analysis be located in the context of production relations (Endholm et al., 1977/8; see also Barrett, 1980, pp. 86-99). Feuchtwang has identified the parallel with the analysis of 'racial oppression' when he comments critically that (1980, p.42): '"Women" and "blacks" are not theorized as differentiated constructions in social and discursive relations, but as naturally occurring categories of human population.' The parallel is not a precise one, as is indicated implicitly in the oft-repeated claim that 'black women' are doubly oppressed, both as 'women' and as 'blacks'. This claim presupposes a 'level' of oppression (i.e. 'racial') which is shared with 'black men' and a 'level' of oppression which is similar to, but still distinct from, that experienced by other 'women' by virtue of 'racial oppression'. The problem of how we are to analyse both the relationship between these 'levels' (or 'forms') and their interrelationship with class relations remains the object of critical attention on which I do not wish to comment at length. What I do claim, however, is that what are popularly defined as 'racial' and 'sexual' oppression/disadvantage should be analysed consistently and exhaustively as social constructions within the context of the reproduction of class relations and that the categories of analysis should reflect more accurately the role of human practice in constructing and reproducing this oppression/disadvantage. This is integral to the task of demonstrating that these oppressions/disadvantages are not naturally part of the organisation of social relations but are socially constructed as part of the process of the reproducing of the material basis of social life. They are, therefore, an element of the real appearance of a given mode of production which should be analysed historically and structurally (cf. Barrett, 1980, pp. 94-6).

Part I
The limitations of
'race relations' theory

To understand and to evaluate realistically one's
adversary's position and his reasons (and sometimes
one's adversary is the whole of past thought) means
precisely to be liberated from the prison of ideologies
in the bad sense of the word - that of blind ideological
fanaticism. It means taking up a point of view that is
'critical', which for the purpose of scientific research
is the only fertile one.

A. Gramsci, 'Prison Notebooks', 1971, p. 344.

The aim of Part I of this text is both expository and critical. I
shall outline what appear as the main justifications, directions
and parameters of the sociology of 'race/ethnic' relations as
developed primarily in Britain over the past two decades. This
sociology is not a homogeneous body of argument and research,
but is nevertheless bound together as a totality by its supposed object, the study of 'race (ethnic) relations'. Most of
the critique will focus on the theoretical adequacy of this
chosen object of study, but it will also consider problems concerning the concept of racism in order to provide a point of
transition to Part II.

1 'RACE': JUST A SCIENTIFIC ERROR?

Human physical variation is enormous. Just a casual glance at passers-by on any street will show great differences in height, eye colour, body shape and colour and type of hair. Moreover, these physical traits do not co-vary in any systematic way. Thus, people who are in excess of six feet tall may have black, brown, blonde or red hair; and people who are fat do not all have green eyes. In other words, the grouping together or categorisation of people by their height will not include the same persons as would a categorisation on the basis of hair colour. Yet some physical characteristics are used to categorise people without regard to other traits that set them apart. One such characteristic is skin colour. This physical characteristic is attributed, relative to other traits such as eye colour, with much greater social significance. It is said to denote a difference of 'race', and on the basis of that difference, unequal treatment can and does follow. In this chapter, the concern is less with social behaviour that follows from such categorisation, but with the categorisation itself. This is because I wish to argue that physical differentiation is rarely of socio-economic significance in itself. Rather, the significance of, for example, skin colour arises from the meaning that is given to it by people. More specifically, the concern is with the fact that people in Britain (in common with many other populations) interpret certain forms of physical variation using the word 'race'.

Reference to 'race' is a common feature of everyday life in contemporary Britain: 'race' is a factor that government is supposed to take account of in political decision-making; the National Front argues that 'race' is the key to national survival; the media report on 'race' riots at home and abroad; and a large proportion of the British population would agree that immigration to Britain since the 1950s has brought about a 'race' problem. Government legislation takes it for granted that 'races' exist: politicians have deemed it necessary to set legal parameters for social relations between 'races' (in the form of the Race Relations Acts of 1966, 1968 and 1976) and there now exists a special commission to encourage equality between the 'races' (the Commission for Racial Equality). Even the academic world records the existence of 'race', as we shall see.

In most everyday discourse, the word 'race' is used loosely and without regard to a formal (scientific) definition. Generally,

9

it will be used when an individual or group believes that the physical appearance (i.e. skin colour, hair type, head shape, etc.) of another individual or group signifies some psychological and/or social difference between them. Thus, much physical variation becomes defined as 'racial' variation, from which is derived the corollary that the world's population can be divided into 'races'. Now it is important to recognise that this process of racial categorisation is rarely an end in itself, but a means to an end. Social significance is attributed to certain forms of physical variation in order to justify or to generate different patterns of behaviour. Often this behaviour will not be formally rationalised, but when it is some reference will be made to the existence of different 'races'.

Two interrelated issues therefore present themselves. First, is there any scientific validity in the attempt to categorise the world's population into different 'races' on the basis of physical variation? Second, is there some deterministic relationship between physical variation and psychological and/or social characteristics? An answer to both questions involves both a historical and a biological dimension.

I shall pursue only the former question below and so the reader is directed elsewhere to follow through the second (e.g. Richardson and Spears, 1972; Rose et al., 1974; Banton and Harwood, 1975; Rose, 1976; Kamin, 1977; Evans and Waites, 1981). Examination of the historical record shows that only in the late eighteenth and the nineteenth centuries did the word 'race' come to refer to discrete categories of people defined according to their physical characteristics. This social construction of 'race' was formally the product of the newly emerging biological sciences as applied to homo sapiens, although, as we shall see later, this should not be taken to mean that the social construction of 'race' was due simply to a scientific error. However, an error was certainly committed. In order to appreciate the nature of that error, it is necessary to enter the world of biology and genetics. Having done so, we can return to a consideration of the world of everyday discourse.

THE SCIENTIFIC CONSTRUCTION OF 'RACE'

The origin of the word 'race' in the English language can be traced to 1508 and for the most of the sixteenth century it was used only to refer to a class or category of persons or things; there was no implication that these classes or categories were biologically distinct. During the seventeenth century a number of Englishmen interested in their historical origins developed the view that they were the descendants of a German 'race' and that the Norman invasion of the eleventh century had led to the domination of the Saxons by an 'alien race'. This interpretation of history gave rise to a conception of 'race' in the sense of lineage. By this it was meant that a 'race' was distinct because it had a separate history: there was little interest in what else might be supposed to be different between such 'races'. Only during the late eighteenth and nineteenth centuries do we find evidence that the word 'race' came to be associated with inherent physical traits. In the same period, the word came to be applied beyond the boundaries of Europe and to the populations of the then ever-expanding world.] Banton summarises this argument as follows (1977a, pp. 18-19): 'There was a social process, which can be called racialization, whereby a mode of categorization was developed, applied tentatively in European historical writing, and then, more confidently, to the populations of the world.'

Banton supports this argument by reference to the content of historical texts of the early nineteenth century, many of which focused on the differences and conflict between the Saxon and Norman 'races'. He concludes from this that 'It looks as if by 1850 a significant section of the English upper class subscribed to a rudimentary racial philosophy of history' (1977a, p. 25). But it was in the application of the term to the growing knowledge about populations outside Europe that it came to refer to distinct biological types whose (supposed) differences were defined as permanent. In other words, it was argued that what set populations apart was not so much their history as their physical appearance.

In order to understand the extension of the application of 'race' and its new meaning, one must take note of the intellectual context of the period in question. The most important characteristic of this context was the centrality of religious belief, the Bible being the key text against which to measure the validity of other ideas. The racialisation of the world developed in the context of a more specific debate about the origin of homo sapiens which, given this broader ideological context, was by implication a debate about the validity of the historical record of human creation provided in the Bible. Those involved in this debate fell into two main camps. On the one hand, there were the monogenists who argued that homo sapiens had a single origin and concluded that all members of the human species must therefore share the same nature. These arguments were justified by reference to and, indeed, seemed to be more in accordance with the Old Testament. On the other hand, there were the polygenists who argued that there were a number of distinct species of homo sapiens, each of which possessed different characteristics. The polygenists were faced with the problem of making their theories compatible with the Old Testament or, alternatively, of rejecting the biblical account in favour of a completely secular explanation for the origin of homo sapiens. Given the predominance of religious thought, the latter was not an easy option, but there were already available certain ideas based on an interpretation of passages of the Old Testament which made the former possible.

Many of those involved in this debate could be described as 'amateur scientists' who had a particular interest in human morphology (i.e. body shape and size). There is neither space nor reason to provide a detailed account of the various arguments and theories that these people formulated. Suffice it here to provide a few examples in order to illustrate the general intellectual trends. For instance, a French anatomist, Georges Cuvier, advanced the idea in the early nineteenth century that homo sapiens could be divided into three distinct types which could be ordered hierarchically (with 'whites' at the top and 'blacks' at the bottom). His evidence was based on the shape and size of skulls, from which he concluded that the physical differences he observed were responsible for the difference in culture and mental attitudes between the 'races' (Banton and Harwood, 1975, p. 27; Banton, 1977a, pp. 32-4). Further studies based on analyses of skulls were published in the United States by a Dr S.G. Morton, one in 1839 on those of American Indians and one in 1845 on Egyptian skulls. In the latter book, it was claimed that Egyptians had a low cranial capacity and that black people in Egypt had always been enslaved. Many of the same themes, along with developments of some of them, appeared in 'The Types of Mankind' in 1854, written by J.C. Nott and G.R. Gliddon. The text made a number of claims, of which the following are a sample: (i) there exist distinct and permanent types of homo sapiens; (ii) there exists a hierarchy of 'races'; (iii) the superior 'races' should not 'breed' with the inferior 'races' for fear of obstructing future progress; (iv) the 'dark-skinned races' were fit only for military government. In a later book, Nott and Gliddon suggested that each 'race' had its own natural, geographical habitat and that its survival would be threatened by moving to a new one (Banton and Harwood, 1975, pp. 27-8; Banton, 1977a, pp. 50-2).

Similar arguments were being advanced in Britain in the same period. A friend of Cuvier, Charles Hamilton Smith, published a book ('The Natural History of the Human Species') in 1848 which repeated the theses of the permanence of racial type and the existence of three discrete 'races', ('Negro, Mongolian and Caucasian'). Smith additionally suggested that the low cranial capacity of 'blacks' in America explained their subordinate position in the social structure. Two years later, Robert Knox published 'The Races of Men' in which he argued that 'races' can be distinguished by anatomical differences as well as by temperament, that the external characteristics of 'races' have been unchanged and that the offspring of the mating of individuals from two different 'races' are infertile. But Knox's major concern was to establish that differences in physical constitution determined cultural variation and that 'race' was the major determinant of historical development. In short, for Knox, 'race' determined both culture and history. This was biological determinism in its most extreme form. But the

articulation of such ideas was not restricted to Britain and the
United States. Throughout the nineteenth century, these same
ideas were being published in book form throughout Western
Europe (Banton and Harwood, 1975, pp. 28-30; Banton, 1977a,
pp. 34-5, 47-8; Biddiss, 1979, pp. 11-35).

It is therefore not surprising that by the middle of the nineteenth century 'race' was a dominant scientific concept. Indeed,
as we shall see in Chapter 5, it was also a dominant political
concept. But there was much about which these scientists
disagreed, particularly when attempts were made to elaborate
and extend the classification of 'races' beyond three. These
disputes concerned not only the number of 'races' but also the
nature of the criteria to be used to identify the different
'races'. These disputes took place, however, against the background of an acceptance of a number of fundamental propositions. These were that (i) the physical appearance and behaviour of individuals was an expression of a discrete biological
type which was permanent; (ii) cultural variation was determined by differences in biological type; (iii) biological variation was the origin of conflict between both individuals and
nations; and (iv) 'races' were differentially endowed such that
some were inherently superior to others. Banton has suggested
that these four propositions can be collectively described as
the 'doctrine of racial typology' (1977a, p. 47).

This typological classification of homo sapiens was consistent
with the general drift and emphasis of the developing biological
sciences of the time. The main concern was to assign each
separately identifiable plant and animal to a type/group within
a species and scientists saw no reason why the same procedure
should not be adopted for the species of homo sapiens. The
first serious challenge to typological classification came with
the publication of Charles Darwin's 'On the Origins of Species
by Means of Natural Selection' in 1859 which was less concerned
with the static nature of formal classification and more with the
dynamic process of biological change. It also laid the foundation for the complete rejection of the arguments of the polygenists. Darwin identified a process of natural selection by
which those members of a plant or animal population which are
best adapted to their environment contribute more to subsequent generations than those less well endowed. Darwin's
emphasis upon selection, process and change, as well as his
concern with environmental influences, contained an implicit
challenge to the idea of static and permanent biological types.
It also contained the potential to provide a monogenic explanation for the very obvious range of physical variation of homo
sapiens. But the assumptions of the exponents of theories of
racial typology were deeply rooted, and the economic and
political circumstances of the latter half of the nineteenth
century were not propitious for a sudden and wide-ranging
change in intellectual direction. The idea of natural selection
became wedded to the existing ideas of racial typology in order

to conclude with the idea of the survival of the fittest. Herein lies the birth of Social Darwinism (Banton, 1977a, pp. 89-100; Biddiss, 1979, p. 20).

In so far as this was so because of scientific reasons, one can point to Darwin's failure to explain the biological basis of natural selection. The explanation was to be found in the work of Mendel who can be regarded as the founder of genetics. In order to understand the implications for our analysis of Mendel's work (and the work of those who followed up his major discovery), a distinction between genotype and phenotype must be introduced. Genotype refers to the underlying and 'hidden' (to the naked eye) genetic constitution or code with respect to a particular characteristic or characteristics. Phenotype refers to a visible appearance of a characteristic or characteristics. Hence, the phenotypical feature of eye or hair type and colour is, other things being equal, determined by the particular form taken by the genetic code. However, at the level of the individual, most phenotypical variation is not the sole product of genotype. Rather, an individual's genotype provides certain parameters within which environmental factors have their effect. Moreover, in the long term and at the group level, genotype is subject to environmental influence.

In order to understand the implications of these developments, it is necessary to recall that the theorists of racial typology based their classifications of the world's 'races' upon factors such as skin colour, cranial capacity and shape, facial angle, and so on. In other words, their classifications were of phenotypical features. Now it was already clear that the various phenotypical features did not co-vary with each other in a consistent way, e.g. not all people with dark skins had black, tightly curled hair and flattened noses. Indeed, it was just such non-correspondence between separate phenotypical features that led to a proliferation of classifications of 'races'. The discovery and subsequent development of genetics provided an explanation for such phenotypical variation. Moreover, because many phenotypical features cannot be clearly separated into discrete groups but in fact exhibit continuous variation, and because the number of genes is insufficient to account for all these forms of diversity, then an explanation for it must give room to environmental factors. The biological determinism of the theorists of racial typology did not allow such a possibility. Genetic analysis has now shown that genes are responsive to environmental influence, thus allowing that phenotypical features are a product of an interaction between genotype and environment. Indeed, for this reason the application of genetics to homo sapiens is extremely complex. One consequence is that any attempt to identify 'races' by reference to phenotypical variation can only ever produce overlapping classifications and not discrete categories (Banton and Harwood, 1975, pp. 47-52).

In a sentence, then, those who proposed a classification of

the world's population into discrete 'races' using phenotypical characteristics were wrong (see Montagu, 1964). Their various claims about hierarchy and superiority were dependent upon the validity of their initial proposition about the permanence of phenotypical type, and this was exposed as false by the development of genetics. But despite the weight of scientific evidence, similar sorts of classifications are still attempted. For example, in 1947 a physical anthropologist proposed a classification of the world's population based on surface phenotypical and skeletal features, from which he identified Caucasoid, Negroid and Mongoloid 'races' (Hooton, 1947). It is this type of argument that the National Front draws upon in order to attempt to argue the superiority of the 'white race' in general and the British in particular (Billig, 1978, pp. 151-2). Moreover, it is just this form of classification which tends to linger in the public consciousness.

'RACE' AND GENETICS

So far, I have argued that there are no scientific grounds for developing a typology of the world's population based on phenotypical variation. But what about genotypical variation? Does this not permit a classification of homo sapiens into distinct 'races'? On the face of it, the answer might seem to be in the affirmative because biologists and geneticists do continue to argue that one can identify systematic genetic variation and that the groups so distinguished should be labelled 'races' (see Bodmer, 1972; Montagu, 1972; Rose et al., 1974; Bodmer and Cavalli-Sforza, 1976). As a specific example, consider Dunn (1959, pp. 90-1): 'a race is a population which differs from other populations in the frequency of some of its genes (a population has already been defined, for cross-breeding species, as a community of genes shared by interbreeding within the group)'. Consider also Dobzhansky (in Osborne, 1971, pp. 16-19):

> Races may be defined as populations which differ in frequencies, or in prevalence, of some genes. Race differences are relative, not absolute ... human populations are racially distinct if they differ in the frequencies of some genes, and not distinct if they do not so differ. The presence of race differences can be ascertained, and if they are present, their magnitude can be measured.

To illustrate this argument, one can cite Bodmer's (1972) reference to the inheritance of non-visible traits, such as blood groups, which are determined by the relevant gene taking one particular form rather than another. These different possible forms are called alleles. In many instances, it is not that one allele is present while the others are absent, but that two

or more are present, although one will be dominant. These are
referred to as polymorphic genes (Bodmer and Cavalli-Sforza,
1976, pp. 307-8). As in the case of the ABO blood group, it
is possible to show that these three alleles occur within different populations with different frequencies. Other poly-
morphisms show even greater variation between populations
than the ABO genetic polymorphism (Bodmer and Cavelli-
Sforza, 1976, pp. 575-6; see also Livingstone, 1964).

Having suggested that the pattern of genetic variation
revealed by such analyses can be used to identify 'races',
Bodmer adds the following qualifications. First, the extent of
genetic variation within any population is usually greater than
the average difference between populations. Second, although
the frequency of occurrence of different alleles does vary from
one 'race' to another, any particular genetic combination can
nevertheless be found in almost any 'race' (from which is
derived the proposition that differences between individuals
should be distinguished analytically from differences between
populations). Third, due to inter-breeding and large scale
migrations, the distinctions between 'races' identified in terms
of polymorphic frequencies are often blurred (1972, pp. 87-9;
also Bodmer and Cavalli-Sforza, 1976, pp. 574-8, 588-91).

Thus, despite the existence of measurable genetic variation,
it is not possible to generate from it a discrete classification
of 'races'. This is Dobzhansky's conclusion (in Osborne, 1971,
p. 16): 'Races ... are not, and never were, groups clearly
defined biologically. The gene flow between human populations
makes race boundaries always more or less blurred.' Bodmer
clearly spells out the implication (1972, p. 90):

> the definition of race in terms of differences of genetic
> polymorphisms is fairly arbitrary. How much difference
> does there have to be between populations before we call
> them different races? ... it is largely a matter of taste as
> to whether one is a splitter or a lumper of population
> groups into races.

Given this arbitrary character, it is not surprising that
geneticists and biologists cannot agree on the meaning to be
assigned to the term 'race'. Montagu, in his discussion of
the definition of 'race' advanced by a UNESCO committee, notes
that biologists continue to use the term in a number of different ways; indeed, some reject its use altogether. His own
conclusion is that 'The term ... at best is at present time not
really allowable on any score in man' (1972, p. 63).

Now let us be clear about what is being claimed. It is not
being denied that there are identifiable, measurable group
differences in the overall pattern of gene frequencies. In other
words, it is accepted that there exist what others have called
gene pools. Montagu himself points out that (1972, p. 68): 'By
the random interchange of genes within (intrabreeding) groups

and other genetic processes, a certain commonality of traits is often established and maintained within such populations.' The formation and maintenance of these intrabreeding populations are not due to genetic or any other biological factors. The determining factors are geographical and socio-economic. Both factors tend to obstruct spatial movement of populations while socio-economic factors discourage or prevent sexual relations between groups which are defined and/or define themselves as somehow distinct from others. The most extreme instance of the latter can be found in South Africa where sexual relations between different 'races' are illegal. However, as has already been emphasised, the different genetic profiles or gene pools that result from these processes do not exhibit absolute difference, only continuous variation (with the consequence that any particular pattern of alleles can be found in any population which is distinguished from another by its overall genetic profile).

In addition, there is no simple or direct relationship between genetic variation and visible physical variation (such as skin colour, height, etc.): many genotypical differences are not evident phenotypically while different geographical populations which share certain phenotypical features do not necessarily share the same genotype (e.g. Leach, 1975). Concerning the latter point, one writer has summarised the evidence as follows (Barnicot, 1964, p. 219):

> we are in no position to say whether populations which are phenotypically similar in these multifactorial characters are also similar genetically ... certain populations which are widely separated geographically resemble one another in skin colour and in various other metrical characters but differ in their frequencies of blood groups and other simply inherited traits. This may at least lead us to doubt whether these anatomical resemblances also imply genetical similarity and indicate the need for caution in accepting these resemblances as evidence of close common ancestry.

Subsequent research has not produced evidence which contradicts Barnicot's conclusion. Bodmer and Cavalli-Sforza refer to the conspicuous phenotypical characteristics such as skin colour and hair and eye pigmentation. They argue that in the case of skin colour, although at the level of the individual this is a characteristic which is largely genetically determined, the distribution of skin colour amongst groups across the world's surface is the result of a long process of natural selection. Other visible phenotypical features more directly reflect climate at the level of the individual, e.g. body build. They comment that the body surface constitutes the interface between the internal and external environment and, because of its important role in the regulation of heat exchange, it must therefore play an important role in adaptation of the body to climate. This has important implications for the way in which phenotypical variation between populations is interpreted. Such variation, because it is probably largely the result of climatic adaptation, almost certainly over-emphasises the genetic variation between populations and may be more of a guide to a population's climatic history than its evolutionary origins (1976, pp. 580-8). In sum, populations which look alike may not share the same genetic profile.

Finally, genotypical differences are subject to ongoing change through gene variability and gene mutation (Montagu, 1964, p. 8) while the traits to which several genes give rise are also the result of the effect of environmental factors, with the consequence that the trait cannot be biologically 'fixed' in advance. An excellent example of this is body build.

It is clear from all this evidence that the interpretation of genetic variation cannot be overlaid with the notions advanced by the nineteenth-century theorists of racial typology. The nature and pattern of genetic variation does not allow one to divide the world's population into a number of permanent and discrete 'races' which can be hierarchically ordered. Neither is there any suggestion by most geneticists that genetic variation is related to some sort of capacity for 'civilisation' as did those in the nineteenth century who were obsessed with the measurement of cranial capacity. In other words, when geneticists and biologists use the word 'race' to refer to genetic variation as described above, its referent is quite different from that of the nineteenth century. And herein lies a fundamental conceptual problem. Is there any reason for scientifically redefining 'race' to mean something which approaches the opposite of its meaning in the nineteenth century?

I believe that there is no valid reason for doing so. Any attempt to redefine a concept will almost certainly involve a transfer effect with the result that the new meaning is 'infected' with aspects of the previous interpretation. One result is analytical confusion. This is evident even in textbooks on genetics. The text cited above by Bodmer and Cavalli-Sforza not only continues to use the term 'race', having cited many of the arguments reported above, but also identifies 'three major racial groups' (1976, p. 565), subdividing at least one of them by reference to 'cultural and physical peculiarities' (1976, p. 567). It is not simply that this involves recourse to the discredited methods of nineteenth-century science, but also that it implies some scientific value in such taxonomic classification. Yet, as the authors themselves argue (see also Dunn, 1959, p. 93), such classifications tell us almost nothing about the frequencies within different populations of genes associated with phenotypical characteristics and so almost nothing of relevance to an appreciation of human evolution. Hence, there is a good reason to agree with Montagu when he argues (1964, p. 23): 'Since what we are actually dealing with in human breeding populations are differences in the frequencies of certain genes, why not use a term which states just this, such as *genogroup*, and the various appropriate variants of this?'

But it is not just a matter of scientific or analytic clarity. If, as Bodmer, as cited above (see also Bodmer and Cavalli-Sforza, 1976, pp. 561-2), suggests, the drawing of scientific boundaries around populations in order to separately identify them as 'races' is arbitrary and a matter of taste, then it is also a matter of politics. The facts that six million Jews were murdered with the intention of maintaining 'racial purity' and that political parties are allowed throughout Western Europe, including Britain, to reproduce these ideas and others derived from nineteenth-century science are good enough reasons for ensuring that twentieth-century science gives absolutely no credence to fascist and other right-wing political philosophies and strategies. In arguing this, I am not suggesting that the refining of scientific terminology will prevent the development of a fascist movement if other circumstances are favourable. But I am arguing that scientific analysis should not give any credence to the discredited theory of racial typology and that therefore, because of the possibility of a transfer of meaning, the term 'race' should no longer be used in science to refer even to populations defined by a distinct gene pool.

THE SOCIAL CONSTRUCTION OF 'RACE'

There is an uneven and unbalanced relationship between the discourse of science and the discourse of everyday life. The development of scientific knowledge about the physical and human worlds only slowly percolates into everyday understanding. What does become 'common knowledge' is selective and not necessarily fully or accurately understood. One consequence is that the subsequent falsification of an idea or theory that has become part of 'common knowledge' does not necessarily also become part of 'common knowledge', displacing what science has come to regard as false. Scientifically discredited notions, therefore, can have a certain life of their own, a relative autonomy. But in claiming that such notions, once lodged in everyday discourse, can be independent of scientific discourse, it is not being suggested that their continued articulation is not without explanation. This argument can be illustrated with reference to the notion of 'race'.

As indicated at the outset, the term 'race' is in regular use in daily conversation and has been given a certain legal status by various Acts of Parliament. But what is being referred to? Ironically, there is little published evidence on which to base an answer to this question, but I can draw on my own previous research (Phizacklea and Miles, 1979, 1980; Miles and Phizacklea, 1981) to suggest one. Rarely, if ever, is reference being made to gene pools. Indeed, given the method of identifying genetic

variation, the fact that many genes do not have a visible phenotypical signifier and that the specific genetic variation within
populations is usually greater than the average between populations, it is not possible for the accepted genetic variation
that does exist to be reliably recognised in social interaction.
For example, it is not possible to identify a person's blood
group from their physical appearance or their behaviour. The
accurate identification of genetic variation is therefore a matter
for the biological sciences.

Rather, when 'race' is used in everyday discourse, it is
usually to refer to or to signify the existence of phenotypical
variation, that is, variations in skin colour, hair type, bone
structure and so on (cf. Bodmer and Cavalli-Sforza, 1976,
p. 580; Banton, 1979, p. 130). In other words, the word 'race'
is used in everyday discourse to refer to those aspects of physical variation which were used by nineteenth-century science
to identify permanent and discrete physical types. It may also
be used to refer to some other alleged or real biological characteristic of an individual or group. But, asks the sceptic, surely
its continued use reflects nothing more than the existence of
'races'? The very terms in which the question is posed are,
however, in error. What exists is not 'race' but phenotypical
variation: 'race' is a word used to describe or refer to such
variation. Moreover, physical differences between people and
groups can only have socio-economic significance if they are
given social recognition and if social interaction is structured
by such recognition. The continued use of 'race' to refer to
phenotypical variation is nothing other than an aspect of such
social recognition. We may, therefore, talk about the social
construction of 'race' or, alternatively, racial categorisation.
This allows us to pose some questions in terms which are somewhat different from those usually employed. For example, why
is social significance attached to phenotypical characteristics?
Why is the 'race' label still used to refer to, or to signify,
phenotypical variation? How is racial categorisation reproduced?

Answers to such questions require historical and structural
analysis. The word 'race' has a history of usage, although the
above analysis suggests that events in the late eighteenth and
nineteenth centuries must have been at work to give it a new
meaning and much wider currency. The development of the
biological sciences can therefore be considered to have played
an important role in the social construction of 'race'. But it does
not follow that the continued use of the term is nothing more
than a result of cultural reproduction. Ideas are not formulated
and reproduced of their own accord. We must therefore ask why
the idea of 'race' was given such great significance in the nineteenth century, by whom, and whether the nineteenth-century
construction of 'race' can be related to preceding ideological
and material processes. And if 'common knowledge' has not
taken up more recent scientific conceptions of 'race', we need
to search for reasons for continuing reference to physical

variation. In other words, why does the social process of racial categorisation continue? The fact that the scientific reconceptualisation of 'race' is not reflected in everyday discourse suggests factors other than the development of the biological sciences were fundamental to the formulation of the notion of 'race' and that similar, or indeed other, factors are fundamental to its continuing reproduction. The identification of these other political and economic factors is simultaneously an analytical shift away from the idealistic tendency of this chapter. This tendency has been necessary to begin the deconstruction of 'race' but must be subsumed by consideration of the material context and antecedents of the development of the theory of racial typology, or in my terms, scientific racism. Some of these questions will be pursued in Chapter 4 in the context of a discussion about the concept of racism, and thereafter in Chapter 5. But before doing this, I want to explore the implications of the above arguments for the way in which the social sciences approach and analyse situations involving social categorisation. One dominant approach is the sociology of 'race relations'.

2 'RACE RELATIONS': A MIRAGE REFRACTED

The sociology of 'race relations' has an institutional existence
in the form of university and college courses of the same title
and an accompanying literature. The starting point of this
literature is with the fact that, despite the scientific falsification of the concept of 'race' (i.e. the theory of racial typology),
social interaction continues to be structured by beliefs about
the existence of 'races'. In this chapter, I want to evaluate
critically that argument which derives a sociology of 'race
relations' from this fact, from which I shall conclude that the
problem that this poses is pointless and misleading. It is, in
other words, a false problematic.

The argument of this chapter is, in essence, a simple one and
can be illustrated by reference to the phenomenon of the mirage.
My claim is not that 'race' can be equated with a mirage, but
that by reference to the example of a mirage we can illustrate
a method of critical analysis which counts as scientific. A
mirage is an optical illusion in which a person sees nonexistent
water or material objects. There is no question that the observer really sees what is described but what is seen is not water
or trees but images of these phenomena. The physical sciences
do not set out to explain this seeing of appearances by reference
to the observer or by utilising analytical categories exclusively
and directly derived from the empirical phenomena (including
statements made by the observer). Indeed, the phenomenon can
only be described as a mirage by beginning an explanation and
using analytical categories which have no direct and immediate
source in the empirical phenomenon. The explanation for the
mirage refers to the effects of the travel of light through an
atmosphere which has a peculiar air density, leading to the
refraction of the wave front and the formation of a displaced
image. These conditions may be described as the essential relations of the phenomenal appearance of the mirage: they explain
why the observer sees the appearance of water or trees. In
other words, the explanation begins with, but does not exclusively depend upon, the observer's perception.

Much of my analysis will focus upon a single text, 'Race Relations in Sociological Theory' (Rex, 1970). There are three reasons for this. First, Rex's text contains some propositions which
are held in common with other writers, although not all of these
writers would necessarily accept Rex's conclusions. Second, it
constitutes a conscious theoretical attempt to delineate a field
of study which is linked with certain, central sociological

22

propositions. For that reason, it is frequently quoted or referred to as a reference point for empirical analysis. Yet, to date,
no one has attempted a sustained critique of its main propositions. Third, in a very general way, this text both derives
from and supports two empirical studies (Rex and Moore,
1967; Rex and Tomlinson, 1979), both of which have been the
focus of critical attention (e.g. Haddon, 1976; Dahya, 1974;
Bourne, 1980; Gilroy, 1980). However, the focus of these
criticisms has either been on a particular facet of Rex's interpretation (e.g. the 'theory' of housing classes) or upon the
validity of his conclusions in the light of his attributed political
presuppositions. Here I want to question the conclusions of
his empirical studies by questioning some of the more general
theoretical propositions and assumptions which underlie them.
This will constitute the focus of the first part of this chapter,
to be followed by a critical exposition of more general issues
arising from attempts to formulate a field of study or theory
of 'race relations'. Given this intention, I here have no direct
interest in those critiques of the sociology of 'race relations'
in general and Rex's work in particular which are concerned
to develop an almost exclusively political critique and which
ignore the theoretical contradictions with which I am concerned
(Bourne, 1980; Gilroy, 1980). Indeed, some of the claims made
against Rex actually express a common articulation of the 'race
relations' problematic (see Gilroy, 1980, pp. 47-8, 51-2).

A SOCIOLOGY OF 'RACE RELATIONS': AN EXPOSITION

Rex defines his starting point as arising from 'an urgent necessity for a reassessment of the role of the race concept in sociological theory' (1970, p.2). He notes the scientific falsification
of the 'race' concept and claims that the focus of analysis
should be upon 'race' as a social category (1973, p. 192):

  Social categories depend for their existence on the subjective definition given to them by social actors. Race is no
  exception. So long as it exists in the minds of men there
  will be race relations problems to study just as there will
  be men who can be helped to fight against the buttressing
  of injustice by the use of pseudo-scientific beliefs.

So, for Rex, the idea of 'race' gives rise to 'race relations'
situations. The task of the sociology of 'race relations' is,
thence, to study such situations, but, first, it is necessary
to identify the boundary that divides such relations from other
sorts of relations (1970, p. 7): 'We are trying to discover which
of the various kinds of social situations, structures and processes which sociologists study belong within the sub-field of
the sociology of race relations.' This is not such an easy task
as it appears at first sight, or so Rex tells us. First, he

argues, the structuring of belief and action by the idea of 'race' occurs only in certain types of social structure and so the sociology of 'race relations' is given the task of identifying and ordering these social structures (1970, pp. 9–10). Second, there is the problem of identifying what is to count as racism, particularly when arguments are not systematically formulated and do not contain explicit reference to biological theories (1970, p. 12). It is upon the first of these problems that I wish to concentrate in this chapter, while the second will be discussed in Chapter 4.

Rex's central claim is that it is possible to identify certain types of historical and social structure in which 'race relations' predominate, that is (1973, p. 203): 'historical situations in which it is frequently the case that the problem of relations between men are defined as problems of race relations'. Ironically, Rex's first typology of 'race relations' situations (1970, pp. 39–40) does not appear in his theoretical text, but the fact that the typology was published in a revised form three years later (1973, pp. 203–4) suggests that the omission cannot be accounted for by some decision on his part to reject or reformulate it. Moreover, one of the types of historical situation (i.e. where unfree labour predominates) receives extended consideration in the theoretical text (1970, pp. 32–58) and is consistent with his claim that the sociology of 'race relations' must begin with an analysis of colonialism because it was in colonial situations that forms of unfree labour (e.g. slavery, migrant labour, indentured labour) predominated. Hence, Rex suggests elsewhere that a central issue warranting attention is a (1973, p. 176): 'fundamental structural and dynamic analysis of British imperial society, including both free labour in the metropolis and ... "fettered labour" in the colonies'.

Rex explicitly claims that the uniqueness of his analysis lies in his emphasis upon unfree labour, this emphasis deriving from the methodological claim that the structure of a society can only be understood by means of an examination of the social relations that characterise its productive institutions. With this as his starting point, Rex proceeds to consider various forms of European conquest under the general concept of colonialism, paying particular attention to the productive systems and the means used to produce a labour supply in each case. This is followed by an analysis of the social stratification of colonial societies which centres on two points. First, he considers the nature of the various social strata which characterise colonial societies (mentioning colonial officials and settlers, secondary colonists, church officials and that population which results from sexual relations between colonisers and colonised). Having identified some of the conflicts that develop between these groups, Rex second considers the social imagery of the colonial society that these different strata are likely to develop and maintain. He concludes that colonial societies are characterised

by a social order which (1970, p. 85): 'as it is subjectively
understood by those who participate in it, is less stable, more
violent, more unpredictable and less easily summed up under
the traditional categories of stratification theory than is any
advanced industrial society in a metropolitan country'.

How, then, is it that relations between men (and women?)
are defined as 'race relations' in such societies? Rex suggests,
first, that colonial societies are distinguished from metropolitan
societies by their 'ethnic pluralism' and greater reliance upon
coercive sanctions, features which (1970, p. 87): 'make it more
likely that the unequal treatment meted out to members of
different groups in the colonial case will come to be characterised by racist ideas and beliefs and by racialist practice'. He
is, therefore, suggesting a determinate relationship between a
certain type of historical and social structure and the ideas
that are used to structure social relations and social conflict
in that structure. Second, bearing on the fact that the metropolitan societies in the post-colonial era now have ex-colonial
populations living within them, Rex argues that (1970, p. 42):
'the low status of the negro in any system of racial or ethnic
stratification in a plural society has much to do with the fact
that he comes from a people who were more unfree than others'.
In other words, one of the structural characteristics of colonial
societies (i.e. unfree labour) structures the entry of people
from ex-colonial societies into metropolitan societies in the
sense that it serves to reproduce imagery of the colonial
worker in the new context (see also 1973, pp. 154-6).

This latter theme is taken up in Rex's discussion of the
structural preconditions of 'race relations' in metropolitan
societies, a discussion which centres on the position occupied
in the stratification system by immigrant minorities and which
places considerable explanatory emphasis upon the concept of
assimilation. The essence of Rex's argument is that immigrant
minorities differ in their chances of assimilation into the stratification system of a metropolitan society (1970, pp. 98-9,
105-8) and that immigrants from colonial societies are especially
disadvantaged. He suggests that (1970, p. 105): 'the stratification system of a society arises from the subjective picture or
model of social relations which comes to men's minds when they
think of their society as a whole'. Consistent with this explanation of the origin of social stratification, Rex then identifies
those characteristics which the citizens of the metropolitan
society consider significant in allocating the colonial immigrant
to a place in the stratification system. These are the political
and economic status of the colonial workers, the perceived stage
in cultural evolution of the colonial workers, the physical
characteristics of the colonial workers and the source of information about the colonial workers. Using these characteristics,
Rex suggests that the colonial immigrant will be allocated a
place 'beneath the bottom of the stratification system' (1970,
p. 107), 'outside the normal stratification system' (1970,

p. 108). Consequently, the stratification system (1970, p. 108): 'becomes extended to take account of additional social positions marked by a degree of rightlessness not to be found amongst the incorporated workers'.

Hence, the colonial immigrant is allocated roles in the backward sectors of the productive system and is confined to certain disadvantaged sectors of the housing market. Unlike other immigrant minorities, colonial immigrants not only begin by being excluded from the stratification system of the metropolitan society, but are likely to be permanently excluded. Thus, according to Rex, assimilation is not a possibility open to the colonial immigrant. Elsewhere, Rex conceptualises this closure of the stratification system as resulting in the formation of an underclass (1973, p. 215; also pp. 156, 165 and with Tomlinson, 1979, p. 275). 'Immigrants share this underclass position with other contingents of the new poor, but the fact remains that the underclass itself remains a structurally distinct element from the established native working class.'

So, for both colonial and metropolitan societies, Rex has argued that there are certain structural features which encourage the development of 'race relations' situations. These are necessary, but not sufficient conditions. The additional sufficient conditions are identified as first, a certain kind of practice towards the immigrant minorities, and second, a certain kind of definition of the situation (1970, p. 116). Such a practice exists when (1970, pp. 116–17): 'all members of a group are regarded by virtue of possessing certain recognizable characteristics of that group, as being entitled to certain defined rights or as being assigned to certain defined roles'. Rex refers to this practice as 'ascriptive role allocation'. The 'certain kind of definition' is racism. So, Rex formally concludes that a 'race relations' situation can be said to exist when three conditions are met: (i) when two or more groups with distinct identities and characteristics are forced to live together by political and economic circumstances in a single society; (ii) when there is a high degree of conflict between these groups, such that hostile policies are pursued and that the group disadvantaged by these policies is identified by ascriptive criteria; (iii) when the practice of ascriptive role allocation is justified in terms of a deterministic theory (1970, p. 160).

FROM LOGICAL INCONSISTENCIES ...

A critique of this argument must begin by acknowledging that Rex has not produced a theory of 'race relations' in any systematic and strict sense. His stated aims are to determine whether 'race' is a concept which has theoretical validity in sociological analysis and the characteristics by which one can identify 'race relations' situations. Thus, 'Race Relations in

Sociology Theory' is a text which aims to map out the subject matter of a sociological sub-discipline, a sociology of 'race relations'. In so doing, Rex does advance certain theoretical propositions. For example, he theorises that 'race relations' in metropolitan societies are in part determined by 'race relations' in colonial societies; that 'race relations' in colonial societies are in part the result of conquest and the introduction of various forms of unfree labour; that there is not a deterministic, one-way relationship between racist belief and discrimination, etc. But other, arguably central, theoretical questions are not taken up, the most obvious being the question of the origin of racism. In sum, Rex's text does not intend to formulate a series of propositions which are intended to explain systematically why all the different 'race relations' situations take the form that they do.

It is, therefore, not valid to criticise the text for not producing a coherent theory, but we can consider the validity of his argument that there is a place for 'race' in sociological analysis and that, consequently, there is space for a sociology of 'race relations'. In this section, I want to consider the internal logical consistency and validity of Rex's argument while in subsequent sections I shall critically evaluate at a more general level the case for a sociology of 'race relations'. This is because a rejection of Rex's analysis does not necessarily mean that a case for such a sociology cannot be made, unless of course, one clearly establishes some general theoretical or epistemological objection.

First, I want to identify and explore a logical inconsistency in the way in which Rex analyses the two poles of the duality he suggests between colonial and metropolitan societies. Given his claim that different social structures give rise to different 'race relations' situations, then we must expect Rex to conclude that these two types of society will be associated with different situations. This, indeed, is his conclusion, but it is reached by analysing the two different societies by different criteria. Thus, it is conceivable that the different 'race relations' situations derive from different premises and analytical categories rather than from some different 'real' structural characteristic. The error is compounded by his unambiguous assertion that the novelty of his analysis of 'race relations' lies in beginning his analysis of social structures with the social relations of production.

In a general sense, there is no novelty in beginning an analysis with the social relations of production, that is, with 'the functions fulfilled by individuals and groups in the production process and in the control of the factors of production' (Godelier, 1972, p. 335). This is for the simple reason that all Marxist explanations must regard this as one moment in their starting point, and Marxist analysis has a history and tradition which extends backwards long before the publication of Rex's text in 1970. And if Rex were a little more conversant with that

form of analysis which he is so anxious to deride, he would
know that to talk of the relations of production necessarily
involves discussion of the forces of production because social
relations between those party to the process of production are
dependent upon there being a certain combination of land, tools,
human labour power, etc.

Indeed, because an appreciation of the relations of production
necessarily requires appreciation of the forces of production,
one finds in Rex's text an implicit recognition of this in his
discussions of plantation labour, domestic labour and compound
labour (1970, pp. 51-5) when he notes in each separate case
the way in which labour is brought into relation with land,
property and tools, etc. But he does not (or cannot) explicitly
theorise this irreducibility of the forces and relations of production, meaning that his analysis proceeds 'blindly', without
the conscious appreciation of its structure and direction. This
is manifest in his clearly articulated concern with unfree labour
and the social institutions of colonialism, i.e. with the social
relations of production, but without drawing any attention to
what is necessarily complementary, the forces of production.
For, as will be demonstrated in Chapter 5, we cannot appreciate, for example, the social relations between the class of
slave-owners and the class of slaves without comprehending
that the owners are simultaneously owners of land and tools
which they bring into contact with labour by means of the actual
ownership of human beings.

The significance of this criticism is 'diminished' by the fact
that when Rex moves from his structural analysis of colonial
societies to metropolitan societies, he completely dispenses with
any concern with even the social relations of production. This
may be expressed in other words by arguing that Rex exhibits
inconsistency in the form and application of his analytical categories. Thus, instead of inquiring as to the social relations of
production, he focuses upon the possibilities of assimilation of
the colonial immigrant into the stratification system. There is
mention of the sectors of production to which the colonial immigrant is confined, but this does not constitute an aspect of the
relations of production which characterise metropolitan societies.
In order to proceed in a way comparable with the analysis of
colonial societies, Rex should have inquired into the way in
which the labour power of the colonial immigrant is procured
and reproduced, an inquiry which would have led to a rather
disquieting conclusion, namely that the colonial immigrant sells
labour power for a wage in the same way as the 'native' worker.
That is to say, the colonial immigrant occupies a structurally
similar position in the social relations of production because
his/her labour power is combined with machinery, etc., in the
same way as the indigenous working class. Such a conclusion
would not support his argument that colonial immigrants constitute an 'underclass', but more about that shortly.

So far, I have come close to implying that Rex's analysis of colonial societies approximates a Marxist analysis but that this approximation fades when he turns his attention to metropolitan societies. It must be emphasised, however, that this approximation is only apparent and not real. This is because his one-sided emphasis upon the social relations of production derives from his focus, not on material production, but on 'race relations', i.e. upon the way in which one 'race' treats or behaves towards another 'race'. Rex's search is for some underlying structural correlate of this social relationship and in so doing, in common with sociology as a method of investigation (cf. Shaw, 1972, p. 43), he abstracts social relations from production by uncritically defining 'race relations' as the necessary starting point and without reference to their structural context. Thereafter, he accords such relations with an objective status as real relations, with the consequence that they come to warrant analytical status. This will be a focus of critical attention in the next section of this chapter.

The second major logical inconsistency in Rex's analysis appears in connection with his discussion of metropolitan societies. Having identified the necessary structural precondition for the emergence of 'race relations' situations in such societies, he then identifies the practice of ascriptive role allocation and the ideology of racism as the sufficient conditions. Thus, logically, we should be able to identify three empirically separate preconditions for the emergence of 'race relations' in metropolitan societies. In practice this is not possible, for one factor in fact 'doubles' as the necessary structural precondition and a sufficient condition. Let me illustrate the claim. The structural precondition is identified as the exclusion of the colonial immigrant from the 'normal' stratification system by means of being restricted or allocated to the backward sectors of the productive system and inferior sectors of the housing market. In other words, exclusion from the stratification system is achieved by means of ascriptive role allocation. Yet this is attributed with the status of a sufficient condition for the emergence of 'race relations'. So, Rex's claim that ascriptive role allocation and racism are themselves dependent upon a certain pre-existing structural characteristic cannot be accepted as applied to his analysis of metropolitan societies because, upon close inspection, the same social process (which might loosely be described as discrimination) is forced to play the role of both necessary and sufficient condition. The argument is therefore circular and so, ultimately, meaningless.

The third problem concerns Rex's inconsistent usage of the notions of class and stratification. The first major discussion of class refers to a usage 'in something like the Marxian or Weberian sense' (1970, p. 74) where class is defined in terms of differential access to control over the means of production (1970, p. 74) or in terms of differential life-chances (1970, p. 88). The comparability of these two usages (i.e. of Marx and Weber) is not an issue here, for they at least share the characteristic of referring to a position or location in an objective structure of relationships. But then we are subsequently informed (1970, p. 105; my emphasis) that: 'the stratification system of a society *arises from* the subjective picture or model of social relations which comes to men's minds when they think of their society as a whole'. In other words, stratification, of which class is a central aspect, is the outcome of individual consciousness. In the absence of any attempt to reconcile these two approaches to class, our minimal conclusion must be that they are obviously contradictory in so far as each constitutes a very different analytical starting point.

For future reference, let us note how this contradiction arises. As we have seen, Rex drops his interest in the social relations of production when considering the structural preconditions of 'race relations' in metropolitan societies, replacing it with the notion of assimilation. By conceptualising the colonial immigrant as having to enter the stratification system ('successful' entry being defined as assimilation) (1970, pp. 105-6), Rex creates a dichotomy between, on the one hand, a class structure in which the indigenous population occupies class positions by objective criteria and which therefore has a fixed reality and, on the other, colonial immigrants who, because they are defined as a 'race' which enters from outside, are conceived of as being allocated a position in that class structure on the basis of the subjective impressions of the indigenous population. In other words, Rex's analytical criteria for conceiving the structural position of colonial immigrants are quite distinct from those used to conceptualise the structural position of the indigenous population. Rex establishes this dichotomy by attributing (and thereby mirroring) an everyday 'recognition' of physical difference with analytical significance, with the consequence that colonial immigrants cannot have an objective structural position in the class structure, only one that is determined by the subjective impressions and beliefs of the indigenous population. In so doing, Rex implicitly accepts and legitimates the apparent existence of 'races' for in his theory the concepts used to analyse the class position of the colonial immigrant are different from those used to analyse the class position of the indigenous population, to which the immigrant is supposed to assimilate. In this way, Rex reflects theoretically the real process of racial discrimination because he wants to retain 'race' as an analytical category.

... TO A FALSE PROBLEMATIC

It might be argued that these analytical and logical inconsistencies in Rex's argument could be resolved, allowing the central thesis to stand. That thesis is that there is a class of social phenomena which can be labelled 'race relations' and which thereby warrant a sociological sub-discipline, the sociology of 'race relations'. However, mindful of this, I have in the preceding paragraph attempted to show that the inconsistencies derive directly from the attempt to establish just this thesis. In other words, the inconsistencies are less the result of failings in Rex's particular analysis and more the result of the more general project. Thus, the critique of the 'race relations' problematic that follows applies not solely to Rex's analysis, but, at a general level, to all those who write within the same framework.

This critique develops from a fundamental distinction made by Marx between phenomenal form and essential relations. By phenomenal form, Marx was referring to the way in which the phenomena of the external, social world are represented in human experience while the notion of essential relations was used to refer to the conditions of existence of the phenomenal forms. Phenomenal forms are, therefore, obvious and apparent to the human agent, such that they may even be regarded as natural and inevitable: they constitute the surface appearance of the way in which the world is organised. Indeed, this surface appearance may actually obscure the real, underlying relations, i.e. the essential relations which explain why the phenomenal form is the way that it appears (see Sayer, 1979, pp. 3-11, 41-2; also Geras, 1972, esp. pp.284-301; Larrain, 1979, pp. 55-63).

This distinction can be illustrated by reference to the wage form. In a capitalist society, a worker labours for an employer and is 'rewarded' by the payment of a wage which is determined in such a way (i.e. by number of hours worked or items produced) as to suggest that an equal and 'fair' exchange occurs. This, however, only obscures the essential relations because the conditions of existence of the wage contract are such that the worker produces for the employer a product whose value is greater than that of the total wage paid. In other words, the worker actually produces a surplus product (which gives rise to surplus value) and, indeed, must be 'forced' to do so in order to maintain the reproduction of capital. Thus, wage labour is not simply a purposive device, but is an essential feature of the capitalist mode of production which, if examined only at the level of phenomenal form, suggests an equal exchange, and so mystifies a process of exploitation (cf. Geras, 1972, pp. 298-301; Larrain, 1979, pp. 56-7).

It follows from this distinction that the concepts which we use to analyse the social world cannot be inductively derived in some direct and unmediated way from empirical observation of the world as it presents itself. To do so entails the possibility of developing an analysis which draws spurious conclusions from apparent relationships because those relationships express and so may hide an underlying or essential relation (see Sayer, 1979, pp. 114-5, 134-5). This is not to claim that phenomenal relations are not the starting point of analysis (for they are, only that the concepts that we articulate to analyse those

relations or forms take full account of both their historical
and essential conditions of existence (see Sayer, 1979, esp.
pp. 114-15, 134-5, 143-9). To fail to do so entails the possibility of constructing the visible, surface relation or structure as the totality of reality and/or analysing phenomenal
forms as if they are natural and inevitable (i.e. of creating a
fetish). Thus (Geras, 1972, pp. 286-7):

> It is because there exists, at the interior of capitalist
> society, a kind of internal rupture between the social rela-
> tions which obtain and the manner in which they are experi-
> enced, that the scientist of that society is confronted with
> the necessity of constructing reality against appearances.

Let me now explain the significance of this apparent detour
into rather abstract matters. Put very simply, the implication
of the previous paragraphs is that we must not unquestioningly
incorporate in a scientific analysis the categories of description
and analysis used in everyday discourse because, in so far as
that discourse is uncritical and confines itself to the direct
experience and appearance of the social world, then there is
the possibility of creating a false and misleading explanation.
Now, it is accepted that those to whom reference has been
made to establish this point have been specifically concerned
with the origin of Marx's economic categories or concepts, but
there is no reason why the same point does not apply to the
development of those categories pertinent to an analysis of
political or ideological relations (cf. Corrigan, 1980; Corrigan
and Sayer, 1981). Indeed, it is because Marx (and Marxist
theory, as opposed to sociology) was emphatic that it is not
possible to explain adequately any aspect of the phenomenal
appearance of the social world by abstracting production relations from political or ideological relations that the distinction
between appearances and essential relations must be appreci-
ated before generating categories or concepts relevant to any
of these relations.
    So, if we analyse social phenomena using concepts derived
solely and exclusively from the world of appearances, one is
open to the danger of reifying the phenomenal forms, that is,
analysing them as if they are real, active subjects. The task
should be to make the phenomenal categories of 'race' and 'race
relations' the object of a critique. That is to say, we must not
use these categories analytically, but rather we should ask
how and why they came to be constructed to give apparent
sense to the phenomenal world. Let me illustrate the point. As
was acknowledged in Chapter 1, there exists a wide range of
physical or phenotypical variation within the species homo
sapiens. This physical variation is real: some people do have
red hair, others have black skin, while yet others are of short
stature. Certain facets of physical variation have been attributed with particular significance and meaning which, once

having been systematised scientifically in the nineteenth century, gave final legitimation to the belief that the human species consists of a number of distinct 'races', each separately endowed with certain cultural qualities and capacities. And it is because this physical variation is real and apparent that 'races' can appear to exist. This idea of 'race', grounded in the world of appearances, is, in contemporary Britain and other capitalist formations, consistently reproduced in everyday discourse. It is part of common sense. Yet it is also false, in the sense that there is no scientific basis for categorising homo sapiens into discrete 'races'.

The analytical problem arises from the continued articulation and reproduction of the idea of 'race' in everyday discourse. Rex, in common with all those who analyse and debate within their own construction of 'race relations' as an object of study, attempts to solve this problem by developing and utilising 'race' as a social category. So, because people believe that there are 'races', then social relations between groups so categorised become described as 'race relations'. Conversely, any everyday, common sense description of a situation as one of 'race relations' implicitly asserts the existence of 'races'. This is then objectified as an area of study.

This conceptual transition from the social category of 'race' to 'race relations' is one mechanism by which 'race' is given an objective status as an active subject, i.e. reified. This happens because the very term 'race relations' can only mean that 'races' have social relations, one with another. So, for relations to occur, 'races' must exist. Indeed, they 'exist' in the sense that human agents believe them to exist, but uncritically to reproduce and accord analytical status to those beliefs is nevertheless to legitimate that process by giving it 'scientific' status. By creating a sociology of 'race relations', one is creating a form of analysis which simply reflects back the phenomenal, everyday world, and, in so doing, the world of appearances is legitimated. Thereby, the sociology of 'race relations' becomes a moment in the reproduction of the appearance of the social world (and, hence, a moment in ideological domination).

In order to demonstrate this, I shall refer to two different texts, the first of which can be classified as a mainstream sociological work, while the second may be described as a radical sociological text, inspired by a feminist perspective. These two texts are purposively chosen to show that the reification of 'race' occurs at all levels of sociological analysis. Consider the following claim (Beteille, 1977, p. 101):

In a racially stratified society the opportunities available to members of disfavoured races are severely restricted. Where one works, what one earns, where one lives, how one brings up one's children - all these appear to be determined by the race into which one is born.

The claim that human agents are born into a 'race' is a claim
that attributes 'race' with the qualities of a biological universal.
This claim is subsequently explicitly confirmed when the author
writes: 'races exist, like other biological taxa, as a part of
nature' (1977, p. 102). There then follows a discussion of the
distinction between genotype and phenotype, from which it
is concluded that 'there is so much overlap between adjacent
populations that the division of a society into its constituent
races is very often a purely arbitrary matter' (1977, p. 104).
This clearly contradicts the previous claim that 'races' have
a biological and universal existence and is subsequently contradicted by his constant reference to the 'Black and White
races' without qualification or explanation. It is not simply that
this analysis has no logical consistency. It also constructs
'race' as an active subject by claiming that 'race' determines
what a human agent earns, etc. Reification is similarly evident
in the following claim (Sharpe, 1976, p. 255): 'Their [i.e.
West Indian parents'] aspirations extend to boys and girls
alike, but in reality both face a similar job selection to that
of the white working class; although their opportunities are
reduced by the interwoven effects of race.' In this formulation,
'race' is conceived as an active agent or subject which in itself
affects the job choice available to children born of West Indian
parents. It is, however, not 'race' which affects job choice for
there is not such a real phenomenon: what restricts job choice
(as well as level of earnings, the type and quality of housing,
etc.) is a decision by an employer not to employ black teenagers on the basis of a belief about the supposed social correlates of a certain complex of physical attributes. That belief
warrants analysis as an instance of racism (see Chapter 4).

Lest it be thought that the work of Rex is for some reason
free from such reification, let us consider his most recent
research with Tomlinson (1979). We find them reporting that
they asked their respondents 'how they thought the races
got on with each other in Birmingham' (1979, p. 85) from which
they attempt to draw conclusions about the degree of 'hostility
between the races' (1979, p. 86). This is a classic instance
whereby the reification of 'race' is directly fed into the very
content of an interview schedule (confirming the world of
appearances), the responses to which necessarily reproduce
the reification. Thereafter, the data is analysed in a manner
consistent with the original question so as to draw conclusions
about the degree of hostility expressed in relations between
the 'races'. There is here a clear process of circular reproduction of categories drawn from the world of appearances which
are 'scientifically' legitimated by practitioners of the sociology
of 'race relations'. Having derived the analytical categories
unquestioningly from the everyday world, these are directly
fed back in the form of questions, the terms of which confirm
the everyday categories, from which data is derived and analysed using these same reified categories. The final result is a

text which, by reproducing an account of the categories and
the way in which they structured the fieldwork (i.e. the
'return' to the world of appearances), comes to constitute yet
another moment in the process of legitimating the world of
appearances by reflecting back on it categories which the
sociologist originally derived directly and unquestioningly from
it (see Figure 2.1).

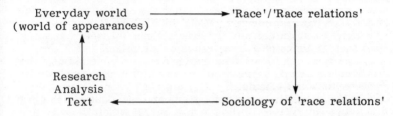

Figure 2.1　The reproduction of 'race'

My argument is not simply that the sociology of 'race relations'
reifies 'race'. It is also that it must necessarily result in misleading and ultimately false conclusions. In this connection,
I want to consider here Rex's project of classifying types of
'race relations' situation, a project which is premised on the
claim that certain structural circumstances ensure that group
conflicts are expressed in terms of 'race relations'. This has
been criticised and justifiably so, because it tends to generate
unproductive controversies about whether a particular circum-
stance meets all the criteria established to identify a 'race
relations' situation (Banton, 1977a, pp. 166-8). My concern is
somewhat different. To claim that a particular set of social
relations at a particular point in historical time are best understood as 'relations between races' is to suggest not only that
that conjuncture is predominantly (even solely?) structured
by 'race' but also that there are types of situation/conjuncture
which are not so structured but which must be structured by
some other factor. Both raise major analytical problems.

The first assumes, but does not attempt to demonstrate, that
the predominant active element in the conjuncture is a categorisation by reference to physical variation, and in so doing
must lead to monocausal explanation. In other words, by labelling a situation as one of 'race relations', one is implicitly
denying that any other force can have an equal or predominant
effect. To anticipate a later argument, this approach means
that if one labels the participants in a process as 'races',
and their interaction as 'race relations', then one is denying
either that they occupy a class position or that their class
position is of significance to the situation and process. Hence,
referring back, we find Rex conceptualising the entry of
colonial immigrants into a stratification system in terms of their
categorisation as a 'race'. Rex thereby rules out, by the very

categories employed, any possibility of understanding the 'colonial immigrant' as occupying a class position in the same manner as the 'indigenous' population.

The second analytical problem is simply expressed. If the analysis designates the existence of 'race relations' situations, then, by implication, there must be other 'types' of situation which the author is therefore obliged to list. In the absence of their being designated at the outset (i.e. in the absence of the conditions of existence of other types of situation being stated) we have no adequate basis upon which to analyse any situation, even though we have the criteria by which to determine the existence of a 'race relations' situation.

In practice, this obsessive search for, and analysis of, 'race relations' situations leads to an empirical and analytical study of the extent and effects of racial discrimination. In Rex's case, this is not the result of chance or some personal interest, but is theoretically grounded in the way in which he sets up the criteria that identify a 'race relations' situation. These include the presence of the ideology of racism and a process of ascriptive role allocation whereby one group restricts another group's access to goods, facilities and resources. Now it is not being denied that study of this process of 'ascriptive role allocation' is important: to be excluded from certain types of occupation and categories of housing must clearly have a substantial effect upon material, social and emotional circumstances. The problem lies in assuming that these circumstances are completely determined by (or the result of) racial discrimination (see Phizacklea and Miles, 1980, pp. 1-4). This error was made in Rex's earliest study (with Moore, 1967), which concentrated upon the position of 'immigrants' in the British housing market. This analysis has been subsequently and justifiably criticised for making unwarranted and unsupported assertions about the extent and nature of racial discrimination in the housing market and for ignoring the analytical importance of the fact that at least some of those 'immigrants' came to Britain with the intention of only a short-term stay, wishing to earn only sufficient money to improve their economic and social circumstances in the country and town or village of origin. Thus, the fact that these 'immigrants' were buying short-lease property which was in (relatively speaking) poor physical condition in Birmingham and Bradford (and no doubt elsewhere) was not only (or not at all) due to their having been excluded from access to all other forms of housing, but also because the purchase of such property was consistent with their 'migrant ideology' (e.g. Dahya, 1974).

This simple, even simplistic, error has been acknowledged and has not been repeated in the same way in Rex's most recent work (with Tomlinson, 1979, pp. 21, 23) but is reproduced at a different level in a different form. This returns us to the last point made in the previous section concerning the way in which Rex analyses the structural position of immigrants in what he conceives of as metropolitan societies. This most recent work poses as its primary question 'what does it mean for an outsider to gain admission to this working class?', from which Rex and Tomlinson derive the intention of demonstrating 'how, in relation to any of the major indicators of class membership, the experience of the average member of an ethnic minority is different from that of the average native-born worker' (1979, pp. 8, 11). Consequently, the empirical project is defined as measuring the 'degree of assimilation or integration of immigrants' (1979, p. 18), and the conclusion that they reach is that (1979, p. 276): 'the immigrant situation ... [is] characterized by a different kind of position in the labour market, a different housing situation, and a different form of schooling'. The predominant emphasis in the analysis is upon the experience of discrimination and racism, with the authors explicitly accepting the notion of (1979, p. 287): 'a cumulative principle whereby the existence of racist beliefs, once they are established, leads to discrimination, and this discrimination produces conditions which further justify the beliefs'. Hence, the conclusion of this 1979 text is to confirm both the form and content of a 'hypothesis' advanced almost ten years previously (1970, p. 110): 'What we are saying is that, where colour discrimination is consistent with the metropolitan culture and value system, it is likely to operate as a means of classifying the colonial immigrant, and placing him in a state of rightlessness outside the stratification order.'

The error has both theoretical and empirical dimensions which will be pursued more thoroughly in Chapter 7. Here I want to do no more than point out that, by analysing the structural position of the 'colonial immigrant' primarily in terms of racism and discrimination, Rex necessarily rules out the possibility of analysing and finding important economic, political and ideological continuities in the position of the 'colonial immigrant' and the 'indigenous' working class. Racism and racial discrimination do not occur in a vacuum, but have their place in a certain sort of society in certain sorts of circumstances. These phenomena cannot be conceived of as the prime determinants of the situation and experience of 'colonial immigrants' without first developing an analytical framework which permits an analysis of that context. Such an analysis allows us to challenge the one-dimensional fetish of the category 'colonial immigrant' who, within the terms of the 'race relations' problematic, is primarily understood as the object of racism and discrimination (and thereby conceived of as standing outside the stratification system). I shall later argue that by entering a 'metropolitan society', the migrant necessarily enters and takes up a position within a set of forces and relations of production. This essential fact is obscured by undue and primary emphasis upon the apparent primacy of racism and discrimination. An analysis which penetrates beyond or below these appearances will conceive the migrant, not solely as a migrant and the object

of political and ideological reaction, but, in the empirical
instance of contemporary Britain, usually also a wage labourer,
an active subject, occupying a class position in a capitalist
mode of production (see also Phizacklea and Miles, 1980, chs 1
and 9).

THE PROBLEMATIC REPRODUCED

As previously indicated, Rex is not the sole proponent of the
'race relations' problematic. Other writers operate within and
reproduce it, and although the specific direction and focus of
their work may differ from that of Rex, the general arguments
marshalled above apply equally to them. For example, Van den
Berghe argues that 'race relations' are an appropriate field
of study and should be analysed in terms of two ideal types.
He then proceeds to distinguish two types of society which
are characterised, respectively, by paternalistic and competitive 'race relations'. He claims that paternalistic 'race relations'
occur in complex pre-industrial societies where the politically
dominant group is in a minority, where roles are sharply
defined on 'racial lines' and where there is 'maximal social
distance'. Competitive 'race relations' occur, he argues, in
industrialised societies where the politically dominant group
is a majority or large minority, where class differences are more
salient relative to 'race' and where 'race' is no longer a major
criterion for job allocation (1978, pp. 29-30). This distinction
is drawn despite the fact that Van den Berghe claims that 'race
acquires meaning only through its social definition in a given
society', that 'the study of race has little claim for an autonomous theoretical status' and that 'race can be treated as a
special case of invidious status differentiation or a special
criterion of stratification' (1978, pp. 21-2). Thus, although
he denies that 'race' has any biological validity or reality, he
is not only prepared to use the concept (along with 'race
relations') analytically (presumably because people behave as
if 'race' has a biological reality), but he utilises it as an active
force in itself, as, for example, when he claims (1978, p. 29):
'In a complex industrial economy ... race is no longer workable
as the paramount criterion for job selection.' Elsewhere in the
same text, he writes (1978, p. 127): 'In the other three societies race continued to be a socially significant aspect of social
stratification and, consequently, there was a clear transition
from a paternalistic to a comparative system of race relations.'
   By giving 'race' and 'race relations' analytical status, he
prepares the ground for according them the same analytical
role, as when he writes (1978, p. 22): 'As a special instance of
stratification, race shares many characteristics with ethnicity
and class.' Thus, class and 'race' are conceived of as sociological categories of equal explanatory significance which can
substitute for one another in particular instances, as when he

suggests that pre-industrial societies (the equivalent of Rex's
'composite colonial societies') are not primarily structured in
terms of class (1978, pp. 27-9). There are important similarities
with the work of Cox (1970), who also conceives of class and
'race' as of equal explanatory significance (for a critique, see
Miles, 1980). In the light of that critique, let me add briefly
that, by virtue of being pre-industrial, such societies are not
thereby classless societies. The colonial bourgeoisie is no less
a bourgeoisie for restricting its 'membership' to those possessing a particular set of phenotypical features while those enslaved are no less a class because only individuals possessing a
different set of phenotypical characteristics are confined to
such a position relative to the forces of production. Van den
Berghe, like Rex, thereby confuses the phenomenal form in
which economic and political conflict appears with the underlying structural characteristics of these social formations.

As another example of an analysis which operates within the
'race relations' framework, I want to consider the more recent
work of Banton (1977a, 1977b, 1979, 1980). This has special
interest in so far as Banton's analysis develops against the
background of the recognition of the importance of studying
the 'work of scholars who did not stand apart from their
subject matter but shared understandings about the nature of
race with the people whom they were studying' (1977a, p. 3).
He defines his task as that of studying the way in which the
idea of 'race' has interacted with the growth of sociological
analysis (1977a, p. 12). His analysis is, therefore, historical;
being concerned to chart the different ways in which 'race'
has been defined and given analytical status. Yet, he himself
fails to make the complete break with the 'race relations'
problematic, despite his assertion that 'race relations' have
nothing to distinguish them from other forms of social relations
(1977a, p. 162). He argues that 'race relations' nevertheless
constitute a special area of academic inquiry in so far as
scholars have established, by their mental labour, a certain
tradition of inquiry, asking certain questions and criticising
the work of others who share the same intellectual heritage
(1977a, p. 166). In my terms, this heritage is the 'race relations' problematic and in asserting the latter, Banton clearly
signals his unwillingness or inability to break completely with
this problematic, despite the fact that he has begun to expose
its inner contradictions. This point stands despite Banton's
more recent acknowledgment of the weaknesses of defining
'race relations' as a field of study by reference to an intellectual tradition because he is still searching for a definition of
this field of study (1979, p. 133).

Yet, because Banton comes close to articulating a critique of
this problematic (because he is aware of both the historical
genesis of what he describes as the idea of 'race' and of the
error that is perpetrated by attempting to distinguish 'races'
as real, biologically defined groups), the contradictions

entailed in nevertheless maintaining an analysis which accepts and gives validity to the objective existence of 'race relations' are nowhere more clear. In other words, having begun to expose the contradictions, yet being unwilling or unable to analyse them through to their logical conclusion, Banton reproduces them in utmost clarity. Of those texts considered in this chapter, these by Banton are therefore the most worthy of close attention. I have only the space for a brief critique to illustrate my claims.

My claim is that although Banton seems to want to break with the 'race relations' problematic, he does not, in fact, do so. Hence, we find him articulating the notion that 'races' are real groups in themselves (1977a, p. 154): 'Races could become autonomous groupings in society only when the previously sub-ordinated groups come to accept racial designations as they accept national ones and the resumption of equality was overthrown.' He infers that a society may be composed of several 'races' when he refers to 'multi-racial societies' (e.g. 1977a, p. 165). He refers to 'race' as a category to be equated with other sociological categories (1977a, p. 8): 'Examination of the history of many minorities shows that it is impossible to separate the influence of race, ethnicity, class, religion, and so on, as if these were factors in an algebraic equation.' Elsewhere, he makes a similar claim ('Because race, class, nation, and other modes of differentiation are so much intertwined in particular communities ...'), from which he concludes that the study of 'race relations' must be historical in nature, but this is then immediately followed by this statement (1977a, p. 164): 'The more the student is led into the examination of particular situations and sequences, the more difficult it is to conceive of race relations as a distinct field of study.' Yet, just two pages further on, we are told that 'race relations' is a 'special area for academic study'!

The contradiction is made evident in crystal-clear fashion in the following claim (1977a, p. 162): 'All the features of race relations, except their label, can be found in some other class of social relations. This may be expressed briefly by stating that inter-racial relations are not different in kind from intra-racial relations.' Let me explain the point. The first sentence of this assertion can be equally well expressed by saying that the only reality that 'race relations' have is as a category of social relations which are grounded in the idea that 'races' really exist. In other words, because people in certain situations in certain societies believe 'races' to exist, the social relations between those groups so designated come to be labelled by them as 'race relations'. But, because this is only a social construction, an apparent reality, then I would conclude, logically, that the categories of 'race' and 'race relations' can have no explanatory or descriptive value (although it would be necessary to refer to these notions in so far as they become the subject of analysis, such reference being made in inverted commas to signal the reproduction of an element of common sense, a phenomenal form). Banton seems elsewhere to have come very close to saying just this (e.g. 1979, p. 130), yet he seems to want to maintain the fiction of 'race relations' as an area of study. Hence, in the very process of trying to deny the existence of 'race relations' as an independent, real phenomenon, he ends up asserting the exact opposite when he claims, trying to prove the former assertion, that relations within 'races' are no different from relations between 'races'. If it is possible for those designated as a 'race' to have social relations, one with another, then 'races' are given a conceptual reality. Again, the real world of appearances is reproduced analytically, serving to legitimate and confirm it.

The contradiction is repeated and intensified by Banton's search for a theory of racial and ethnic relations which (1977a, p. 1): 'must account for the distinctiveness of its subject matter. It must explain in what ways relations between two people of different race (or ethnicity) are distinguished from relations between two peoples of the same race.' Here we find Banton implying at the very outset that 'race' is some quality inherent within persons which can set them apart. The category of 'race relations' is accorded analytical status when 'race relations' are later described as having different patterns (1977b, p. 28) while 'race' is again accorded with an objective status when it is claimed that (1977b, p. 32): 'The significance of race is that it can be used to draw a very hard boundary and it is usually difficult for a person of inappropriate characteristics either to join or leave a racial category.' Moreover, it is difficult to see how Banton's search for a number of different 'models of racial and ethnic relations' (1977b, pp. 44-62) is in any way different from Rex's search for a typology of 'race relations' situations. In both instances, the self-defined task is to generalise across different historical periods and modes of production in order to establish an ahistorical classification of types of situation where 'races' are relating one with another. So, despite Banton's explicit rejection of Rex's project of designating situations where social relations are relations between 'races' (1977a, pp. 166-8), he sets himself a very similar aim in his search for a general theory of what have become designated as 'racial and ethnic relations'.

A final illustration of my argument can be derived from a more recent contribution. He explicitly states a distinction which is fundamental to the argument of this text and with which I can completely agree (1979, p. 130):

People do not perceive racial differences. They perceive phenotypical differences of colour, hair form, underlying bone structure and so on. Phenotypical differences are a first order abstraction, race is a second order abstraction....It just so happens that Western European culture in a particular phase of its history was ordered pheno-

typical variations in what have been known as 'racial' classifications. I should have kept the first and second order
abstractions separate in order to introduce a discussion of
racial classification as something culture-bound and historically bound.

Consistent with this recognition, he states that (1979, p. 134)
'the social scientist cannot safely take his concepts from the
popular consciousness', but later states that the social scientist
is forced to do so (1979, p. 136): 'Because of its use in popular
speech the word 'race' seems likely to remain prominent as a
folk concept....It is a hopeless task to try to reserve for them
technical meanings within social science.' In similar vein, he
writes (1979, p. 137): 'Just as there is a folk concept of race,
so there is a folk concept of race relations, but that need not
prevent the latter expression being used as a name for a field
of study.' The objection to this is stated by Banton himself by
way of analogy (1979, pp. 135-6): 'I do not think it irrelevant
to remark that medical science would not have made the progress it has, had doctors accepted the patient's conception of
his complaint as a definition of the disorder from which he was
suffering.' In other words, because the world is not always as
it appears, or even as it is constructed to appear, we cannot
successfully analyse it as it appears, using concepts derived
from common sense (i.e. folk concepts). It is necessary to
generate first and second order abstractions, but not to necessarily refine common sense categories: if critical analysis shows
them to be misleading, not to have a real object, then we must
reject them (and the problematic from which they derive), and
then ask why and how it is that they have been generated and
reproduced.

CONCLUSION

In sum, I recognise that people do conceive of themselves and
others as belonging to 'races' and do describe certain sorts of
situation and relations as being 'race relations', but I am also
arguing that these categories of everyday life cannot automatically be taken up and employed analytically by an inquiry
which aspires to objective or scientific status. The first task
is to put these categories to the test of critical analysis, asking
the question whether they refer to real phenomena and, if not,
inquiring as to the conditions which account for both their
existence and their reproduction. Thus, because 'race' has no
biological reality (but is a social construction), we must ask
the following interrelated questions:
1 How, and for what reasons, was the category of 'race' generated and reproduced?
2 How, and for what reasons, is the category reproduced in
contemporary social formations? In other words, why is it that

certain social relations are conceived as relations between 'races'?

3 Why does sociological analysis give analytical status to 'race relations'? In other words, what are the conditions of existence of the 'race relations' problematic?

An answer to these questions must be sought in historical analysis (and in this respect, Banton's work is of considerable importance), but that analysis must not only distance itself from common sense categories, but must also have the means to generate its own analytical categories. I want to suggest that only with an analysis based on the principles and procedures of historical materialism is it possible to break completely with the 'race relations' problematic. Without doing so, and despite recognising that 'race' has no objective reality, the idea of 'race' and its derivatives (e.g. the idea of 'race relations') will inevitably retain a certain analytical role. 'Race' will become thereby an analytical fetish, a supposed independent and real factor which has its own supposed 'real' effects. In reality, 'race' (and relations between 'races') does not do anything (or have any consequences). Both are no more than ideas; although let it be admitted that they are ideas which seem to have an apparent, everyday foundation in reality (i.e. in the existence of human phenotypical variation). But, as ideas, they must be generated and reproduced by real human beings in certain real conditions and circumstances with certain aims and with certain consequences. It is these real human beings and these real conditions and circumstances that should be the focus of our attention. Thus we may ask not only under what circumstances the three Race Relations Acts (of 1965, 1968 and 1976) were passed through parliament, but also why legislation was given such an ideological focus: this is of central significance because the fact of 'race relations' law apparently legitimates the existence of 'races' and their supposed mutual relations (cf. Corrigan and Sayer, 1981).

The analytical task is, therefore, neither to try to locate a place for a concept of 'race' in some theory nor to try to develop a theory of 'race relations' but to identify the conditions for the generation and reproduction of the idea of 'race', which is to explain why certain sorts of situation and relations appear (i.e. are socially constructed) as 'race relations'. In Part II of this text, I shall begin to show how this might be attempted in the historical instance of Britain. In the next chapter I shall go on to examine critically a parallel or alternative problematic, that of 'ethnic relations', which has been developed partly as a response to some of the limitations identified above.

3 'ETHNIC RELATIONS': THE 'DISCOVERY' OF CULTURE

The related concepts of 'ethnic group' and 'ethnicity' have achieved academic and political prominence only in the past decade. Indeed, belonging to an ethnic group (and hence the sense of ethnicity) has been proposed as major new social phenomena of the 1970s, occupying a place on world stage alongside class and nation. For example, Glazer and Moynihan do not deny that class and nation are central concepts to be used to analyse contemporary societies (1975, p. 18): 'but it is also true that we must add ethnicity as a major new focus for the mobilization of interests, troublesome both to those who wish to emphasize the primacy of class, and those who wish to emphasize the primacy of nation'. In explaining the emergence of this new phenomenon, others have identified what they believe to be 'major macro-social trends in the world today' such as a tendency to more inclusive identities, a decline in authority and a shift in ideology (Bell, 1975, pp. 142-52). For these writers, some momentous change has been happening in the social world in recent years.

The ripples of these changes seem to have reached even the insular shores of Britain. Within the political arena, there is now talk about identifying the special needs of 'ethnic minorities' in, for example, education, social services and housing, etc. Thus, within the education system, there is pressure to ensure that teachers and administrators are aware of the distinct language and culture of 'ethnic minorities' and of the implications for teaching in schools. Hence, in some areas, there has been consideration of the implications for religious instruction and for co-educational schooling given that Muslim children now attend British schools. At another level, one can refer to the change to the law concerning the compulsory wearing of crash helmets by riders of motor cycles to take account of the religiously required practice amongst Sikhs of wearing a turban at all times. In the context of these concerns, it is therefore not surprising that political parties have begun to consider the nature, size and possible impact of the 'ethnic minority' vote, and what they might do to ensure that they can win it. It would seem that sociologists of the British scene must now add to their conceptual apparatus these 'troublesome' concepts of 'ethnic group' and 'ethnicity'. And, indeed, some of them have done so. I want to critically evaluate their efforts.

A MULTIPLICITY OF MEANINGS

Before proceeding with this critique, it is necessary to docu-
ment the fact that the concept of ethnic group has its origin
in anthropological literature and has undergone a transformation of meanings, particularly since anthropologists and sociologists have put the concept to work in 'industrial' and 'urban'
contexts (e.g. Cohen, 1974). The introduction of the anthropological 'tradition' into analysis of 'industrial/urban' societies
parallels the migration of labour from non-capitalist modes of
production and so reproduces an anthropological concern with
documenting cultural differences within capitalist societies.
   So, what is an ethnic group? By reference to what criteria
do we identify such a group from others? The following criteria
are mentioned in the literature:
1 Cultural difference: an ethnic group is identifiable by reference to its distinct culture and corresponding way of life, the
distinctiveness being in contrast to other groups with which it
shares some relationship in the same society (e.g. Lyon, 1972,
1973).
2 Interests: an ethnic group is recognised in terms of its having a distinct set of interests and needs which require collective
organisation in order that they be pursued or defended (e.g.
Glazer and Moynihan, 1975).
3 Personal identification: an ethnic group consists of those
persons who identify with a way of life which is shared with
others (e.g. Barth, 1969).
4 Affectivity: an ethnic group consists of those persons who
feel an affective attachment to a way of life which is shared
with others (e.g. Epstein, 1978, pp. 104-6).
   These different meanings are not mutually exclusive. They
have been articulated sequentially, one being a response to
some identified inadequacy in a previous definition. Thus,
definition 3 arises out of Barth's critique (1969, pp. 13-15) of
studies which defined an ethnic group in terms of cultural
difference (definition 1). He concluded that an ethnic group
be defined as self-identified groups and by reference to the
maintenance of difference (i.e. the boundary of difference)
rather than the content of the difference. Similarly, Epstein
has criticised the analysis of Glazer and Moynihan (1975),
who defined ethnic groups as interest groups (definition 2),
claiming that it underemphasises the fact that an ethnic group
regulates informal social relationships by virtue of the members'
affective attachment to the group (1978, p. 104). Epstein builds
on the work of Barth to produce definition 4.
   I do not wish to pursue the implications of these different
definitions. I simply note them. This is because the differences
are matters of emphasis and because the various authors nevertheless share a concept, a similar set of interests and therefore
a problematic. It is the shared interests and perspective with
which I am concerned, and in the context of my preceding

critique of the 'race relations' problematic. I want to argue
that the attempt to differentiate ethnic groups from other
groups gives rise to a number of logical contradictions, with
the result that the concept cannot usefully be used for descriptive or analytical purposes. Moreover, all these definitions
abstract either the fact of cultural difference or the process
of the maintenance of social/affective difference from its historical and material context: thus, ethnic groups are defined
without reference to or in opposition to the class structure
of the social formation in which the identified persons live.
Finally, I shall suggest that the attempt to advance some of
these definitions has been partly motivated by an awareness
of the analytical limitations of the sociology of 'race relations'.
The identification of these limitations is significant, but the
implications have not been fully understood and developed,
with the result that 'ethnic relations' studies tend either to
replicate (or stand for) 'race relations' studies or to lead to a
simplistic cataloguing of cultural difference.

RACIAL CATEGORY OR ETHNIC GROUP?

The language of ethnic group and ethnic relations suggests
the existence of an area of inquiry which is distinct from
'race relations' research. However, many of those who contribute to these areas do so in such a way as to suggest
some overlap or even identify between the two. Thus, we have
both Banton (1977b) and Gordon (1975) proposing a theory of
'racial and ethnic relations'. Banton's work proceeds on the
basis of an explicitly defended proposition that racial and
ethnic groups are analytically distinguishable and separate
sorts of collectivities (1977a, pp. 148–9) but Gordon writes
as if the two are synonymous (1975, p. 104): 'Many of most
ethnic groups within a given society or state have ancestral
ties of language, religion, race, or national origins with some
other sovereign state.'
   That there might be ethnic relations and 'race relations'
implies the existence of two different types of group, ethnic
groups and 'race' groups. Some writers have attempted to
express such a distinction analytically. Lyon, for example, suggests a distinction between an ethnic group and what he calls
a racial category using two criteria: (i) the source of categorisation (i.e. whether the group is self- or other-defined);
(ii) the character of the criteria employed in the categorisation.
Thus, a racial category is the consequence of categorisation
by an outside group using physical criteria while an ethnic
group is the consequence of self-categorisation using the
criteria of culture and ancestral descent (see Figures 3.1 and
3.2). The process of categorisation establishes a social boundary between the group categorised and all others: correspondingly, a racial boundary is defined and maintained from without

while an ethnic boundary is self-defined and self-maintained
by the members of the group.

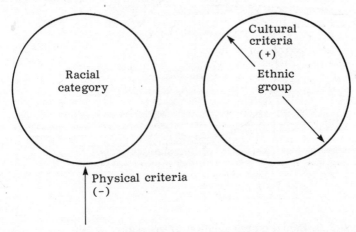

Figure 3.1 Racial category   Figure 3.2 Ethnic group

Lyon builds into his definition of ethnic group, the characteristic of collective organisation. He claims that, by definition,
an ethnic group must be characterised by collective aspiration
by virtue of its members' identification with the distinctive
culture. A racial category, by way of contrast, must lack this
characteristic because it is other-defined: it therefore does
not even warrant description as a group because there cannot
be a positive, collective self-identification. In other words,
all that binds the persons together is the other-identification
in terms of supposedly distinct physical criteria, e.g. skin
colour (Lyon, 1972, pp. 257-8).

The concept of ethnic group is further developed when Lyon
argues that it has the following three characteristics: (i) a
historic culture and ancestry; (ii) a distinctive pattern of interaction; (iii) a corporate organisation on the basis of beliefs and
values which are sufficiently coherent to permit the collective
pursuit of common goals. Additionally, he suggests that an
ethnic group may also be the object of categorisation by others
using physical criteria. In other words, an ethnic group may
also be a racial category (Figure 3.3). But the alternative possibility is specifically denied on the grounds that a racial category is no more than a residual category, the consequence of
categorisation by an out-group. Because it does not have a
historic culture which supports a distinctive pattern of social
interaction and corporate organisation, then it lacks the means
to resist the categorisation of the out-group. An ethnic group,
by virtue of these characteristics has a social basis for asserting its own identity against that imposed from outside (1972,

pp. 257-8).

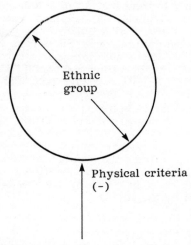

Figure 3.3 Racial categorisation of an ethnic group

   In applying this distinction to the example of Britain, Lyon
argues that West Indians constitute a racial category. He
acknowledges that West Indians share a number of cultural
characteristics, but argues that they are the consequence
of slavery and colonialism. The negative connotations of this
past means that such characteristics cannot serve as an alternative focus of identification in reaction to their racial categorisation within Britain (1972, p. 260). The colonial structure
of the West Indian islands entails a close correlation between
phenotypical variation and class position: the ruling class was
white and the rural peasantry and nascent working class was
black, between which was a group of administrators and bureau-
cratic officials who were lighter skinned than the latter. Hence,
economic and social advancement required a 'whitening' of skin
colour and this could only be achieved through a subsequent
generation after marrying a person with a lighter skin colour.
To the extent that West Indians aspire to 'whitening', they
accept the definitions of the dominant class and must negatively
evaluate their own physical appearance. West Indians therefore
arrive in Britain with the experience of racial exclusion, and,
as a racial category, they lack any cultural basis for an alternative positive identity. They therefore lack any means to
challenge their economically and politically subordinate status
(1972, pp. 259-62; 1973, pp. 334-8).
   By contrast, the migrants from India and Pakistan constitute
a number of different ethnic groups. Lyon identifies three main
'Asian' groups in Britain: West Pakistanis (now more likely to
be called Bangladeshis since the coming into existence of the
separate state of Bangladesh), Indian Gujaratis and Indian

Punjabis (1973, p. 345). The West Pakistanis identify and interrelate according to their district of origin, permitting distinctions between Mirpuris, Cambellpuris, Pathans and Kashmiris (1973, p. 346). Indian Gujaratis share a common language and regional culture, while Sikhs from the Indian Punjab constitute a religious and linguistic collectivity. Both groups are culturally homogeneous and contain within them a sub-caste which has a tradition of migration. This has, in turn, ensured a basis for and tradition of collective organisation (1972-3, pp. 6-7). This collective tradition is not yet reflected in effective national organisation, but is limited to single or small groups of towns (1973, p. 347). Nevertheless, for all of these groups, there is a historic culture and pattern of social interaction which constitutes the basis of positive identification with the group. Having such an identification, members of these various 'Asian' ethnic groups are able to 'resist' the 'race' label applied by the British.

THE CONCEPT OF BOUNDARY

Lyon's distinction between a racial category and an ethnic group owes much to the work of Barth, who defines ethnic groups as 'categories of ascription and identification by the actors themselves' (1969, p. 10). Consequently, he is concerned with the social processes by which ethnic groups identify themselves and maintain a difference from other groups. He grasps this process with the concept of boundary maintenance. An ethnic group is therefore to be defined not by its cultural characteristics, but by reference to the process of boundary maintenance. An ethnic group is always a self-defined group and consequently analysis should focus upon (1969, p. 15):

> the ethnic *boundary* that defines the group, not the cultural stuff that it encloses. The boundaries to which we must give our attention are of course social boundaries, though they may have territorial counterparts. If a group maintains its identity when members interact with others, this entails criteria for determining membership and ways of signalling membership and exclusion.

Clearly, Lyon has taken the notions of boundary and ethnic group as an ascriptive group from Barth's work. But his analysis diverges from Barth in two respects. First, he notes that social boundaries can be established and maintained from within and from without. Second, he maintains that social boundaries established and maintained from without can be drawn only by reference to phenotypical criteria. These divergencies would seem to constitute a refinement and advancement of Barth's analysis, but closer examination reveals that they point to a logical contradiction and a misreading of the empirical evidence that pertain to Lyon's attempt to distinguish between an ethnic group and a racial category. We can locate the source of these contradictions in the fact that Lyon ignores the most novel characteristic of Barth's analysis, that is, his claim that ethnic groups are defined by the process of boundary maintenance and not by the fact of cultural difference per se.

THE CRITERIA OF INCLUSION/EXCLUSION

Lyon's emphasis is upon the direction from which the boundary of inclusion/exclusion is established and maintained. He pays less attention to the nature of the criteria used to establish and maintain social boundaries. In particular, he makes no attempt to justify the assumption that the criteria of inclusion/exclusion are always empirically separable. He asserts, but does not defend, the position that cultural boundaries are always and only self-defined whereas racial boundaries are always and only other-defined. Yet, employing the criteria that Lyon has used to draw his distinction between an ethnic group and a racial category to the full extent of logic, it is conceivable that cultural boundaries can be other-defined (see Figure 3.4) and that racial boundaries can be self-defined (see Figure 3.5).

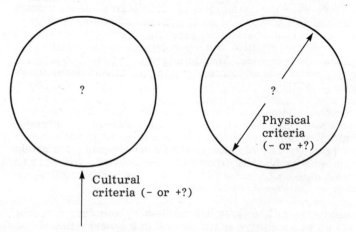

Figure 3.4 Categorisation using cultural criteria

Figure 3.5 Categorisation using physical criteria

Put another way, if there are two main criteria employed, logically they can be combined to produce four possible cases or options (see Figure 3.6). Lyon arbitrarily limits the combination to produce just two options which are mutually exclu-

sive and which therefore permit a precise and absolute distinction between an ethnic group and a racial category.

	Self-defined	Other-defined
Physical criteria	?	Racial category
Cultural criteria	Ethnic group	?

Figure 3.6 Criteria of categorisation

This distinction is difficult to maintain, despite the fact that
one can accept an analytical distinction between the use of
cultural and phenotypical criteria in processes of social categorisation. The historical and contemporary record both suggest that cultural and phenotypical criteria are consistently
used together. The 'scientific racism' of the nineteenth century
(along with contemporary expressions of that racism) insisted
that there was a deterministic relationship between phenotypical
variation and cultural difference. Additionally, that contemporary racism which 'apparently' eschews reference to racial
typologies nevertheless suggests that there is something about
the behaviour or belief (i.e. culture) of a group which is
identified in terms of some phenotypical characteristic which
warrants exclusion. In other words, racial categorisation (using
real or imagined phenotypical and/or genotypical variation)
consistently involves reference to cultural criteria. The point
is simply illustrated by reference to the fact that much racist
sentiment in Britain focuses upon the maintenance on the part
of migrants from the Indian sub-continent of cultural practices
which are the norm in their country and region of origin.

The same point is made in a different way by Wallman (1978,
pp. 203-4):

> The 'racial' differentness of West Indians is, in Lyon's
> terms, the principal, if not the only threat they present
> to Englishness....The *significant* difference between the
> same white English and people from the Indian sub-continent
> is, on the other hand, said to be a difference of culture.
> And by inference, of course, it is *Asian* culture which makes
> the difference, Asian *culture* which is a threat to English-
> ness.
> 　But both the 'racial' and the 'ethnic' classifications are
> external to the groups being classified. As such they

ignore divisions within those groups and disregard shifts in context and changes of meaning which affect the boundary from inside.

In other words, cultural boundaries can be other-defined and, moreover, the criteria employed by the out-group can categorise persons who, themselves, do not recognise those criteria as being the most significant and who draw very different social boundaries by reference to different (and, to the out-group, 'hidden') cultural criteria. Hence, the group of persons defined as 'Asian' and an ethnic group by large sections of the 'British' population only recognise such a boundary in very limited circumstances (see Figure 3.7). Wallman concludes that Lyon's attempt to distinguish between a racial category and an ethnic group should be set aside in favour of studies of the criteria that are used to make social boundaries, the process of boundary maintenance and the conditions under which boundaries shift.

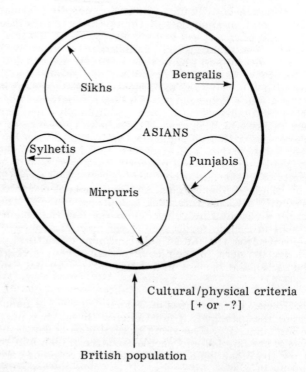

Figure 3.7 British categorisation of 'Asian' migrants

These criteria might be phenotypical or cultural in nature: for Wallman they have equal analytical status and they can be applied internally and externally. Ultimately, Wallman is arguing that the focus of investigation should pursue the recommendation of Barth, that is, that it should be upon the process of boundary construction and maintenance and not upon an application of the distinction between racial categories and ethnic groups. I shall later criticise such a focus. The point established here is that both phenotypical and cultural criteria can be applied externally and usually they are applied together.

CONCERNING TRANSITION FROM 'RACIAL CATEGORY' TO 'ETHNIC GROUP'

The second set of problems facing Lyon's analysis concerns his claim that a 'racial category' does not have the cultural resources to transform itself into an 'ethnic group' and is therefore unable to challenge effectively the racial categorisation of the 'out-group' (1972, p. 262): 'Minorities which are "purely racial", such as West Indians in Britain, lack corporate organisation and are weakened by majority disesteem, so that they have little control over their fate, which accordingly must depend upon the racialist policies of British society.' It must be noted that this claim necessarily follows from the nature of the distinction Lyon has drawn between a 'racial category' and an 'ethnic group': racial categorisation, argues Lyon, is always externally applied and so is not a resource available to the persons so categorised.

Despite the fact that Lyon argues that 'minority problems' in Britain cannot easily be compared with those in the United States, the evidence that he draws upon to support the claim that a 'racial category' cannot come to behave as and constitute an ethnic group is drawn from the United States. Moreover, the evidence clearly contradicts the initial distinction between a 'racial category' and an 'ethnic group', dependent as it is upon the presupposition that social boundaries referring to phenotypical variation are always and can only be applied externally. Lyon, by referring to the development of 'black pride' in the United States (1972, pp. 259-60), is implicitly acknowledging that the persons who constitute the 'racial category' have the option of 'accepting' the 'racial label' and can also invert it and give it a new and positive evaluative content. In other words, racial boundaries can be self-defined (cf. Wallman, 1978; Banton, 1977a, pp. 136-55).

Lyon seems unaware of having contradicted one of his fundamental presuppositions. His argument continues by claiming that despite the attempt of some American blacks to use 'race consciousness' as a means of 'ethnic mobilization' there is no possibility of the 'racial category' transcending this status to constitute itself as an ethnic group (1972, p. 259). The following reasons are advanced: first, black Americans do not have new and increasing opportunities for economic advancement;

second, black Americans have failed collectively to mobilise
the black vote and thereby achieve political power; and third,
'racial dishonour, deference and division are too powerful for
ethnic honour, pride and solidarity' (1972, p. 260). The argument develops on the basis of a comparison between black
Americans and the white immigrants to America in the nineteenth and twentieth centuries and hangs ultimately upon the
claim that black Americans have failed to overcome racial discrimination.

But that failure is as much to do with the changing pattern
of labour demand by American capital as it is with collective
mobilisation. The demand for low wage and low skill labour in
the second half of the nineteenth century was arguably met by
'white' immigration (i.e. immigration from Europe) because the
debate over slavery and the consequences of eventual abolition
in the context of the widespread articulation of racist ideology
ruled out any possibility of the growing demand for labour in
the northern states from 1850 being met by encouraging the
migration of labour from the south. Moreover, the southern
landowners had not completely relinquished their ideal of re-
establishing the slave mode of production, if not in name,
then in effect, and so were unwilling to sanction or encourage
internal migration northwards. Consequently, the economic
and social 'advancement' of the 'white' immigrants was as much
to do with economic factors as it was with political and ideological factors. The economic, political and ideological circumstances were rather different in the 1920s and 1930s when a
new demand for labour in the northern states was then met by
encouraging labour migration from the southern states (Piore,
1979). The possibility of collective mobilisation in a similar
context to that of the 'white' immigrants was therefore historically delayed.

Moreover, and equally significant, the evidence that Lyon
presents tells us only that the collective mobilisation of American 'blacks' has, to date, been unsuccessful in overcoming
discrimination and not that they have failed to mobilise. To
attribute the failure to eliminate racial discrimination completely
to some supposed group characteristic is to ignore the impact
of the material advantages accruing to American capital from
such discrimination and to denigrate the long history of struggle against that same discrimination (e.g. Genovese, 1975; also
Blauner, 1972, pp. 124-61). This is not to deny the inhibitory
effect of 'racial dishonour' but it is to assert that the events
of the past two decades in the United States are perhaps a
rather inadequate guide to the potential for 'ethnic mobilisation'
given the collective experience of more than a century and a
half of slavery.

And what of the validity of the argument as applied to England? What sense is there to the claim that West Indians in
England are a 'purely racial' minority, without the basis for
'ethnic' mobilisation? The failings of a static, formal distinction

become very clear when we consider the available evidence
relating to the Caribbean migration of the 1950s and 1960s.
Migrants from the West Indies did not arrive with a predominant
conception of themselves as West Indians. Their self-identity
focused on their community and island of origin. When mixing
socially with fellow islanders, their identity focused on the
village and parish of origin while when with other West Indians,
their identity focused on the island of origin. These island
identities were particularly significant as is evident in the
extreme rivalry between 'big islanders' and 'small islanders'
which reproduced itself in England. And cutting across island
identity was an urban/rural distinction (Pearson, 1977, pp. 375-
6; also 1981, pp. 148-75). The significance of these island
identities is apparent in the geographical and residential distribution of West Indian migrants throughout English cities:
evidence from London, for example, demonstrates a not incon-
siderable degree of 'island concentration' in particular boroughs
(Philpott, 1973; Midgett, 1975).

These distinctions were either not perceived or not considered
to be relevant by the English with whom they were in contact.
They identified the migrants as 'coloured' and West Indian.
From the perspective of the migrants, both were inadequate:
the former label took no account of the social significance
attributed to shades of 'blackness' while the latter imposed a
geographical/cultural label (which in turn signified phenotypical variation) which had little meaning in so far as there
was no homogeneous political or cultural entity to which 'West
Indian' could apply. Hence, the 'West Indian' identity was, in
the early phase of the migration, of far greater significance
to the English than to the Caribbean migrants (Midgett, 1975,
p. 76). However, given the extent of hostility and racial discrimination, Caribbean migrants, despite their regional and
island identities, were faced with common experiences and
problems and this has been an important factor in encouraging
the development of a West Indian self-identity. To what extent
this is a positive black identity in addition to being a geo-
graphical/cultural identity is not easy to say: the fact that
a Caribbean migrant identifies him/herself now as both black
and West Indian does not necessarily mean that either definition
is positively evaluated (cf. Phizacklea and Miles, 1980,
pp. 176-88). It has been argued that Caribbean migrants identify with the struggles of black Americans and have developed
a racial consciousness which draws upon the symbols of 'Black
Power' (Sutton and Makiesky, 1975, p. 128), but if this is so,
it has not been given significant organisational expression,
either at a local or a national level.

But this seems to prove the point that Lyon is making; or
does it? Let us begin by accepting the distinction that he
draws between migrants from the Caribbean and the Indian
sub-continent, but suggest that the apparent lack of communal
organisation (compared with migrants from the Indian sub-

continent) may be due to factors additional to the impact of racism and racial discrimination. Pearson, for example, stresses the internal social divisions within the Caribbean population which derive from length of residence in England and generational and gender differences. Moreover, regional and island identities lead to continued social differentiation and this is evident in the existence of locally based status systems which still form within the boundaries of island communities (Pearson, 1977, pp. 375-7; also 1981). This makes it difficult to determine the potential scale of communal organisation: will it be limited to 'island' communities or does it extend to a 'West Indian' community? Clearly, then, there are a number of bases of communal fragmentation which make application of the concept of a West Indian 'community' rather difficult to apply. These same bases of fragmentation may then help to explain what appears as a relative absence of communal organisation.

Expressed in different terms, Lyon begins by assuming the existence of some homogeneous West Indian community, then acknowledges that this 'community' is racially categorised and finally concludes that it is the latter which obstructs communal organisation. It is the initial assumption that is problematic because, as I have already argued, Caribbean migrants did not arrive with a ready formed West Indian identity but more as Jamaicans, Bajans, etc.: this, along with other lines of social differentiation, obstructed the development of communal organisation. It is therefore arguable that there is no, or only limited, communal organisation because there was no West Indian 'community'.

But, then, is Lyon correct to argue that West Indians lack the capacity of 'collective organisation for the pursuit of common goals' (1973, p. 345). It must be acknowledged that several writers have referred to a relative absence of voluntary and political organisations amongst the West Indian population (e.g. Midgett, 1975, p. 64; Pearson, 1977, p. 371). But this is not the same as saying that such organisations are absent. The pentecostal church, island associations and mutual savings groups (usually organised amongst persons from the same island) are all examples of West Indians' communal organisations (Midgett, 1975, p. 64; Philpott, 1977, pp. 110-11). It may be that such organisations only rarely transcend island boundaries but, as previously established, Lyon's emphasis upon a racial boundary marked by the concept of West Indian ignores the bases of internal social/cultural differentiation within the West Indian population and therefore the basis of communal organisation.

In the light of this evidence of communal organisation, the contrast that Lyon wishes to draw between West Indian and 'Asian' migrants seems overdrawn. We need to consider carefully the other half of the comparison, the nature and extent of communal organisation amongst 'Asian' migrants, because it is this that permits the attribution of 'ethnic'. We have already

noted Lyon's distinction between West Pakistanis, Indian
Gujaratis and Indian Punjabis. He then sets apart the first
group on the grounds that it exhibits little communal cohesion
or organisation! Then, having analysed certain features of the
two Indian populations, he offers the following reservation
(1973, p. 347): 'Asian communalism in Britain is not at present
geographically extensive. Punjabi and Gujarati organisation
tends to be confined within one two or group of nearby towns,
and personal knowledge based on face-to-face contacts stretches
across ethnic networks only in particular townships.'

Lyon's observation about the lack of communal organisation
amongst Pakistanis is confirmed by other researchers. Khan
suggests that Pakistanis in Britain fall into four social/
regional groups. Most of the migrants from these different
areas are rural village dwellers and should be distinguished
socially from urban, educated Pakistanis (1976, p. 224). The
most significant focus of social interaction for Pakistani rural
migrants is the village/kin network and there is only limited
contact with Pakistanis who are not part of that network. Consequently, there is no prominent, day-to-day identity as a
Pakistani amongst the village/kin network.

This is partly a result of the character of communal organisation in the villages in Pakistan. Dayha notes that there is considerable suspicion of 'outsiders' who come to Pakistani villages,
particularly those seeking political office or some other form
of support. It was generally believed that such people were
primarily seeking personal gain. This ensures that there is no
social basis for collective action with people who are neither
kin nor previously established allies in the same village. Consequently, and this applies in both Pakistan and Britain, there
is a general indifference to voluntary organisations and those
that do exist usually include only friends and kinsman. Such
organisations are usually formed by Pakistanis of urban origin
and, in the context of personal and kinship rivalry, the formation of one organisation will usually stimulate the formation of
alternatives. These organisations may claim to speak for and
lead the local or even national Pakistani 'community' but the
reality is often rather different. However, elected representa-
tives and administrators within the British political structure
commonly accept these claims of 'national' leadership and con-
sult the 'leaders' accordingly. Thereby, they play a part in
creating them as 'leaders' of the Pakistani community (1972-3,
pp. 258-61). Only in situations of perceived collective threat,
when a 'national' identity as Pakistanis emerges, might the
rural Pakistanis then look to the urban-educated 'leaders' for
representation (Dahya, 1972-3, p. 262; Khan, 1976, p. 226).

How far these features of Pakistani 'communalism' apply in
the case of Indian migrants is difficult to assess in the absence
of research findings. Lyon suggests that Indian migrants do
not constitute such a fragmented population, but his final
qualification (quoted above) implies that in so far as there is a

notion of common ancestry and culture amongst Punjabi Sikhs
and Gujaratis, it is not sufficiently strong and extensive to
lead to anything other than local community organisation. This
is confirmed by a study of Sikhs in Gravesend, Kent (Helweg,
1974). I am, therefore, arguing that the contrast between West
Indians and 'Asians' which is drawn on the basis of some suggested absolute difference in the capacity for communal organisation is mistaken. There may be some difference of degree,
but this empirical evidence cannot support Lyon's distinction
between a 'racial category' and an ethnic group which requires
that West Indians (qua racial category) lack any basis for
communal action.

My final criticism focuses on Lyon's static conception of culture which lies behind his identification of an ethnic group in
terms of its historic culture. There is no notion of culture as
referring to beliefs, values and practices which are socially
created, sustained and changed. This constrains any analysis
derived from Lyon's definitions from acknowledging that the
cultural characteristics which developed in the Caribbean in
response to colonialism and slavery can be invested with new
meanings in a different context in order to mark and maintain
a sense of social difference which is positively valued in reaction to racial categorisation. This is clearly evident in the
instance of a group of West Indian men playing dominoes: the
rules, language and style of the game effectively exclude anyone unacquainted with those rules, etc., in much the same way
as an Islam prayer meeting. My point is that there is a wide
range of cultural practices which West Indians can employ to
serve as a boundary of inclusion/exclusion. This is even more
the case in the instance of their British-born children, a significant proportion of whom have drawn upon mainly Jamaican
symbols of revolt against colonialism and invested them with a
meaning specific to their experiences in Britain (see, Johnson,
1976, 1980/1; Miles, 1978; Cashmore, 1979; Hebdige, 1979;
Clarke, 1980).

THE IMPOSSIBILITY OF THE RACIAL CATEGORY/ETHNIC GROUP DISTINCTION

Before broadening the argument, it is necessary to make clear
the very specific claims being made against Lyon's case for
drawing what is in effect an absolute distinction between a
'racial category' and an 'ethnic group'. First, I am arguing
that the distinction is drawn abstractly by reference to two
distinct criteria and that Lyon does not justify why all the
possible logical combinations of those criteria are not analysed.
Second, the absolute distinction between the use of cultural
and of phenotypical criteria cannot be maintained: that social
categorisation which warrants description as racist always
combines reference to both cultural and phenotypical character-

istics (cf. Rex, 1970, pp. 136-61). Third, this same abstractly
drawn opposition, which must maintain the impossibility of
'communal' or political mobilisation of those persons defined as
a racial category, cannot be sustained in the light of the evidence of West Indian and 'Asian' political mobilisation in Britain.

Specifically, Lyon misrepresents the evidence concerning the
social identities of West Indian migrants; ignores the significance
of alternative explanations for what might appear as a low level
of 'communal' or political organisation; inaccurately records the
existence of 'communal' organisation amongst the West Indian
population in Britain; overemphasises the cohesiveness and
extent of such organisation amongst 'Asian' groups; and operates with a static conception of culture which blinds him to
the process of 'reworking' a cultural past to provide a new
political identity and thereby a basis for political mobilisation.

Two additional points of clarification are required in order
that the above claims are not misinterpreted. First, I do not
want to suggest that there are no significant distinctions concerning politically relevant cultural characteristics to be drawn
between migrants from the Caribbean and from the Indian sub-
continent. Migrants from the Caribbean come from societies
which were the direct product of colonialism and the slave mode
of production whereas those from the Indian sub-continent
came from societies which have a historic culture which was
well-established before colonial intervention. Consequently,
although the colonial intervention was not without effects in
the Indian sub-continent, it cannot be said that the intervention
decisively shaped those societies in the way that it did in the
Caribbean (Lowenthal, 1972). Thus, many migrants from the
Caribbean came to Britain with the positive image of Britain as
'the Mother Country' and a land of opportunity for all (e.g.
Pryce, 1979, pp. 2-5), whereas many migrants from the Indian
sub-continent came with a more pragmatic and detached image,
their attachment to their region, town or village of origin
constituting a very much more positive focus than Britain.
Thus, a migrant from Mirpur, immersed in a Moslem way of
life, will immediately develop a much more profound sense of
difference once in Britain than will a migrant from Jamaica who
will have to create anew a positively evaluated culture, building on those cultural differences that become apparent as a
consequence of migration as well as reinterpreting the racial
label which was externally imposed. But these differences,
and others, can be acknowledged for what they are without
necessitating a distinction such as that drawn by Lyon.

Second, I do not wish to suggest that a distinction cannot
be made between the use of phenotypical and cultural criteria
in the process of social categorisation. Clearly, for analytical
clarity, it is necessary to recognise such a difference, not
least because the significance of the difference is a key component in the debate about the nature of racism and its contemporary mode of expression (see Chapter 4). Moreover,

the sorts of labels that people apply to others clearly have
implications for the way in which both the 'labellers' and the
'labelled' react to each other, and that cannot be ignored. My
criticism is aimed at the subsequent attempt to reflect simplis-
tically that difference of labelling criteria in a secondary classification of 'types' of group ('racial category' and ethnic
group). To do so, I am arguing, requires that the history of
the ideology of racism and of the New Commonwealth migrants
themselves must be misinterpreted.

FROM ETHNIC GROUP TO ETHNICITY

As previously indicated, the distinction suggested by Lyon
has been the object of criticism from others who would nevertheless see themselves as working within the field of 'ethnic
relations'. The source of their critique lies in the work of
Barth, upon which they wish to build in developing their investigation of 'ethnic relations' in Britain. Their work signals a
rejection of static classification (is this group a 'racial category'
or an 'ethnic group'?) and a focusing of concern on what might
be termed the process of cultural difference. It also entails use
of the concept of ethnicity, introduced in part to emphasise
the subjective dimension of the process of the recognition and
maintenance of cultural difference. I shall outline these arguments briefly, and then move to a critique of the problematic
from which they derive.
    Khan defines ethnicity as being about (1976, p. 223): 'people
of one culture realizing its distinctiveness and utilizing its distinctive resources (be they emotional, symbolic, cultural,
political, economic, etc.) in interactions with outsiders. Both
presuppose an awareness of difference and a degree of contact
and interaction with non-ethnic outsiders.' What is of interest
to Khan is not the fact of cultural difference, but the process
by which, for example, migrants from the Indian sub-continent
become aware of their differences once in social contact with
sections of the 'indigenous' population. Put another way, ethnicity is used to refer to the development and maintenance of
ethnic awareness/identity. The analytical focus thereby shifts
to the social boundaries that are drawn on the basis of the
recognition and maintenance of cultural difference. Research
must therefore begin with people's perception of a sense of
difference in relation to others who are perceived to be 'not
us'. Khan therefore argues that one cannot speak of 'Pakistani
ethnicity' in any meaningful sense because migrants from
Pakistan rarely perceive themselves as sharing characteristics
in common with each other. Rather, the sense of difference
with 'Britishness' has as its positive identification what is
perceived as common to kin and fellow villagers from the same
region. This subjective component refracts the considerable
social differentiation within the population of Pakistani migrants

in Britain (1976, p. 228).

A similar but more developed analysis is offered by Wallman (1978, 1979). Wallman claims (1979, p. ix): 'Ethnicity refers generally to the perception of group difference and so to social boundaries between sections of population. In this sense *ethnic difference* is the recognition of a contrast between "us" and "them".' Later, and similarly (1979, p. 3): 'Ethnicity is the recognition of significant difference between "them" and "us". Neither the difference nor its significance is set.' For Wallman, social boundaries can be marked by a number of different criteria and these can change from one social context to another. What is important is not that there may be some objective basis of differentiation between groups because these can only ever be potential boundary markers. Rather, it is the perception and attribution of significance to such difference which is the foundation of ethnicity. And, in common with Khan, Wallman stresses that ethnicity is reactive (1979, p. 6): 'It is culture in-adaptation-to, in-response-to, up-against "others" within a context shared by both sides of the ethnic boundary, and it is shaped by the aims, constraints and opportunities of that context as they pertain to each side.'

These claims clearly lead to a rather different sort of analysis than that which would follow from Lyon's distinction. Significantly, they meet one of my principle objections to Lyon's analysis, his bifurcation of the utilisation of phenotypical and cultural criteria in the process of social categorisation. Wallman argues that one should not make a priori assumptions about what criteria will be used in the process of categorisation: for example, it does not follow from the fact that two persons, each with distinct phenotypical features and engaged in social interaction, will attribute any social significance to those phenotypical differences. The conclusion drawn is that (1978, p. 205): 'it seems to me useful to set the racial/ethnic quibble aside and to consider simply how social boundaries are marked, how they are maintained and when they shift'. These arguments seem to promise a radical shift away from usage of the terms 'ethnic group' and 'ethnicity' to refer simply to the fact of cultural difference. At one level, this promise is realised in so far as Lyon's dichotomy is jettisoned. But there remains a fundamental contradiction between the continuing usage of the notion of ethnicity and the reality to which it is made to refer. Behind this fundamental contradiction lies the fact that the focus of the perspective remains at the level of phenomenal relations. Let me first identify the contradiction.

By using ethnicity to refer generally to the perception of group difference, the term is being made to refer to any criteria by which one group may distinguish itself from another. What is thereby promised is some general theory and analysis of the development and maintenance of social boundaries. Accordingly, we might therefore expect studies of, for example, any and every group which defines itself as different in some way from some other group. This produces a conceptual problem of considerable dimensions because of Wallman's 'hidden' assumption that cultural difference is synonymous with ethnic difference and that ethnic difference constitutes the boundaries of ethnic groups (for example, Wallman, 1979, pp. 5-14). Either we must then define any group which identifies itself ('us') in relation to some other group ('them') as an ethnic group (e.g. mods, the working class, feminists, punks, trade union negotiators, students, and so on) or we require some means by which 'ethnic groups' can be distinguished from other types of group. By virtue of the former possibility, all social groups defined by some common identity shared amongst their members become ethnic groups, with the result that the terms ethnic/ethnicity lose all specific meaning and therefore have no analytical value. In relation to the second, we are offered no such means of identification, only an assumption that an ethnic group is a culturally distinct minority. Yet, that is similar, if not identical, to Lyon's definition of an ethnic group. Accordingly, we arrive back at the very point from which Lyon departs.

Additionally, the scope of the analysis offered by 'ethnicity theorists' is limited by its predominant focus upon phenomenal relations. This is evident in the concentration upon what people believe to be the characteristics which typify them as a group which is distinct and separate from others. Hence, we have Khan's claim that Pakistanis in Britain cannot be conceived of as an ethnic group because they lack any continuous, conscious sense of identity as a common collectivity. Rather, the prime focus of personal identity is the village/kin network. The empirical validity of such claims are not here disputed. But what is criticised is the fact that the development of the primary categories by reference to social consciousness means that underlying historical and structural processes are passed over in silence and so receive little or no analytical attention. These processes set the parameters of class boundaries and of fractionalisation within classes, parameters which are not necessarily evident in social consciousness.

The point can be made by analogy. In the course of the 1960s, much sociological attention was devoted to attempting to demonstrate that the British working class could no longer become a radical political force because it lacked any widespread consciousness of itself as a working class with a radical mission. Such arguments were shown to have grave limitations not only by specific events of the later 1960s (e.g. Blackburn, 1967; Westergaard, 1970), but also by the very obvious intensification of class struggle in the early 1970s. The latter originated in part with the attempt of a Conservative government to restore profitability, a policy that was necessitated by the historical decline of British capitalism (e.g. Glyn and Sutcliffe, 1972). Underlying that crisis was a class structure which was (and continues to be) evident in widespread material and political inequalities (Westergaard and Resler, 1975). Such

inequalities are in toto rarely the object of the conscious attention of the working class. Yet there are occasions when particular events bring some aspects of these inequalities to widespread attention and large numbers of workers recognise in
some way the structural realities which determine their class
position. The fact that these realities are not the object of
permanent conscious attention does not make them any less
important determinants of the economic and political circumstances of the working class. Even more certainly, we would
discover little about their determination of the parameters of
the working class and its internal divisions by studying only
the sense of 'us' consciously articulated within the working
class.

Similarly, it is now well-established that the extent of racial
discrimination is much greater than that 'imagined' by those
who are its object (Smith, 1977, pp. 127-42). The extent of
racial discrimination is an important determinant of the economic and political circumstances of those subject to it because
it places limitations on the occupations that can be obtained
and on the type and quality of housing that can be entered
(Smith, 1977, passim). Consequently, groups of persons come
to share structurally determined interests. The fact that they
are not necessarily widely recognised at the level of everyday
consciousness does not mean that those interests do not exist,
but rather that we need to explain why these essential relations
are not reproduced within phenomenal relations. There is no
simple answer to that question, but in the absence of it being
posed, analysis must remain at the level of simply documenting
ethnicity, that is 'the recognition of significant difference
between "them" and "us"' (Wallman, 1979, p. 3), irrespective
of how misconceived and inaccurate that process of recognition
might be.

However, it should be recognised that these 'ethnicity theorists' do avoid reifying 'race'. This can be illustrated by the
following claim of Wallman (1978, p. 204):

> The difference between two aggregates of people will be
> *objective* to the extent that an outsider can list items that
> mark it, but it is inevitably *subjective* to the extent that
> none of these markers has any necessary or precise signi-
> ficance outside the perception of the actors.

This is a clear acknowledgment of the social construction of
'race' by virtue of signalling that the fact of real phenotypical
difference only has social 'effects' when some social significance
is attributed to difference. Consequently, analytical attention
must focus upon demonstrating that it is the process of the
attribution of significance that is the 'active' element and not
the fact of phenotypical difference (or in some cases the alleged
fact of genotypical difference).

But there are significant limitations to an analysis which does not or cannot attempt to proceed beyond analysing the perception of (phenotypical or genotypical) difference. Wallman claims, just prior to the above quotation (1978, p. 204): 'It is the *perception* of colour or phenotype or nose-form or culture as a sign of immutable and socially *significant* difference which is the basis of racism.' This claim is a dangerous half-truth in that it passes off the necessary recognition of the fact that meaning has to be attributed to phenotypical/genotypical difference for such difference to 'intrude' upon social relations, as being the basis for the generation and reproduction of racism. It is insufficient to recognise the social categorisation of 'race' if one does not simultaneously inquire as to why that process of categorisation has occurred only in specific contexts and at specific points in historical time. The basis of racism is to be found not in the attribution of meaning to phenotypical difference, but in identifying the economic, political and ideological conditions that allow the attribution of meaning to take place. And such an analysis necessitates proceeding beyond cataloguing people's perceptions of difference (i.e. phenomenal relations) in order to inquire about the material basis of the reproduction of social life and, in particular, the reproduction of ideological relations. In the case of Britain, this requires consideration of the essential relations of capitalist production, both historically (and therefore with respect to colonialism) and in their contemporary form.

'RACE RELATIONS' VERSUS 'ETHNIC RELATIONS'

Nevertheless, the theoretical parameters and empirical concerns of 'ethnic relations' research constitute a breaking of the mould of 'race relations' research in a number of important respects. First, 'ethnic relations' studies have encouraged consideration of the migration of groups to Britain whose phenotypical characteristics are very similar to those of the 'majority, indigenous population' e.g. the Irish, Italians and Cypriots (Watson, 1977a; Khan, 1979). Despite the fact that these groups of migrants cannot be identified so immediately and definitively as phenotypically distinct in the way that migrants from the New Commonwealth can be and have been, some of these groups have experienced a similar process of ideological, political and economic exclusion. This clearly supports the contention that skin colour or any other phenotypical characteristic is not itself an active determinant of social conflict, but that such differences can serve as a focus for or symbol of conflict which has an origin in other, quite distinct characteristics. Consequently, in the absence of clear group phenotypical difference and of those factors which ensure that certain phenotypical differences are attributed with social significance, other characteristics or criteria (e.g. cultural) can be made to play the same role (Miles, 1981, 1982).

Second, by virtue of the emphasis upon personal or group identity and upon the maintenance of cultural difference, 'ethnic relations' studies conceive of members of ethnic groups as active subjects and not as simply the objects or 'victims' of racism and discrimination. The obsession of 'race relations' research with the extent and impact of racial discrimination to the exclusion of most other factors encourages a perspective in which West Indians, Pakistanis, Indians, etc., come to be viewed undimensionally as the objects of other people's beliefs and behaviour. They come to be portrayed as lacking any capacity for self-activity or, where such a capacity is allowed for, it is solely in terms of reacting to discrimination. The implication is that, as 'victim' or even as active participant, the sole determinant of the group's experience and structural position is racial discrimination. By stressing identity and the facts of cultural difference, 'ethnic relations' research presents West Indians, Indians, and other migrant groups in a context in which they have at least some capacity as active subjects. Moreover, the inter-related concepts of 'chain migration' and 'migrant ideology', (see MacDonald and MacDonald, 1964; Philpott, 1973; Watson, 1977a; Piore, 1979) by virtue of their stress on intention, both direct attention towards the migrants as active participants who, because of their own beliefs and behaviour, can have some impact on their destiny.

Third, 'ethnic relations' studies have encouraged an awareness of the nature and extent of cultural heterogeneity amongst New Commonwealth migrants. One does not necessarily have to deny or ignore a common experience of racial discrimination in order to recognise this heterogeneity amongst New Commonwealth migrants. But this heterogeneity has the potential of constituting significant barriers against the development of a shared political perspective and evaluation amongst all those who share that experience of discrimination. In other words, once cultural heterogeneity is recognised, one cannot automatically assume that what seems to be a similar experience leads to a common outcome. By reference to cultural heterogeneity, the Pakistani migrant from a village in rural Mirpur might conclude that he has as little in common with a migrant from Kingston, Jamaica, as with a person born in Britain who has quite distinct pheno-typical characteristics.

Fourth, because of its concern with the actor's definition of the situation, 'ethnic relations' research tends to refer to migrants rather than immigrants. This research is, therefore, emphasising that many of those who came to Britain in the 1950s and 1960s came not with the idea of permanent settlement, but with the intention of earning sufficient money to improve their economic and political position in the area from which they migrated. Hence, if their intentions are seriously taken account of, the groups in question cannot be conceived of as immigrants, people who were breaking most or all ties with the country of birth in order to live permanently elsewhere. Rather, their

migration to Britain was motivated by an intention to return to
the region and country of birth. For this reason, economic,
political and ideological links with that region and country are
maintained and the maintenance of those links has important
implications for the decisions and strategies the migrants
pursue in Britain (Watson, 1977a, passim; Helweg, 1979).

But this is the limit of 'ethnic relations'/anthropological
concern. These themes require development for they suggest
the need for, but do not constitute the framework for consideration of, the relationship between the actual or aspired class
position of the migrant in the country of origin and the class
position occupied whilst in Britain. It is commonly asserted
that many migrants are motivated in their migration by a desire
for economic advancement and this often means in practice that
land ownership must be attained or extended, or that capital
be obtained and invested in some sort of public service, e.g.
a taxi or shop (e.g. Philpott, 1977, pp. 98-100). In Britain,
these migrants may be working towards such an aim by selling
their labour power for a wage or they may have established
some petit-bourgeois enterprise in Britain. The implications
and even contradictions that arise from these similar and different class positions has not even been adequately considered,
let alone actually studied (cf. Moore, 1977).

Fifth, and following from the previous point, 'ethnic relations'
research points to the significance of studying the political
economy of labour migration. By conceiving migration as a chain
which connects the country of the migrant's origin with Britain,
there is a clear suggestion that the reasons for and effects of
migration have to be considered in relation to both ends of the
chain (e.g. Philpott, 1973; Watson, 1977a). Hence, we find in
one recent volume of research findings several writers referring
to the economic reasons for migration and the resulting economic
impact of large-scale migration on the area from which the
migrants have come: migration from Pakistan, Montserrat, Hong
Kong and North Italy has left these areas to varying degrees
desirous, if not dependent upon, financial remittances from
the migrants (Watson, 1977a, pp. 70, 95, 100, 187, 208, 261).
At the extreme this can mean a new form of neo-colonial dependence, whereby the rural areas on the periphery of the metropolitan capitalist economy become dependent upon the money
remitted by the migrants working in that capitalist economy.
Research on Western Europe shows that this dependence is
'limited' not only to cash income, but to employment per se:
if the migrants had remained (or are forced by the metropolitan
capitalist formation to return) they would have been unable to
obtain any form of wage labour (Castles and Kosack, 1973;
Paine, 1974). However, this issue is not pursued systematically
(nor even in these terms) within 'ethnic relations' research.
But it is clearly placed on the agenda, partly because of the
traditional anthropological concern with studying 'small-scale'
societies as totalities. This has the result of encouraging direct

consideration of the complex interconnections between social life and production relations.

These characteristics of the 'ethnic relations' problematic may constitute an advance on the perspective of the 'race relations' problematic, but they must also be assessed, in turn, in terms of the former's own limitations. I have outlined several very specific criticisms of the work of particular authors whose work falls within this framework: I now want to make a more general critical comment. The 'advances' outlined above all derive from the fact that the central feature of 'ethnic relations' research is its emphasis upon culture. Expressed simply, 'ethnic relations' research replaces the emphasis upon 'racial minorities' as primarily the objects of racism and discrimination with an emphasis upon 'ethnic groups' as self-defined groups whose beliefs and behaviour have to be assessed in terms of their culturally determined distinctness. In so doing, it tends to abstract the facts of cultural differentiation in the course of making them the primary object of inquiry. At one level this can lead to a simple cataloguing of cultural difference (a dictionary of the 'exotic'), while at another it presents an analysis of the interaction between culturally distinct groups either without reference to or even in direct opposition to class relations. Thus, culture comes to be portrayed as a universal, collectivist characteristic and is used to explain the totality of the belief and behaviour of the individuals who constitute the 'ethnic group'. A simple cataloguing of cultural difference may satisfy a sense of curiosity, but it cannot by itself solve any analytical problems. And it is when attempts are made to grapple with such problems that the primary emphasis upon cultural difference comes to exhibit its most general limitation (e.g. Williams, 1980).

By abstracting cultural differentiation, and the notion of group identity which derives from this difference, from production relations, the consequence is either a failure to identify class divisions within the culturally distinct populations or, if this is suggested, these are nevertheless isolated from the class divisions within the other culturally identified groups (that is, from the social formation as a whole). This must happen in the case of research which focuses upon the establishment and maintenance of ethnic boundaries: the analytical emphasis is upon identifying and explaining the cultural signifiers of the ethnic boundaries (e.g. language, dress, diet, etc.) irrespective of production relations.

This is not to deny that the owner of a small clothing workshop who migrated from Pakistan in the early 1960s may share with his employees a fundamental faith in Islam (and so on). But this sharing of a common identity tells us nothing about the conditions under which the production of commodities (shirts, coats, dresses) proceeds and therefore about the factors governing the purchase and sale of the labour power of the fellow 'ethnics'. We therefore cannot know anything about the material basis upon which the owner of the workshop is able to maintain that ownership and, therefore, his petit-bourgeois class position. One factor of particular significance in maintaining that position is the price paid for wage labour. This is of significance not only because it remains a major variable in determining the profitability or otherwise of the enterprise, but also because it is an important determinant of the relationship with his employees. Yet the price paid is not a whim of the owner (perhaps dependent upon his cultural characteristics) but is cruicially determined by the conditions pertaining in the whole sector of clothing production (and indeed beyond). We must therefore explore not only the facts of cultural difference but also the economic relations in which these 'ethnics' are enmeshed.

I am not wishing to claim crudely that there is some permanent, clearly identifiable conflict between these owners of small businesses and those whom they employ, when the latter share and identify with a number of socially significant cultural characteristics. Indeed, that common sense of cultural identity might well serve to obstruct the development of such conflict. But this sense of identity can only have a marginal impact upon the continuing reproduction of the positions in production relations that those persons occupy: of fundamental importance to that reproduction is the condition of the market for the commodities produced and for the purchase and sale of labour power. And those market circumstances always have the potential of bursting the ideological (i.e. 'ethnic') bond between employer and employee if the conditions of production necessitate the imposition of terms and conditions upon the employees which for material and/or political reasons they find unacceptable. In this sense, therefore, there is little difference between class relations 'within' the Pakistani (or any other 'ethnic') population and those 'within' the 'majority' population: there is always some form of ideological bond between employer and employee in any wage labour situation.

But if we begin with class relations, rather than with the facts of cultural difference, we first identify a population of migrants who came to Britain from the New Commonwealth and entered class relations as wage labourers. We must here acknowledge the meshing of the collective motivation and aspirations of the migrants and the requirements of British capital. This same meshing is evident in the process by which the establishment of migrant communities led to the development of petit-bourgeois enterprise within them (e.g. Dahya, 1974), some of which has developed to serve a wider market (as in the case of the restaurant trade). But in this process, it is not the direct needs of British capital that support the formation of a petit-bourgeois class amongst the migrants but the needs of the migrant population, with the result that the Indian and Pakistani petite-bourgoisie certainly comes to constitute a distinct fraction of petit-bourgeois capital in Britain. There are some

interesting exceptions to this. For example, the migrants from
Italy and Hong Kong entered Britain with the intention of
establishing themselves as a petite-bourgeoisie in the catering
trade, meeting a demand not from fellow migrants but from the
resident population (Palmer, 1977; Watson, 1977b). At least a
proportion of the political refugees from Kenya and Uganda
constitute another exception by virtue of their petit-bourgois
and even bourgeois class position in Africa before they were
forced to leave (e.g. Bristow et al., 1975). And in investigat-
ing the position of these different groups of migrants in these
different petit-bourgeois class locations, our first consideration
must be the nature of the material conditions that permit the
formation of such a class. The research that has been done
under the rubric of 'ethnic relations' fails to recognise this
and consequently has failed to provide us with any substantial
information about the petite-bourgeoisie within the migrant
population (as well as with any substantial information about
the larger working class qua working class). There is therefore no doubt about the validity of endorsing the following
admission of Watson (1977a, p. 4): 'To date, most anthropologists - including the contributors to this volume - have not
really come to grips with the problem of class in complex
societies.'

But the issue does not concern only the class position that
migrants come to occupy in British capitalism. It also concerns
the material forces which determine the migration. Watson's
edited text claims to offer a new perspective on 'ethnic relations' by virtue of both studying ten different ethnic minorities
and considering each end of the migration chain (1977a). What
is striking about most of these groups of migrants to Britain
is not so much the facts about their cultural difference from
each other and from the 'majority' population but rather the
similarity of the material circumstances that they experienced
before their migration and of the experience of the migration
process itself (cf. Piore, 1979). With the exception of the Poles
(who constitute a political refugee population) and the West
Africans (most of whom have migrated to Britain to pursue
further education), all of the populations referred to originate
from rural and (with one exception, the Italians) ex-colonial
social formations. The rural areas from which they have come
have been unable to provide adequate material support for their
populations, with the result that migration has become in the
course of the twentieth century (if not earlier) a traditional
means of both ensuring the material reproduction of the population and providing a mechanism for improving some people's
class position within it. This is achieved by migrating to and
occupying a vacant economic position within metropolitan capitalist economies, whether it be to staff its health service or to
provide cheap restaurants. These positions then become the
sites for a (temporary?) class position in the metropolitan
capitalist economy.

How temporary that position is depends not only on the intention of the migrant but equally upon the possibility of the migrant realising the material ambitions which prompted the migration. This is not simply a matter of how hard the migrant is prepared to work because there will remain definite material limits to that by virtue of the migrant's class position in Britain and the sector of production that the migrant enters. In the case of New Commonwealth migrants to Britain, a combination of the latter features and the effects of racial discrimination (Smith, 1977) have ensured that a very large proportion of the migrants have become, in effect, settlers. But this is not in itself a new phenomenon, as a comparison between the Italian migration to the USA in the late nineteenth century and the Sikh migration to Britain in the 1950s and 1960s shows. If one compares the respective accounts of these migrations by the McDonalds (1964) and the Ballards (1977), one discovers that these two groups (distinguishable in terms of the historical period of the migration, the country to which they migrated and their cultural characteristics) underwent and experienced a very similar social and economic process (see Table 3.1).

Table 3.1   Phases of migration

Late nineteenth-century Italian migration to USA	Mid-twentieth-century Sikh migration to Britain
Phase 1 Migration through padroni	Phase 1 Pioneers
Phase 2 Serial migration	Phase 2 Mass migration
Phase 3 Delayed family migration	Phase 3 Family reunion
	Phase 4 Second generation

The two groups' specifically distinct cultural characteristics are of little assistance in explaining this process, although the facts of difference are relevant to the formation of distinct patterns of interaction in each case. The migration process has to be assessed and explained in terms of the concentration of capitalist relations of production at certain locations in the world economy (the USA and Britain rather than southern Italy and north-west India) and the related internationalisation of the labour market. If it were not for those two facts, the persons who did migrate could not otherwise have done so. In sum, the 'discovery' by 'ethnic relations' research of culture constitutes an analytical trap if it is divorced, as it has, from its historical and material context, that of the development of capitalist relations of production.

CONCLUSION

These critical considerations have, of course, played no part
in the process by which the terms 'ethnic relations' and 'ethnic
minorities', and so on, have become threaded into 'everyday'
debates. However, the 'discovery of culture' is signalled by
the switch to, or combination of, 'ethnic relations' language
with 'race relations' language in those debates. It is, in other
words, an admission by politicians, policy-makers, and so on,
that the facts of cultural difference constitute a valid parameter
for their deliberations. The same cannot be said in the case of
the terminology of 'race' and 'race relations' because the facts
of phenotypical difference have no intrinsic significance for
such deliberations for the reasons stated in Chapter 1 (although
the facts of racism and racial discrimination do). There is,
therefore, a sense in which the emergence of 'ethnic relations'
language constitutes a major and significant step in the direction of a valid analysis. But it is only one step in the right
direction, and it is taken from an almost lost position. Yet,
one is naive to expect those same individuals to accept the
criticisms of this 'discovery of culture' because it would necessitate making a complete break with their analytical starting
point.
    And what of the conceptual fate of 'ethnic relations'? There
can be no place for it as a distinct area of investigation per
se for the reasons argued above. However, a place has to be
found for the notion of 'ethnic group' in so far as one must
recognise the existence of a sense of common identity amongst
groups of people who wish to recognise and maintain their
cultural difference vis-à-vis others. This phenomenal process
has real political and ideological effects on, inter alia, the
development of class struggle and the formation of class consciousness. But, equally, one must recognise that the persons
who constitute a group which is formed and identified on this
basis also have a position in essential relations. That is, they
have a position in production (and, thereby, class) relations.
It is this fact that 'ethnic relations' studies cannot recognise,
account for and assess the significance of.
    In this and the previous chapter I have been arguing that
the analytical frameworks that have been developed within
British sociology over the past decade and a half in order to
construct a certain field of study ('race/ethnic' relations) contain a number of analytical, logical and empirical contradictions
and/or errors. On the basis of these arguments, I wish to go
on to argue in Part II in support of a different analytical perspective. In order to ease the transition from critique to exposition, I want, finally, in this part to outline and critically evaluate the main arguments about the nature and genesis of
racism.

4 RACISM: THE DEBATE ABOUT ITS NATURE AND GENESIS

INTRODUCTION

The concept of racism provides us with a conceptual and a historical problem. As we shall see, the way in which we define racism affects the scope of any historical analysis of its origin and continued existence as an ideology. Some writers have defined racism in such a way as to limit its application to those scientific theories developed during the nineteenth century. Others have argued that the origin of racism lies not with the development of biological science but with the important role played by colonialism in the development of capitalism. However, not all who have entered this debate have wished to restrict their definition of racism to a set of ideas or ideology and have extended the term to refer to social behaviour and social structures. My aim in this chapter is to outline and discuss the adequacy of the main definitions of racism and the predominant explanations of the origin of racism. The analysis that follows does not pretend to provide an exhaustive catalogue of the multitude of available definitions but, rather, aims to discuss the general trends in the arguments that have occurred over definition. I shall attempt to define racism in a way which resolves the problems that I identify, stressing that it should apply to an ideology. The problems that arise in the course of examining explanations for the origin of racism will be pursued in Chapter 5.

DEFINING RACISM

In the late 1960s, Banton defined racism as (1970, p. 18): 'the doctrine that a man's behaviour is determined by stable inherited characters deriving from separate racial stocks having distinctive attributes and usually considered to stand to one another in relations of superiority and inferiority'. This definition derives from his preliminary analysis of 'scientific' ideas about 'race' which were formulated and developed in the late eighteenth and nineteenth centuries. As we have seen in the first chapter, these ideas have been scientifically discredited, allowing Banton to claim that racism originates in a scientific error (1970, p. 28. See also 1977a, p. 169): 'it was the product of a movement in biology that has been left far behind. As a biological doctrine, racism is dead.' Whether this claim is valid in the light of the work of Jenson and Eysenck, amongst others, is not of concern here (see Kamin, 1977; Richardson and Spears, 1972). What is more important is the argument that we limit the parameters of the concept of racism to refer to those 'scientific' ideas that were developed in the nineteenth century which purported to explain cultural varia- tion as being a product of supposed biological variation. This is an issue that faces not only Banton's definition but also that advanced by Van den Berghe who, like Banton, uses the con- cept to refer to a set of ideas which assert that (1978, p. 11): 'organic, genetically transmitted differences (whether real or imagined) between human groups are intrinsically associated with the presence or absence of certain socially relevant abili- ties or characteristics, hence that such differences are a legitimate basis of invidious distinctions between groups socially defined as races.' In essence, this definition of racism limits the application of the concept to those arguments which explicitly assert that 'race' determines culture. As we shall see, and as Banton recognised, this is a restrictive definition. Banton pointed out in the late 1960s that emotional identification with one group often involves the expression of hostility towards others but that this is now rarely justified by the group con- cerned in terms which allege the 'racial inferiority' of the defined 'out-group'. Instead, reference is usually made to some cultural attribute of the group, a reference that may be sup- ported by drawing upon psychological or sociological arguments. Banton therefore concluded that where the 'out-group' is not specifically identified as a 'race', the hostility shown towards it should be seen as an expression of ethnocentrism and not racism (1970, pp. 29–31). It follows logically from this definition that racism is a historically limited phenomenon, appearing only in the late eighteenth century and weakening (disappear- ing?) after 1945.

Rex criticised Banton's definition on the grounds that, first, biological theories may have functional substitutes, and, second, that expressions of hostility and the justification of unequal treatment may not take the form of explicit, logical theories but consist of (1970, p. 12): 'stereotypes, proverbs, symbols, folklore and so on, which while it may be seen to have an inter- nal logic of theoretical assumptions, does not at any point have these assumptions set out'. He develops his first objection by pointing out that when groups are in conflict, attempts are usually made to explain and justify the conflict. These justifica- tions may involve reference to different bodies of theoretical ideas, including the natural sciences, religion, history and sociology, with the result that it is not necessary to draw upon biological or genetic ideas. Rex is therefore arguing that racism is to be defined not by reference to arguments about supposed biological variation and its relationship with culture (i.e. about the content of beliefs) but by the form that the beliefs take (1970, p. 159):

In our belief the common element in all these theories is that
they see the connection between membership of a particular
group and of the genetically related sub-groups (i.e. families and lineages) of which that group is compounded and
the possession of evaluated qualities as completely deterministic.

So, although Rex agrees with Banton in using racism to refer
to a set of ideas, for Rex, those ideas have to assert or imply
a deterministic theory about a given group and its supposed
characteristics; for Rex, the content of the theory and the
coherence with which it is expressed are not relevant to the
identification of racism (1970, p. 160). Such a definition must
include a much wider set of beliefs and arguments within the
parameters of racism than is allowed by Banton's definition.
The differences between the respective definitions of Banton
and Rex have not been resolved satisfactorily, primarily
because neither author has felt it necessary to reply directly
to the other's arguments. With the exception of the publication
in 1973 of a letter written to Banton, Rex (1973, pp. 223-9)
has not subsequently taken up Banton's arguments. Banton has
mentioned the points of difference between himself and Rex,
but in the context of a wider discussion of the way in which
the concept of racism has been loaded with additional meanings
and explanatory tasks (1977a, pp. 159-62). In this more recent
work, Banton has argued that his late 1960s definition of racism
can now be conceived of as referring to the doctrine of racial
typology. In the light of this, and given that he also argues
that extending the application of the concept of racism cannot
be successfully defended (1977a, pp. 158-9), Banton seems
to be concluding that there is no longer any place for a concept
of racism in sociological analysis. Rather than use the concept
of racism, Banton seems to wish to refer to the doctrine of racial
typology which developed in the late eighteenth and nineteenth
centuries. This is evident when he defines a 'racial minority'
as existing when (1977a, p. 148): 'opposition to the social
incorporation of a minority is justified on the grounds of the
minority members' hereditary characteristics, particularly those
associated with skin colour and nineteenth century doctrines
of racial typology'. This shift from racism to doctrine of racial
typology in no way alters his claim that what is important is
the content of arguments (1977a, p. 156). But Banton does not
take up Rex's specific criticisms of his earlier position and so
this more recent statement seems to be little more than a termin-
ological sleight of hand which absolves him from considering
the problems involved in the use of the concept of racism.
With these points of difference between Banton and Rex
unresolved, other arguments have entered the field of discussion. Blauner, for instance, has argued that the concept of
racism should not be limited to referring to ideas or 'prejudiced
attitudes' because racism has become institutionalised (1972,

pp. 9-10):

> The processes that maintain domination - control of whites
> over nonwhites - are built into the major social institutions
> ... Thus there is little need for prejudice as a motivating
> force. Because this is true, the distinction between racism
> as an objective phenomenon, located in the actual existence
> of domination and hierarchy, and racism's subjective con-
> comitants of prejudice and other motivations and feelings
> is a basic one.

So, rather than use the concept of racism to refer to an ideology, Blauner is suggesting that it refers to a social process
which results in a certain form of social structure. Hence, he
claims at one point (1972, p. 112) that racism is 'a propensity
to categorise people who are culturally different in terms of
nonculture traits, for example, skin colour, hair, structure
of face and eye'. Elsewhere in the same text (1972, p. 41) he
suggests that:

> racism is an historical and social project aimed at reducing
> or diminishing the humanity or manhood (in the universal,
> non-restrictive meaning of the word) of the racially oppres-
> sed....The tendency of racism is to convert the colonised
> into objects or things to be used for the pleasure and profit
> of the coloniser.

A previous student of Blauner has extended some of these
arguments. Wellman, too, begins with the claim that racism
should refer to more than 'prejudiced arguments'. He claims
that prejudiced attitudes are usually identified by their being
overt, prejudgments and hostile. He then suggests that some
attitudes do not share these characteristics but are nevertheless worthy of being described as racist. For example, traditional institutional structures are often defended in terms which
do not include any reference to 'race' (1977, p. 8): 'While
these sentiments may not be prejudiced, they justify arrangements that in effect, if not in intent, maintain the status quo
and thereby keep blacks in subordinate positions.' Additionally,
he points out that both the prejudiced and the unprejudiced
are often inconsistent in their thought and behaviour in ways
which are inconsistent with their beliefs. Wellman suggests
that these limitations follow from the assumptions that racist
attitudes are rarely rational, that these attitudes have a life
of their own (i.e. are independent of the social structure) and
that the 'racial organisation of society' is a consequence of
racism (1977, pp. 14-15).
Wellman's definition of racism follows from his alternative
focus upon the material benefits that accrue to those who occupy
a dominant position in a 'racially stratified' society. He suggests
that 'racial stratification' is a phenomenon similar to class

stratification and then argues (1977, p. 35):

> The subordination of people of colour is functional to the
> operation of American society as we know it and the colour
> of one's skin is a primary determinant of people's position
> in the social structure. Racism is a structural relationship
> based on the subordination of one racial group by another.

Clearly, Wellman is not limiting the concept of racism to refer
to a complex of ideas and beliefs, but rather is broadening
it to refer to a structural feature of a social formation. Indeed,
it would seem that, for Wellman, racial stratification, racial
subordination and racism are synonymous concepts. However,
Wellman goes on to reintroduce the idea of racism as referring
to a set of ideas. He subsequently claims that racism takes a
number of different forms: it can appear as personal prejudice,
as an ideology to rationalise the superior position of whites,
or as an institution in the form of systematic practices which
exclude blacks from access to scarce resources. Thus, the
concept of racism is to refer to beliefs, behaviour and structure
(1977, p. 236):

> A position is racist when it defends, protects, or enhances
> social organisation based on racial disadvantage. Racism is
> determined by the *consequences* of a sentiment, not its
> surface qualities. ... White racism is what white people *do*
> to protect the special benefits they gain by virtue of their
> skin colour.

Let me summarise the analysis so far. I have outlined the
definitions of racism advanced by a number of different authors,
a comparison of which indicates that there are clear discrepancies and contradictions between them. I now want to identify
these discrepancies and contradictions more clearly and to go
on to attempt to resolve them. The first and most obvious is
between those who wish to define racism as an ideology and
those who want to extend the definition beyond that of ideology to refer to social practices and even to a type of social
structure. Second, should we limit the application of the concept to ideas which are systematically formulated? Third, is it
the subject matter or the character (or structure) of the ideas
which should warrant them being described as racism? Fourth,
should the concept be limited to negative beliefs about black
people which are held by white people?

Concerning the first problem, I suggest that the extension
of the application of the concept to refer to both ideas and
social practices must lead to analytical confusion. This is
because the same concept is being used to refer to two different
phenomena, ideas and action. Perhaps the only logical defence
of such a move would be to claim that ideas and action always
occur together, but such an argument is difficult to defend.

At the level of individual behaviour, there is no necessary reason for a person who articulates racist beliefs also to discriminate actively against individuals who are the object of those beliefs. This may be because the individual is never in a situation where discrimination is possible or because in such situations other factors intervene to neutralise or negate the determination of action by belief. Conversely, as Rex has argued (1970, p. 118): 'there may be situations in which a practice emerges which is not supported by any kind of explicit theory. And lastly there may well be cases in which a practice continues after its theoretical justifications have become disreputable and have been abandoned.' Rex's former point is well illustrated by reference to the fact that the slave mode of production existed in the Caribbean for at least a century before it was justified by arguments about the inherent inferiority of the enslaved (see Chapter 5). Wellman's analysis seems unaware of, and incapable of accounting for, such possibilities. His concern, as he explicitly states, is to reject the argument that 'racial stratification' is the consequence of racism but to substitute for it the equally deterministic formulation that 'racial stratification' produces racism (1977, pp. 35-44). In so doing, he is clearly making an unwarranted assumption. Consequently, it seems preferable to use the concept of racism to refer only to a set of ideas. But to what ideas? How is racism to be distinguished from other sets of ideas or ideologies? It is with this problem that the other three issues are concerned.

So, second, do we describe as racism only those ideas which are explicitly and logically formulated? Banton's late 1960s definition seems to imply an answer in the affirmative. According to that definition, racism refers to ideas presented in the form of an explanation, i.e. racism refers to the argument that, in brief, 'race' determines culture. It follows that the simple ascription of supposed and negative characteristics to a group (e.g. 'blacks are lazy and don't want to work'), that is, statements of supposed fact, which are not accompanied by an argument which justifies such a claim, cannot count as racism. This means that such a definition must exclude from consideration much 'everyday' conversation about New Commonwealth migrants and their British-born children, characterised as it is by the ascription of negatively evaluated attributes without recourse to explanation (cf. Rex, 1970, pp. 147ff, 160). We shall return to this point shortly, but let us conclude for the present that racism should be defined in such a way as to include more than logically and clearly expressed theories or doctrines.

Third, can we accept Rex's claim that racism exists when a group is identified as inevitably possessing certain fixed qualities (1970, p. 159): i.e. racist ideas are characterised by their deterministic correlation of characteristics? This claim arises from Rex's valid concern to broaden the definition offered by

Banton. But Rex strays too far in the other direction because
he allows the inclusion of all statements/arguments which deterministically attribute the negatively evaluated qualities to any
group. For example, the claim that 'manual workers could
never themselves administer the production process because
their position as manual workers reflects their inherent inability
to make complex decisions' involves the deterministic attribution of characteristics to a group. In Rex's terms, this must
qualify as racism. (Wellman's view that racism is to be identified on the basis of the consequences of ideas produces an
equally sweeping inclusion of statements and arguments. If a
racist belief is one which has as its consequence the defence
or maintenance of the existing structure of 'racial stratification',
then any defence of the existing social formation must count as
racist. On these terms, a study of racism would include all
ideas except revolutionary ideas.) In order to avoid such an
all-encompassing definition, it is necessary to specify the
content of the ideas, along with their referent. And this leads
to the final problem.

   This is evident explicitly only in Wellman's analysis and arises
from his claim that (1977, p. 4): 'racist beliefs are culturally
sanctioned, rational responses to struggles over scarce resources; that they are sentiments which, regardless of intentions,
defend the advantages that whites gain from the presence of
blacks in America'. In other words, racism is the prerogative
of 'white people' and only 'black people' can be the object of
racist beliefs. This is an unnecessary and misleading limitation
of the concept because it must exclude from consideration the
development and expression of (racist?) beliefs about the Jews
amongst the (white?) populations of Europe. It must also
exclude consideration of the way in which the Irish have been
categorised by the English and the Scots as an inferior 'race',
even though the two groups cannot be distinguished by skin
colour (Curtis, 1968, 1971; but see Gilley, 1978, for a critique,
and Chapter 6).

   In the light of these comments, racism should be defined in
such a way as to refer to a set of ideas/ideology which need
not be coherently formulated, which have a specified referent
or content and which are not constrained by terminology of
'white/black' social relations. My solution (with Annie Phizacklea: see Phizacklea and Miles, 1980) to these analytical problems is to define racism as an ideology which ascribes negatively evaluated characteristics in a deterministic manner
(which may or may not be justified) to a group which is additionally identified as being in some way biologically (phenotypically or genotypically) distinct. Put another way, the concept of racism refers to those negative beliefs held by one
group which identify and set apart another by attributing
significance to some biological or other 'inherent' character-
istic(s) which it is said to possess, and which deterministically
associate that characteristic(s) with some other (negatively

evaluated) feature(s) or action(s). The possession of these supposed characteristics may be used to justify the denial of the group equal access to material and other resources and/or political rights.

RACISM AS AN IDEOLOGY

Having formally defined racism as an ideology, it is necessary to devote some attention to the concept of ideology in order to elaborate more fully how racism is to be understood and used as a concept. This is fraught with problems because the meaning and use of the concept of ideology is much contested. I have no intention of directly entering that contest, but wish to draw upon some strands within it in order to clarify my definition of racism and to assist an understanding of its origin and reproduction.

Problems concerning the use of the concept of ideology stem from the fact that it has been used to refer to a complex of 'facts' which were organised as a theory, that is, as an explanation for, usually, the socio-economic organisation of a society, or some facet thereof. The fact that those who were the first to have said to have formulated an 'ideology' were the intellectuals supporting the French Revolution has meant that the term has subsequently been used with scorn and derision by those 'out of sympathy' with notions of social change and revolution. Subsequent usage of the term within some Marxist theories has intensified these problems. Ideology has become associated with the notions of falsity and manipulation: bourgeois ideology has been said to be the conscious product of the ruling class which aims to mystify and thereby subdue the working class. This notion is often combined with or gives rise to the base/superstructure metaphor: ideology is said to be a superstructural phenomenon, the form and/or content of which reflects the nature of or developments within the economic base. The reader is directed elsewhere to pursue these issues 'in and for themselves' (e.g. Lichtheim, 1967; Williams, 1973, 1977; Seliger, 1977; Centre for Contemporary Cultural Studies, 1978; Larrain, 1979).

In order to proceed, let us first draw a formal distinction between ideology 'in general' and 'in its specific forms'. This is to signal the possibility (and necessity) of analysing ideology as a structural characteristic, with its own pertinent effects, of and within a social formation. Such analysis should produce generalisations which are applicable to and are supported by a study of specific instances of ideology (such as racism). But to what does the term 'ideology' refer? It refers to a complex of ideas about socio-economic organisation and includes statements of 'fact' and of explanation. Consequently, 'ideology is a genetic term for the processes by which meaning is produced, challenged, reproduced, transformed' (Barrett, 1980, p. 97).

A further distinction is now required, this one drawn from the writings of Gramsci. He distinguished between systematic ways of thought (which he variously, even inconsistently, called philosophy or ideology) and eclectic, disjointed and contradictory ways of thought (which he called common sense) (1971, pp. 323-43).

As Hall et al. (1978, pp. 48-52) emphasise, Gramsci was consciously attempting to break with the notion that ideology simply reflected economic relations and wanted instead to analyse the process by which ideology is formed and articulated. The concept of intellectual was central to this latter task and it enabled Gramsci to (Hall et al., 1978, p. 51): 'analyse the organisation and production of ideology as a specific practice that is not reducible to the classes to which the intellectuals are linked. Hence ideas are not expressive of classes but comprise a field in which class conflict takes place in particular forms.' To suggest that intellectuals have a role in generating and systematising ideas is to give ideology a 'relative autonomy'. However, once generated and articulated, ideas can be appropriated by classes for their own ends. They can be 'integrated' into the common sense of a class, but not necessarily in a logical and consistent manner. And because classes are always fractionalised (see Chapter 7), then different fractions may take up and combine such ideas in different ways for different ends. But the common sense of a class, or a class fraction, is not the simple product of an appropriation of ideas produced by intellectuals. As Gramsci emphasised, there is a sense in which all men and women are philosophers: from their own lived experience, they generate notions about the structure of the world which become part of common sense. Moreover, the common sense of a class can include ideas previously appropriated by other classes and articulated in order to advance their own class interests. Finally, common sense has a historical dimension in that it is both the partial product of the ideas of the past and is also offered to future generations.

None of this should be interpreted to mean that Gramsci conceived the ideology as 'free-floating'. Although he rejected a mechanistic Marxism, he consciously remained a Marxist and insisted on a material basis for ideology. This is evident in at least two senses. First, in arguing that all men and women are philosophers, he was allowing that common sense would refract the material basis of social life: in the case of the working class, this means that it directly experiences and conceptualises the power of capital through wage labour. Second, by suggesting that ideology, which has its own conditions of existence and reproduction, is nevertheless the site of conflict between classes and class fractions, one can argue that class ideologies will appropriate those themes and ideas which it is considered will most adequately express and advance their (class, that is, their material) interests. This process is, however, not without its own effects upon the production and reproduction of ideo-

logies. Indeed, one of the conditions of existence and reproduction of ideology is class conflict. We shall return to this
point shortly.

But let us first summarise certain relevant claims about the
nature of ideology. First, ideology/ideologies is/are rarely
'imposed from above' with the conscious aim of deception.
Rather it/they has/have its/their own conditions of existence
and reproduction (although these are not independent of
material forces). Second, ideologies are not fixed and given
forms, but have to be produced and reproduced, with the
implication that their content and object is subject to change.
Third, ideologies, particularly in the form of common sense,
are not necessarily integrated and logically coherent. So, when
I claim that racism is an ideology, I am doing so with these
specific points in mind. The significance of this will become
apparent through a consideration of the ways in which some
writers who have claimed to articulate a Marxist perspective
have written about racism.

MARXISM AND THE ORIGIN OF RACISM

Most Marxists who have taken account of, or who have specifically analysed, racism have established a simple problematic:
their interest has been in formulating an explanation for the
origin of racism. In other words, the problem they have set
themselves is to identify the cause of racism. In the main, their
answer to this question has been correspondingly simple. They
have concluded that the ideology of racism was and is the direct
product of the development of the capitalist mode of production.
The consequence is a functional definition of racism which also
'explains' its origin, namely that racism was an ideology formulated by the bourgeoisie to exploit black labour in the colonies
and to divide the working class at home. What we have here
is a classic instance of a mechanistic, economistic Marxism.
Before examining some instances of such arguments, I should
add that not all Marxist analyses take this form (e.g. Genovese,
1969; but see Gabriel and Ben-Tovim, 1978).

Cox (1970) is usually credited with having written a, if not
the, Marxist analysis of 'race relations'. I have argued elsewhere (1980) that the attribution of Marxist status to 'Caste,
Class and Race' is perhaps ill-advised, but this is of only
peripheral concern at this point. Here I want to consider
Cox's argument about the origin of racism, or rather, as he
prefers to term it, race prejudice (1970, p. 482). Cox argues
that (1970, p. 322):

> racial exploitation and race prejudice developed among
> Europeans with the rise of capitalism and nationalism, and
> that because of the world-wide ramifications of capitalism,
> all racial antagonisms can be traced to policies and attitudes

of the leading capitalist people, the white people of Europe and North America.

He claims that prior to the discovery of the Americas (and so including the period of initial European expansion which was characterised by the development of trade without settlement), the religious view of the world was the crucial factor in obstructing the development of 'race prejudice' because Christianity (in the form of Catholicism) stressed that those with whom contact was made should receive the word of God and, consequently, they came to share the status of human beings (1970, pp. 327-8). Such status was not to be accorded to those populations 'discovered' at the time of, and after, the development of capitalism. Cox is sufficiently bold to date the emergence of 'race prejudice' to the end of the fifteenth and the early sixteenth centuries (1970, pp. 331, 334) and argues that it arose from the need to exploit labour in the form of slave labour (1970, pp. 330-2). Hence (1970, p. 333):

> racial exploitation is merely one aspect of the problem of the proletarianisation of labor, regardless of the color of the laborer. Hence racial antagonism is essentially political-class conflict. The capitalist exploiter, being opportunistic and practical, will utilise any convenience to keep his labor and other resources freely exploitable. He will devise and employ race prejudice when that becomes convenient.

As an ideology, 'race prejudice' is therefore viewed as the direct product of the bourgeoisie, formulated to justify the exploitation of labour power. Thereby Cox is able to link the origin of 'race prejudice' with a material factor, namely the means of extracting surplus product from labour power. This is clearly expressed in the following claim (1970, p. 476): 'Race prejudice, then, constitutes an additional justification necessary for an easy exploitation of some race. To put it still another way, race prejudice is the social-attitudinal concomitant of the racial-exploitative practice of a ruling class in a capitalistic society.' But this 'attitudinal justification' did not emerge 'fully formed' in the early sixteenth century (1970, pp. 399-400) but developed with and alongside the growing dominance of capitalism and nationalism over a period of three centuries (1970, p. 330):

> Racial antagonism attained full maturity during the latter half of the nineteenth century, when the sun no longer set on British soil and the great nationalistic powers of Europe began to justify their economic designs upon weaker European peoples with subtle theories of racial superiority and masterhood.

In addition to the materialistic nature of Cox's argument, there are two other characteristics that should be noted. First, it specifically links the origin of racism with the development of the capitalist mode of production: as an ideology, it did not exist prior to the development of capitalism. Second, the ideology was formulated as a means to an end: it constituted a justification for the exploitation of labour power. This leads Cox to define 'race prejudice' in functionalist terms. For Cox, 'race prejudice' is (1970, p. 393): 'a social attitude propagated among the public by an exploiting class for the purpose of stigmatising some group as inferior so that the exploitation of either the group itself or its resources or both may be justified'.

In as much as Cox's argument has come to be regarded as definitive of Marxism, both by Marxists and non-Marxists (e.g. Banton, 1970, p. 21; Rex, 1970, pp. 15-16), one would expect to find its main postulates reproduced in other Marxist explanations for the origin of racism. For example, Nikolinakos, who refers to Cox in an approving manner, proclaims an intention to develop a Marxist theory of racism (1973, p. 365). Such a theory should be economic, he claims, and (1973, p. 366): 'should explain the different historical forms in which it (i.e. racism) has appeared till now and reveal the function racism serves in a capitalist system'. Nikolinakos suggests that racism, which he defines as a 'social attitude', did occur in precapitalist formations (so, on this issue, he disagrees with Cox) but, unlike in capitalist formations, it was not coherently expressed for the purpose of exploitation. Only with the rise of colonialism and then imperialism did it become necessary that racism be systematically formulated and utilised for material or economic ends (1973, p. 367): 'Racism served in this way as a justification and at the same time as a means for the Europeans to exploit the indigenous peoples. This exploitation facilitated the capital accumulation of the imperialist countries.'

In other words, racism, although not the specific creation of the rising bourgeoisie, only took on economic, political and ideological significance when merchant-capitalists wished to justify their exploitations of labour in the colonies. And because racism was thereby a means to the realisation of class interests, the conflict to which it gave rise is class-based (1973, p. 368): 'It is therefore evident that racial conflicts appear as racial only on the surface. In reality, they are class conflicts and they have always appeared as such both in cases where racial groups have been dominated and where they have been dominant.' Finally, Nikolinakos implies that the utilisation and articulation of racism is the sole prerogative of the bourgeoisie. This is evident in the attention that he gives to the function of racism not only as a justification for colonial exploitation, but also as a means to divide the working class and intensify the exploitation of labour 'at home' (1973, p. 369).

A similar argument is advanced by Castles and Kosack in their study of migrant labour in Western European capitalism. They claim that migrant labour has both an economic and a socio-political function for capitalism: first, as a new reserve army of labour, and second as a means of dividing the working class. Developing this second point, the authors locate the origin of racism in capitalist expansion (1972, p. 16):

> Racialism and xenophobia are products of the capitalist national state and of its imperialist expansion. Their principal historical function was to split the working class on the international level, and to motivate one section to help exploit another in the interests of the ruling class.

Again, Cox is approvingly quoted in connection with this claim.

A final example will emphasise my point. Sivanandan, too, traces the 'root' of racism to (1973, p. 384): 'the colonial phase of capitalist expansion when the opportunity to amass vast profit from the enslavement and proletarianisation of whole continents of people required a commensurate philosophy of justification'. Again, racism is analysed in terms of its function in a capitalist society, the most important of which is the division of the working class and the blurring of class boundaries (1973, p. 385; 1976, pp. 350-1). Of greater significance, for Sivanandan, than this political and ideological function of racism is its function of ensuring the super-exploitation of black labour (1976, pp. 350-1, 358). But here Sivanandan's argument adds a new dimension for he recognises that the super-exploitation of black labour has repercussions at the level of political and ideological relations. In Britain, these repercussions have taken the form of black militancy amongst black youth which he believes threatens to stimulate radical political action amongst black workers and even the working class as a whole. But let us note for the purposes of later analysis that the relationship between these 'levels' is posed as deterministic and one-way (1976, p. 367):

> For capital requires racism not for racism's sake but for the sake of capital. Hence at a certain level of economic activity (witness the colonies) it finds it more profitable to abandon the idea of superiority of race in order to promote the idea of the superiority of capital. Racism dies in order that capital might survive.

In other words, racism is no longer functional for capital and consequently its articulation is abandoned.

In so far as these arguments reproduce the main themes to be found in Cox's analysis, a critique of Cox is simultaneously a critique of Nikolinakos, of Castles and Kosack and of Sivanandan. There are several general criticisms that will be made here (while the historical arguments will be pursued in Chapter 5). The first concerns the functionalist character of

the explanation for the origin of racism: the arguments developed against the functionalist school of sociology (e.g. Cohen,
1968) apply equally to this 'explanation'. In practice nothing is
actually explained because, as with all functionalist arguments,
the cause of a phenomenon is held to lie in its effect. Logically,
this means that the effect is also the cause, and so the argument becomes circular: it follows from defining racism as the
means by which capitalism exploits 'black' labour that the exploitation of 'black' labour 'causes' racism which 'causes' the exploitation of 'black' labour which 'causes' racism which 'causes' ...
etc. The approach is ultimately vacuous because we are given
no explanation as to how racism originated; that is to say, we
are not told of the antecedent conditions that were necessary
for the formation and articulation of those ideas which qualify
as racism.

Second, Cox's analysis approximates to a conspiracy theory.
He specifically claims that the ideology of racism was devised
or produced by the capitalist class, an argument which, in the
absence of statements to the contrary, implies that this class
consciously and collectively decided to formulate a set of ideas
to achieve a certain end, i.e. to facilitate the exploitation of
'black' labour. Not only is no historical evidence provided to
support such a view, but it also runs counter to the fact that
members of that class have also articulated anti-racist ideas.
As with all conspiracy theories, unwarranted and unsupported
(by evidence) claims are made which assume a homogeneity of
interest and purpose within the class in question.

Third, racism is analysed as if it were the prerogative of
the bourgeoisie or ruling class. Where recognition is given to
the fact that racism is articulated within the working class,
it is suggested that this is the successful outcome of the ruling-
class strategy to divide the working class. The working class
is therefore portrayed as an empty vessel into which have been
poured bourgeois ideas. Such an argument not only gives a
simplistic and misleading notion of the means by which ideology
(in both of the senses mentioned by Gramsci) is created and
reproduced but also fails to appreciate that ideas articulated
within the working class can have their origin in and/or be
reproduced for material reasons which are specific to that class
(see Phizacklea and Miles, 1979; 1980, pp. 127-32, 163-5,
173-6).

Fourth, Cox's analysis assumes a linear development of
racism. He places great explanatory significance on two separate events in the late fifteenth and early sixteenth centuries
in order to support the contention that racism emerged simultaneously with the development of capitalism and he separately
states that racism reached 'maturity' in the nineteenth century.
There is no discussion of what happened in the intervening
three to four hundred years. In addition to objecting to locating the rise of capitalism in the late fifteenth century, it can
be claimed that the only basis upon which one can assume such

a linear development is by assuming a linear development of capitalism and a mechanical determination of the political and ideological by the economic relations. As we shall see, there are theoretical and historical reasons for objecting to both assumptions.

Fifth, in locating the origin of racism with the simultaneous rise of capitalism and colonialism, Cox makes the fundamental error of limiting the analysis to the ideas about 'black people' held by 'white people'. He does make an attempt to distinguish analytically between racism and anti-semitism, but the distinction cannot be maintained (see Miles, 1980). This point will be pursued further in Chapter 5.

It is possible to summarise these objections to Cox's argument into two general criticisms. His argument and the arguments of his followers are deterministic and fail to make adequate reference to the historical record. In addition, there are a number of conceptual errors, but they concern us less in this context. Similar criticisms of Cox and others are beginning to be voiced from within the framework of Marxist theory. For example, Gabriel and Ben-Tovim (1978) seek to apply some of the more recent developments within Marxist theory and in so doing they find good reason to reject the economic determinism and reductionism evident in Cox's work. Concluding their analysis, they argue that racism is a 'determinate ideological practice' with its own 'theoretical/ideological conditions of existence' (1978, p. 139):

> Only subsequent to this process of ideological production do specific racial ideologies intervene at the level of political practice and the economy. These levels themselves cannot be held responsible for the production in the first instance of racist ideology, although there is a sense in which they can be said to determine in the last instance the *mode of reproduction* of racism.

In other words, racism is not the direct product or reflection of capitalism but can be explained by reference to factors quite separate from economic relations. However, the effect of racism as an ideology is structured by economic relations, as well as by political relations.

Ironically, this particular article shares with the work of Cox a disregard for historical analysis. The method of the paper is to criticise theoretically (and often correctly) the definitions and analyses of other writers by a mechanical application of some of the insights of Althusser and Poulantzas (for an exposition of their arguments, see Centre for Contemporary Cultural Studies, 1978) without any attempt to substitute any specific solutions to the problems they raise. This can be illustrated with two examples. First, they criticise (1978, pp. 129-32, 138) those analyses which have attempted to define racism solely in terms of the content of the ideas (i.e. reference to (supposed) biological features of a group), but fail to specify the meaning that they give to racism. Second, they exclude theoretically the possibility of economic relations having any determinant effect on the formation of racism, confining the impact of the economic to the reproduction of the ideology, but fail to specify the factors responsible for the development of racism. In other words, the analysis shields itself from all criticism other than that which is exclusively theoretical by failing to offer any specific solution to the identified problems. It is only by giving substance to theoretical criticism through reference to the historical record that it is possible to explain more adequately the nature, origin and development (or reproduction) of racism as an ideology (see Chapter 5).

SOCIOLOGY AND THE ORIGIN OF RACISM

It is ironic that writers who would prefer to identify themselves as sociologists rather than Marxists have appropriated the field of systematic historical analysis in considering the origin of racism. There are only a few exceptions (e.g. Genovese, 1969; Kiernan, 1972). I now wish to contrast the type of analysis and argument described above with the sociological contribution.

Some sociologists have questioned the determinism and functionalism that characterises much Marxist analysis. For example, Banton wishes to question the view that (1977a, p. 13): 'Western conceptions of race arose out of the contacts between white people and black people that followed European voyages of exploration to America, Africa, and Asia in the fifteenth and sixteenth centuries.' He is quick to state that these contacts, and the exploitation of labour that followed from them, helped to shape the 'racial categories' that were developed by Europeans, but adds that other factors were also important. He then explicitly denies the possibility of being able to disentangle the influence of each of the factors involved (1977a, p.14). This having been said, he subsequently sets out to concentrate on one particular 'influence', on the grounds that other writers have paid it little or no attention. This influence is identified as the impact of social change within Europe, and, more specifically, the way in which the English came to view themselves as a 'race'.

As indicated in Chapter 1, Banton claims that during the seventeenth century, English political writing expressed the view that the English were descended from the Saxons, and that this historical interpretation constituted an embryonic racial theory of history. His analysis then 'jumps' to the beginning of the nineteenth century, notably because the word 'race' begins to change its meaning from that of lineage to a physically defined category. During the course of the nineteenth century, this new notion of 'race' was applied beyond Europe to the

populations of the world as a whole. A central feature of this
process was the development of a scientific theory about the
nature of 'race', a theory which Banton labels the theory of
racial typology. For my purposes, I now wish to label the
theories developed in this period as scientific racism.

How does Banton account for the development of scientific
racism (in his terms, the doctrine of racial typology)? He
argues that the principal source was the development of ideas
about the world's prehistory and explanations for the origin
of species while a number of other factors are attributed with
a supplementary influence, namely (i) the limited knowledge
of Europeans about non-Europeans; (ii) the material advancement of Europe relative to the rest of the world; and (iii) contacts between Europeans and non-Europeans overseas (1977a,
p. 54). Mindful, no doubt, of Marxist arguments, Banton ela-
borates on the significance of the latter factor, arguing that
the attack on the slave trade in the late eighteenth century
had only a limited impact on the development of scientific racism.
Of greater significance, he continues, were various events in
the mid-nineteenth century (the China War, the Indian 'Mutiny'
and the American Civil War), although he argues that this
should not be interpreted to mean that there was a connection
between imperialism and the development of scientific racism.
He justifies this by claiming that the mid-nineteenth century
was not a period of colonial expansion, as was the late nineteenth century, adding that imperialist sentiment in the late
nineteenth century focused on support for the 'white colonies'
and not upon the rule of 'black men by white' (1977a, p. 60).
However, he seems to contradict this last claim later in the same
text (1977a, p. 96):

> At the end of the nineteenth and in the early twentieth
> century the British saw race relations in an imperial con-
> text as involving them with backward races overseas. Social
> Darwinism flourished both in this context and in discussions
> of the relations between social classes at home.

There are a number of points to be made about this argument.
First, given that Banton equates racism with the theory of
racial typology (i.e. scientific racism), his analytical task is
to explain the emergence of a certain set of ideas in the mid-
nineteenth century. He acknowledges that a number of factors
were at work, but claims that it is impossible to distinguish
the relative importance of each one. He then contradicts this
by arguing that the principal factor was the evolution of English ideas about themselves as a 'race'. Moreover, he offers no
evidence which would allow us to evaluate his claim that this
factor was more important than the others.

Second, the argument is idealist: that is to say, the ideas of
nineteenth-century racism are explained as being primarily the
product of other ideas (e.g. the ideas of the English as a

'race'). Such an argument implies both an infinite regress
(ideas lead to ideas which lead to ideas, etc.) and the determination of socio-economic structures and processes by ideas.
It is here that we confront a major conflict between sociology
and Marxist analysis because, as Marx argued (Marx and
Engels, 1965, p. 50):

> This conception of history depends on our ability to expound
> the real process of production, starting out from the material
> production of life itself, and to comprehend the form of
> intercourse connected with this and created by this mode
> of production (i.e. civil society in its various stages), as
> the basis of all history; and to show it in its action as
> State, to explain all the different theoretical products
> and forms of consciousness, religion, philosophy, ethics,
> etc., and trace their origins and growth from that basis;
> by which means, of course, the whole thing can be depicted
> in its totality (and therefore, too, the reciprocal action of
> these various sides on one another). It has not, like the
> idealistic view of history, in every period to look for a
> category, but remains constantly on the real *ground* of
> history; it does not explain practice from the idea but
> explains the formation of ideas from material practice.

How is this error manifest in Banton's argument? The answer
lies partly in his implicit denial of the material basis for the
development of science in the nineteenth century for, as
various writers have stressed (e.g. Hobsbawm, 1969, pp. 59-
60, 173-4), the development of industrial capitalism posed
and required the solution of many technical problems. But in
arguing that the production of scientific knowledge answered
at least some of these questions, it is not being suggested
that the process and product of science was determined by
capitalism. Rather, capitalism created a terrain within which,
and which structured the way in which, scientific knowledge
was produced (cf. Rose and Rose, 1976). But the process of
generation of knowledge has its own effects on the product of
knowledge. Moreover, those involved in the production of
knowledge are themselves subject to the influence of not only
economic, but also political and ideological factors and these
are likely to be of particular significance when the object of
science is social relations. Consequently, if scientific racism
was a scientific error, as Banton claims, then it cannot be
viewed as a 'simple' product of error internal to the production
of scientific knowledge (i.e. a product of a 'wrong' observation
or an 'invalid' explanation). In this connection, it is pertinent
to ask why it was that science posed, as a question for analysis,
the socio-economic significance of phenotypical variation. It is
even more pertinent to inquire into what factors were involved
in the formulation of an answer which proposed a hierarchy of
'races' (see Chapter 5).

Now Banton does attempt an answer to these questions, but his analysis remains primarily at the level of intellectual production. For example, the evidence he cites to support his argument is primarily in the form of the written word (ideas), i.e. ideas about the English 'race', ideas about the inferiority of 'black' people. Hence, his historical analysis is circumscribed, in effect, to a history of ideas. Here, Rex misses the point when he tries to suggest that Banton's work is not sociological (Banton, 1977a, pp. 161-2). Rather, the error lies in failing to pay at least equal attention to the history of real, material relations (between classes, between different modes of production, etc.). But before I go on to show in Chapter 5 that this sort of historical analysis is both possible and necessary, it is important to consider briefly other sociological explanations about the origin of racism.

Van den Berghe's analysis shows certain similarities with that of Banton, but there are some important differences between them too. Van den Berghe claims that racism is neither universal nor a unique invention of nineteenth-century European culture during a period of colonial adventure. However, he believes that the racism that developed in Europe during the nineteenth century was of special political significance and thereby worthy of special attention. He traces its origin to the 1830s/1840s, claiming that it reached its peak between 1880 and 1920, since when it has been in decline. He suggests that three factors have to be taken into account in explaining the genesis of nineteenth-century racism. First, although racism was congruent with capitalist exploitation (in the forms of New World slavery and colonial expansion in Africa), there can be no direct causal relationship between the two phenomena because the institution of slavery preceded the development of racist thought. Second, he claims that racism was congruent with the Darwinism which was evident in biological thinking and which was applied to social relations in the late nineteenth century. Third, the egalitarianism of the American and French Revolutions both conflicted with and assisted the development of racism, the latter because in the light of the contradiction between the treatment of slaves and the rhetoric of equality, Europeans were led to distinguish between men and savages (1978, pp. 12-18).

This explanation leaves much to be desired. In the absence of supporting evidence and argument (of which there is none), tracing the origin of nineteenth-century European racism to the 1830s/1840s is arbitrary. Moreover, if racism is not a phenomenon unique to the nineteenth century, then there is no logical reason to assume that the form that racism assumed in the nineteenth century was not the result of processes that pre-dated the nineteenth century and which may account for the earlier appearances of racism. Finally, there is only limited emphasis upon material factors as opposed to ideas, while the emphasis that is made is negative in that the aim is only to deny 'any

simple, direct, causal relationship that makes racism an epi-
phenomenal derivative of the system of production' (1978, p. 17).

So, despite recognition being given to the need for an historical analysis of the development of racism, and to the
'congruence' of racism and capitalist exploitation, Van den
Berghe's analysis fails to develop either of these lines of
investigation and explanation. The former cannot be said of
Jordan, who, concerned to trace the historical origins of
racism in America, begins with consideration of the reaction
of the English to their first contacts with Africans from the
middle of the sixteenth century to the end of the seventeenth
century. He stresses that the first contact was not with Africans as slaves, but as other sorts of men. He argues that four
factors structured the English view of the African, a view that
subsequently came to structure the perception of the African
as a slave. First, the English noted the African's skin colour,
this occurring in a cultural context in which blackness was
loaded with intense negative meaning. Second, the African was
considered to be a heathen, a feature that was considered to
be inseparable from other attributes and which led to the conclusion that the African was not civilised. Third, the African
was viewed as a savage beast. Because initial contact with
the African was simultaneous with initial contact with the chim-
panzee, there developed speculation about both the origin of
the African and the possibility of sexual relations between apes
and Africans. This related to the fourth characteristic attributed to the African, sexual potency. Jordan argues that the
attribution of these characteristics to the African occurred in
a period marked by the Protestant Reformation when the guid-
ing principles were adventure and control. Overseas 'adventure'
in the form of mercantilism brought material prosperity to a
few but the social changes consequent upon that prosperity
led others to worry about social and moral control at home.
They became concerned about the need for discipline, and if
self-discipline failed, then it had to be applied externally.
Jordan suggests that the conception of the African as a heathen,
a savage beast and sexually potent made them candidates for
a special kind of discipline (1974, pp. 3-25).

This analysis constitutes a double challenge, both to other
sociological accounts, and to the form of Marxist account discussed in the previous section. The sociological accounts outlined above have limited the existence or appearance of racism
to the nineteenth century, either by the manner in which
racism is defined (e.g. Banton) or by the arbitrary fiat (e.g.
Van den Berghe) and so have avoided systematic consideration
of the historical development of negative ideas about other
populations identified as being biologically distinct. Jordan's
argument suggests that to do so is to ignore an important determinant of the image constructed by the English of (black)
Africans as 'early' as the mid-sixteenth century. By implication,
this means that there may be at least a link, if not a determinate

relationship, between the scientific racism of the nineteenth century and the imagery of the African developed in the late sixteenth and early seventeenth centuries. As far as economistic Marxism is concerned, Jordan's argument suggests that there cannot be a simple, deterministic relationship between capitalism and racism because the content of Western European culture, with its overlapping dichotomies of meaning (black/white: sin/purity: dirt/cleanliness, etc.), contained within it a predisposition to a negative evaluation of populations with a darker skin. By the same token, Jordan's analysis is congruent with those Marxist accounts which wish to locate the origins of racism outside the late eighteenth and nineteenth centuries. The significance of some of these points will be pursued in Chapter 5.

CONCLUSION

This chapter has had an expository and critical aim in that it has been concerned with the adequacy of definitions of, and accounts of the origin of racism. I have identified a number of problems with existing definitions of racism and, in the light of these, have suggested an alternative definition. In arguing that the concept should be used to refer to an ideology, I have attempted to specify the sense in which this latter term should be used by reference to the work of Gramsci. I then went on to contrast sociological and certain Marxist accounts of the origin of racism, in the process of which I was able to identify their respective and similar shortcomings. One of the key conclusions to emerge from this discussion is that much greater significance and scope should be given to historical analysis: economistic Marxism effectively disregards such analysis while sociological analyses tend to limit the focus of their historical scope, either by their idealism and/or by their emphasis upon the development of scientific racism in the nineteenth century. But in drawing this conclusion, I am not suggesting that a simple recounting of the historical record in detail will reveal the origin of racism. Of crucial significance is the formulation and use of the concepts with which the historical record can be analysed. It is with these questions in mind that I move on to attempt to use the historical record and contemporary sources to provide some answers which avoid the limitations of 'race/ethnic' relations analysis.

Part II
The significance of
political economy

Man's reflections on the forms of social life, and consequently, also, his scientific analysis of those forms,
take a course directly opposite to that of their actual
historical development. He begins, post festum, with
the results of the process of development ready to hand
before him.

K. Marx, 'Capital', vol. 1, 1970, p. 75.

The problem is, therefore, to de-construct the idea of 'race'
and to reconstruct, historically and with due regard to the
limitations placed upon social processes by production relations,
the way in which racial categorisation has become a significant
feature of not only political and ideological relations, but also
economic relations. The process of analytical reconstruction
must accord due significance to the fact that 'race' and 'race
relations' are not the given realities that they now appear but,
rather, are ideological forms which have been articulated and
reproduced by persons within classes, with consequent determinate effects upon economic and political relations. The nature
of these effects ensures that 'race' and 'race relations' appear
to (and, in a certain sense, do) have an object to which they
refer. But the object is not an essential reality, rather an ideological construction which has been developed within the constraints of certain material parameters. The three chapters that
follow make no pretence of being a complete analysis of that
process. They are three interrelated essays which address
three key dimensions of the process within Britain. They pay
particular attention to the historical record and to developing
an analysis critically, by reference to the limitations of alternative sociological explanations.

5 CAPITALISM AND COLONIALISM: THE IDEOLOGICAL LEGACY

The aim of this chapter is to reconsider the nature of the relationship between capitalism, colonialism and racism. This will proceed at two levels: first, attention will be given to theoretical matters in order to specify the sort of conceptual framework within which to understand the relationship between racism (understood as an ideology) and capitalism and colonialism; second, I shall consider the historical record with the intention of indicating the possibility of constructing a Marxist account of the generation and reproduction of racism which avoids the error of economism as identified in Chapter 2. But, by virtue of referring to historical evidence, it becomes necessary to indicate some historical parameters for study. In this chapter, the focus is upon Britain, primarily because it was Britain which first underwent the transition from feudalism to capitalism, the transition being dependent upon, inter alia, the development of a colonial empire. This must not be interpreted to mean that racism is a specifically British or perhaps English (cf. Nairn, 1977) phenomenon, although, as we shall see, the specificity of the British development does have specific implications for an explanation of the generation and reproduction of racism.

IDEALISM, REIFICATION AND PSYCHOLOGISM

I want to begin by identifying a number of errors that are commonly made in non-Marxist accounts of the generation and reproduction of racism. This will allow the reader to appreciate more readily the distinctiveness of a Marxist analysis. The first error is that of idealism which, because it has been discussed in Chapter 4, requires only brief mention here. An idealist analysis attempts to explain the emergence and effects of ideas in terms of preceding ideas. The consequence is that historical analysis comes to focus upon the history of certain ideas, into which 'real' events only intrude as consequences. One can further illustrate this tendency by referring to a text by Poliakov (1974) which attempts to explain the origin of the Aryan myth. Poliakov argues that this myth was the product of the development of a new science which was in the throes of attempting to rid itself of religious beliefs (1974, pp. 202, 328). In other words, racism emerged from a conflict between two other ideas.

The second error is that of reification. By this I mean that some writers have characterised racism as an active subject in the historical process in such a way as to suggest that racism brings about certain consequences 'by itself'. For example, Mosse writes (1978, p. xii): 'Racism annexed every important idea and movement in the nineteenth and twentieth centuries and promised to protect each against all adversaries.' Elsewhere, he talks about racism 'creating myths' (p. xiii) and racism allying itself with social movements (p. 112). Now it is not here denied that an ideology has real effects on economic, political and ideological relations, but this has to be understood in a very specific sense. Ideologies have effects only because they are constructed by human actors in order to give meaning to and to structure human activity. They are therefore social constructions and have effects not 'in themselves', but by virtue of their creation and articulation by human actors in certain circumstances. Hence, an ideology cannot, in itself, have any effect, but is the means by which people evaluate or stimulate an outcome or event (although the outcome may not be the one that the actors intended). The active agent is, therefore, not the ideology but the person or group generating and articulating the ideology. Consequently, our analysis of racism must avoid reifying (i.e. making a thing of), ideology, but, rather, should regard it as a social product which has real effects only through human agents.

The third and final error is that of psychologism, by which I mean the tendency to explain socio-economic phenomena as the outcome of some universal psychological characteristic or desire. This is evident in Poliakov's text when he claims in the course of a discussion of the various ideological strands that contributed to the generation of scientific racism that (1974, p. 204): 'In the last analysis, however, we believe that all these debates and contradictions lead us back to a permanent conflict which dwells in the heart of every human being.' This permanent conflict is identified as being between 'regressive maternal influences' and 'identification with the paternal image'. Consequently, the origin of racism is ultimately located in a psychoanalytic conflict which is common to all human beings, the corollary being that racism is both a necessary and universal phenomenon.

The objection to all three of these tendencies is both epistemological and empirical. The epistemological objection can be summarised in the following claim by Marx and Engels (1965, pp. 37-8):

We set out from real, active men, and on the basis of their real life-process we demonstrate the development of the ideological reflexes and echoes of this life-process. The phantoms formed in the human brain are also, necessarily, sublimates of their material life-process, which is empirically verifiable and bound to material premises. Morality, religion,

metaphysics, all the rest of ideology and their corresponding forms of consciousness, thus no longer retain the sem-
blance of independence. They have no history, no development; but men, developing their material production and
their material intercourse, alter, along with this their real
existence, their thinking and the products of their thinking.

Following from, and guided by this claim, the empirical objection lies in the fact that it is possible to trace, historically and
by reference to human agents, the generation and reproduction
of an ideology of racism. That ideology has not been a universal and psychologically determined phenomenon, but has
developed out of the real activity of human agents in given
conditions. In so far as it has become like any other ideology
a 'material force' (Marx, 1971a, pp. 122-3), this has been
because its articulation in certain socio-economic conditions by
particular groups has had real effects upon material and social
relations.

It is to the historical record that I now want to turn, but not
yet to account for the generation and reproduction. of racism.
Before that, I wish to demonstrate empirically the inadequacy
of one strand of Marxist explanation, economism (see Ben-Tovim,
1978).

THE REJECTION OF ECONOMISM: THE HISTORICAL RECORD

In his 'Prison Notebooks', Gramsci wrote (1971, p. 407):

The claim, presented as an essential postulate of historical
materialism, that every fluctuation of politics and ideology
can be presented and expanded as an immediate expression
of the structure, must be contested in theory as primitive
infantilism, and combated in practice with the authentic
testimony of Marx, the author of concrete and political
works.

To pursue the theoretical contestation is diversionary in the
present context; the 'concrete and political' is not. I now
want to argue that the historical evidence cannot support the
claims of some Marxist writers (see Chapter 4) that the appearance and articulation of racism can be traced directly and
deterministically to the development of capitalism as a mode of
production. The specific vehicle for this deterministic relationship is said to be colonialism. The argument runs as follows.

The development of the capitalist mode of production was
dependent upon, inter alia, a process of primitive accumulation
which, historically, was ensured by colonialism. Colonialism
involved at its earliest stage, plunder and trade, but later
assumed a productive aspect in that territory was acquired and

raw materials and agricultural goods were produced from within
that territory. The goods produced entered into a cycle of
trade, to the material benefit of merchant capitalists who were
able to thereby generate sufficient capital to initiate industrial
production. But in order that agricultural commodities could
be produced in the colonies, labour power was required. For
a variety of reasons, the demand for labour could only be
satisfied by importing labour into the various territories. Hence,
those persons supplying the labour power were taken from
Africa to the Caribbean islands and, later, to the North American mainland. For our purpose, what was significant was the
means by which labour was procured in Africa and the means
by which labour power was appropriated in the colonies. These
are usually understood as the slave trade and slavery respectively. These processes, the argument continues, had to be
justified and so the ideology of racism was formulated, presumably by the planters and merchants. The conclusion, as we
have already seen in Chapter 4, is that racism is a direct product of the development of capitalism (e.g. see Cox, 1970,
pp. 321-45).

Using the historical evidence, one can formulate the following
objections to this argument. These are additional to the criticisms outlined in the previous chapter. First, a respected
historian of the slave trade and the relevance of the slave
mode of production to the development of capitalism has recor-
ded the following conclusion to his historical study of the
British Caribbean (Williams, 1970, p. 204): 'these seventeenth
century arguments in favour of slavery acknowledged, directly
or indirectly, that the Negro was a man, and that they were
not based on any alleged inferiority - except the implied
inferiority of power - of Negroes'. Williams argues that it was
not until the second half of the eighteenth century that the
central issue in the debate about slavery became the alleged
inferiority of black people. Thus, if there was such a long
'delay' in developing a justification of slavery in terms of the
alleged inherent inferiority of Africans, then it follows that
the ideology of racism could not have been an immediately
necessary product of and/or condition for the continuation of
the slave trade and the slave mode of production. Moreover,
if the development of capitalism did not immediately give rise
to racism at the point that it became dependent upon this
trade and mode of production and was able to continue without
a theory of alleged natural inferiority, then some other fac-
tor(s) must have intervened to stimulate the generation of the
ideology. Racism, understood as an ideology alleging the
inherent inferiority of the African, was not, therefore, the
'immediate expression of the structure'.

Second, in so far as the ideology of racism places great
explanatory and evaluative significance upon physical appearance (or phenotypical variation), and in particular upon skin
colour (i.e. blackness), we have to take account of those

elements of British culture which placed an evaluative premium
upon whiteness and associated a range of negative characteristics with blackness (Jordan, 1968, pp. 4-11). This point takes
on special significance when one recalls that initial contact
between Europeans and Africans was not in connection with
the slave trade or with Africans as slaves (Jordon, 1968,
p. 4). Walvin notes that information about Africans has been
available in Europe for several hundred years before the middle
of the sixteenth century in the form of manuscript and, later,
printed accounts of foreign travel. In so far as the African's
blackness was a matter of comment and considered worthy of
explanation, the Bible was commonly used to provide an answer
(Walvin, 1973, p. 3; also Jordan, 1968, pp. 17-18). These early
accounts and explanations took on new meaning and significance
when Englishmen produced their own, contemporary accounts
of contact with Africans from the mid-sixteenth century onwards
as a result of their own direct experience as explorers and
traders. These people took particular note of the African's
blackness and nakedness, characteristics which challenged
their values. As Walvin states (1973, pp. 21-2): 'The existence
of the African placed a strain on a series of fundamental English
beliefs: the genesis of mankind, the nature of beauty and,
most perplexing of all, the reliability of biblical explanation.'
   This imagery of the African, focusing on blackness and nakedness, and the challenge that it posed for English values, developed when English involvement in the slave trade was very
limited and in the absence of control over any colonial territory,
let alone involvement in production using slave labour. It was
not until the first half of the seventeenth century that English
merchants gained control over a large part of the West Indies
and not until the second half of that same century that English
involvement in the slave trade became formalised and extensive
(the Company of Royal Adventurers being formed in 1663 and
replaced by the Royal African Company in 1672). Clearly, there
was time and opportunity for negative evaluations to develop
in the English mind about the African, given the cultural values
symbolised in the black/white dichotomy, without the pressing
incentive of having to justify either involvement in a slave
trade or slave mode of production. In sum, these basic cultural
dichotomies in English culture were an important predisposition
for the later (i.e. late eighteenth-century) development of
theories of inherent inferiority. In so far as the conditions of
existence of these dichotomies have to be located in a time and
place before the sixteenth century, these are certainly prior
to the colonial beginnings of that long process that was to
result in the development of the capitalist mode of production.
Clearly, then, we cannot conclude that racism is a simple and
direct consequence of the development of capitalism.
   Third, any argument that locates the origin of racism firmly
and completely within a capitalism/colonialism problematic has
little or no scope for explaining the development of racism in

Western and Central Europe. The same point may also be
expressed by arguing that economistic explanations, by their
focus upon colonialism and reactions to blackness, are unable
to account for the development of racism which has its focus
on the Jews. Consequently, it is quite possible to read texts
on the history of racism within Europe which make no mention
of the role of colonialism (cf. Mosse, 1978). This is not necessarily because their authors reject Marxist explanations, but
because the development of racist ideology which focuses upon
Jews cannot be grounded in the development of colonialism.
In this connection, Poliakov notes (1974, pp. 209-10) that,
compared with the rest of Western Europe, the Aryan myth
never gained a great deal of popular attention or support in
England and that the history of colonialism was a more important
factor in the genesis of racism in England. Later, he refers to
the 'special climate of opinion that prevailed in England' (1974,
p. 223). Lorimer also suggests that the development of racism
in England took a different course than that in the rest of
Europe, although his explanation refers to the absence of a
major cultural division within the 'middle class' (1978, p. 208).
The difficulty of explaining European racism by reference solely
to a history of colonialism may be the very reason that English-
speaking Marxist analysis often attempts to distinguish analytically between racism and anti-semitism (Cox, 1970, pp. 393-4),
although it is difficult to see how this distinction can be justified and sustained (Miles, 1980, pp. 178-81). This is an
instance when the specificity of English capitalism and its off-
shoots (e.g. USA) is neatly refracted in the analytical focus of
its Marxism. Other, non-Marxist writers simply postulate that
imagery of the Jews in Britain has a different source to that of
imagery of 'coloured immigrants' and so fall prey to the contradictions of idealism (Thurlow, 1980, p. 42).

But this means neither that a Marxist explanation for the
development of European racism is not possible nor that there
were no important continuities between ideological developments
in England and the rest of Europe. Indeed, the fact that there
were continuities and that, at a certain level, they were related
to the formation of capitalist nation states means that a Marxist
explanation is not only possible, but necessary. As we have
already seen, the development of scientific racism was a phenomenon common to Western Europe and the United States in the
nineteenth century (Gossett, 1965) and as Poliakov emphasises
(1974, p. 225), this was accompanied by the declining significance attributed to religious explanations and evaluations of
the material and social world. A Marxist analysis would develop
Poliakov's reference (1974, p. 225) to the developing nationalism
throughout Europe in the nineteenth century stimulating a
search for, or, more accurately, creating in thought, separate
and distinct 'races', by arguing that the appropriation and
development of these ideas was carried out by the aspiring
capitalist class who saw the formation of a nation state as a

central requirement for the successful development of capitalism.
It was therefore possible for the ideas of European writers such
as Gobineau to be taken up by both those whose racism was
articulated with the African as its object and by those who
were concerned with the position and circumstances of the
Jews in Europe: Gobineau's writings had a similar relevance
to sections of both the English and German ruling class,
despite the fact that their focus and specific interests were
different in the mid- and late nineteenth century.

So, the historical evidence suggests that the origin of racism
cannot be explained simply as a direct reflection within the
superstructure of the emergence of capitalism by means of the
colonial exploitation of African labour. I want now to consider
some of the implications of this rejection of economism for an
alternative analysis.

SOME IMPLICATIONS OF THE DEMISE OF ECONOMISM

The fact that the development of racism within the mainland
of Western Europe has a somewhat different genesis to the
racism that developed within England should warn us against
conceiving of racism as a fixed ideological entity or 'package',
having an unchanging focus and content. Those engaged in
analysis of contemporary social formations are most likely to
commit this error if they assume that the ideological patterns
that they identify are either the consequence of a singular
development or have remained in existence in their current
form since they first appeared. But this error is also implicit
in the terms in which the problem is posed for analysis. The
object of analysis is usually to locate the origin of racism. The
clear implication is that there was a period when those ideas,
which warrant description as racism, did not exist, with the
consequence that the analytical aim is to date and explain their
first appearance. As we have seen, an economistic explanation
both dates and explains the origin of racism in a deterministic
way with the emergence of capitalism. I believe this to be a
false starting point not only because, in the light of the historical evidence, it is difficult to claim that the ideas which the
concept of racism describes have had the same content and
form over a long period of historical time, but also because of
the nature of the historical record (cf. Gutzmore, 1975–6,
p. 282). By the latter I mean that attempting to assess the
nature and extent of ideas and explanations over a long period
of time has to confront the facts that the written record may
not correspond in any clear way with what people actually
thought in the given period and that what was written down
may not have had wide circulation because of not only the cost
of buying printed material but also of the extent of literacy.

For these reasons, I would argue that it is analytically more
useful to pose the problem in somewhat different terms. Rather

than be concerned with locating the origin of racism, I argue that the aim should be to explain the generation and reproduction of racism. By the former notion I mean that we should trace the conditions for and the manner in which certain ideas and arguments were and are articulated by certain groups (conceived of as classes or class fractions). In saying this, I make no assumption that these ideas are necessarily novel. Rather, the concern is with the fact that they have appeared and given social support in a given context. By the latter notion, I mean that we should trace the conditions under which these ideas are repeated and spread beyond the group that articulates them. The processes of ideological generation and reproduction are, in fact, complementary and overlapping because, in the process of reproduction, new ideas can be generated or existing ideas subtly or even dramatically changed. Hence, in posing the issue for analysis as the generation and reproduction of racism, I am suggesting that we are concerned with an ideological process in which the content and structure of and support for ideas described as racist are defined at the outset as variable and subject to change.

None of this necessarily involves admitting that it is impossible to locate the origin of racism, or that racism is a universal phenomenon. The latter may, in fact, be true, but this can only be finally demonstrated if the evidence relating to the origin continually points to an ever further receding date. The nature of the historical record makes that a very difficult task and I see little point in engaging in what must inevitably become speculation without adequate recourse to systematic evidence.

But of what significance is this redefinition of the problematic for Marxist theory? Recent developments in Marxist theory (e.g. Gramsci, 1971; Althusser, 1969; Althusser and Balibar, 1970; Hall, 1977a, 1977b) have been concerned explicitly with a rejection of economism and, consequently, have moved on to a somewhat different theoretical terrain. Hence, it 'matters' less to Marxist analysis that racism is not a direct product of capitalism when ideological relations have been allocated a 'real' relative autonomy. What has become of much greater interest is not only the more general question of the way in which ideological (and political) relations are determined (or have their limits established – see Williams, 1973, 1977) by economic relations in the last instance, but also, and equally important, the way in which economic relations are themselves determined by ideological (and political) relations. What does this mean specifically for an analysis of racism? It means, first, that we should ask how, and for what reasons, and with what effects, is racism generated and reproduced. But, second, these processes of ideological generation and reproduction must not be conceived of as occurring in a vacuum. Rather, as Marx and Engels wrote (1965, p. 36): 'Empirical observation must in each separate instance bring out empirically, and without any mystification and speculation, the connection of the social and political structure with production.' This 'connection' must not be interpreted in a mechanistic manner because although material production may prepare the terrain for particular ideological trends to be generated and reproduced, this can rarely, if ever, be a sufficient condition for their generation and reproduction. Hence, political and ideological factors must also play a central role in the generation and reproduction of racism. Moreover, by the very fact of its reproduction, racism must, in turn, structure the terrain of material production in specific instances.

Using this general framework, a Marxist analysis should be able to demonstrate the validity of the following propositions. First, it must be shown that, as an ideology, racism refracts and obscures the socio-economic world. In other words, as an explanation for the way in which the world 'works', racism is false. This has already been partly achieved in Chapter 1. However, second, following Sayer (1979, p. 8):

> If, like Marx, we assume an internal relation between people's action in, and consciousness of the world, we imply that all consciousness, including ideology, possesses a minimum of what I will term practical adequacy. It must, in other words, allow men and women to conduct and make sense of their everyday activity....If ideological accounts of the world are false, then their falsity must be explained in terms of the nature of the experience which is capable of sustaining such illusions, illusions, moreover, which must be assumed to be practically adequate in the face of the experience of the knowing subject.

This requires us to show that racism is generated and reproduced as a real, lived phenomenon and is not simply (although it may sometimes be) an ideological imposition of and by the ruling class (i.e. what I call the 'ideological baggage' thesis) in the logical pursuit of its economic interests.

Not all of these questions can be answered in the remainder of this chapter which, as stated at the outset, has a particular and limited aim. I now want to go on to provide an account of the generation and reproduction of racism which is grounded in material production but which also gives full regard to the determination of ideological and political relations. This account will conclude that the economic relationship between British capitalism and colonialism does have an ideological legacy which has to be taken into account when examining the generation and reproduction of racism in contemporary Britain. The latter is, however, not the subject matter of this chapter, but will be taken up in Chapter 7. I must also add that what follows is not the definitive and exhaustive account of the generation and reproduction of racism, but it does constitute the framework for such an analysis.

AFRICA, THE SLAVE TRADE AND PLANTATION PRODUCTION

Too often, slavery and the slave trade are written about primarily in terms of the experience of those enslaved (e.g. Elkins,
1968). The emphasis is upon the harshness and cruelty of
slavery, and hence upon the effects of these features upon
the character of the slaves. The implication would seem to be
that slavery and the slave trade were the products of uncaring,
even evil, merchants and planters who placed little premium
upon human life. It is not denied here that the slave trade and
slavery were both characterised by much suffering on the part
of those enslaved, but it is to be argued that an analysis of
the slave trade and slavery is ultimately misleading if it remains
confined to such issues. What all such analyses ignore is that
slavery, sustained by the slave trade, was introduced and
spread through the Caribbean and the English colonies on the
American mainland as a solution to a material problem (Mintz,
1966, 1974). In order to appreciate the significance of this,
let us reflect briefly upon the notions of slave and slavery
because their common sense usage has moral overtones which
blind us to a materialist analysis.

The notions of slave and slavery usually give rise to images
of 'black' men and women who have become the property of other
(white) men. Consequently, the owner has direct control over
very many aspects of the lives of those enslaved. What thereby
becomes of significance for contemporary observers is the
apparent lack of freedom of the slave. Both these images are
the legacy of not only the British involvement in slavery and
the slave trade, but also of the anti-slavery movements of the
late eighteenth and nineteenth centuries. What is ignored or
confused in this imagery is, first, that slavery was not the
sole form or expression of 'unfreedom' or bondage in the seventeenth and subsequent centuries. Indeed, in so far as the comparative reference point is the 'freedom' of contemporary Western Europe, then that freedom/unfreedom is relative rather than
absolute. Second, historically, it has not just been the misfor-
tune of the African to be enslaved. Summarising these two
points in slightly different terms, there is, historically, no
deterministic relationship between blackness and the condition
of slavery or other forms of unfreedom.

In order to express this argument in positive terms we have
to begin from a different star'ing point, from that of production
(cf. Hindess and Hirst, 1975, pp. 125-48). This is because
slavery was a means of procuring labour: planters in the Caribbean bought Africans as (human) commodities primarily in order
to provide a source of labour power, to be brought into combination with land and tools with the aim of producing tobacco,
sugar and later (on the American mainland) cotton. This means
of procuring labour power was a response to both the scarcity
or absence of other forms of labour supply and to, at the early
stage of colonisation, the availability of large areas of fertile

land. Because of the latter condition, indigenous populations, where they existed, would only engage in colonial agricultural production if coerced by the colonists, while free migration from England would have led only to the migrants themselves occupying an area of land and producing for themselves. Hence, a condition of production in the Caribbean was forced or unfree labour. Thus, the first source of labour power was the forced labour of the indigenous populations, to be followed by the use of indentured labour from England. In addition, English convicts were deported to the New World in large numbers and forced to work. Slavery was therefore only one means amongst several of solving a problem of production. All of these means shared the characteristic of coercion and the people so coerced did not all share the same physical characteristics. Hence, as Mintz has concluded (1974, p. 66): 'It should be stressed that the relationship between slavery and Africans was rooted fundamentally in demographic and economic forces, not in the physical type of the slaves themselves.' Moreover, in order to retain this material emphasis, it is necessary to either discard the notion of slavery as an analytical concept and refer instead to the slave mode of production (e.g. Hindess and Hirst, 1975, ch. 3) or ground it in some reference to plantation production (e.g. Mintz, 1974) or plantation economy (e.g. Mandle, 1972, 1978).

But why did slave labour become the predominant means of supplying and exploiting labour, and why did Africa become the predominant source of that labour? The questions and the answers to them are interrelated. Most indigenous labour either resisted forced labour or suffered the consequences, often resulting in death from over-work or disease. Indigenous labour was replaced by indentured labour (Williams, 1964, pp. 9-19; also Sheridan, 1969, 1974). Production by means of slave labour had advantages over indentured labour, however, in that it was cheaper and ensured greater coercive control, and for the life-span of those enslaved. Moreover, and significantly, the supply of persons to be enslaved could be integrated into a structure of trade and production which ensured not only a profit for the merchant at each of three points of what became a triangular system, but also, and ultimately, the primitive accumulation of capital that was to permit the development of industrial capitalism in England (e.g. Williams, 1964; Mandel, 1968, pp. 106-10; Genovese, 1969, pp. 25-6; Hobsbawm, 1969, pp. 34-54, 57-8; Barrett Brown, 1974, pp. 73-95). In sum, the development of the slave mode of production (made possible and initially sustained by the trade in slaves) was neither direct cause nor consequence of racism in the form of some theory of natural or inherent inferiority of the African. Rather, the slave (or plantation) mode of production was a solution to a problem of production in a certain economic and political situation. In so far as this solution had ideological effects, these took the form of reproducing traditional religious and

philosophical justifications for slavery which focused on ideas
of original sin and the supposed just consequences of heathenism (Davis, 1966, pp. 88-9, 108-9, 165-6). But this is not to
be interpreted to mean that this interdependent relationship
between capitalism and colonialism was not without its effects
upon the generation of racism. Such effects as they were cannot, however, be understood without recognising that, as
argued above, there existed an image of (but not a systematic
theory about) the African in England prior to development of
the slave mode of production and the slave trade. This image
negatively evaluated the African's blackness and heathenism
and interpreted nakedness as a sign of excessive sexuality.
This imagery was to be reproduced and given both new meaning and new dimensions as a consequence of the material developments in the Caribbean colonies.

One particularly important outcome of the establishment of
the slave mode of production and the slave trade was that,
during the course of the eighteenth century (i.e. the period
of the economic dominance of the slave trade and plantation
production in the Caribbean and American colonies), the
African was dehumanised by means of being treated as a commodity. As a commodity, the African became an object to be
bought and sold. Walvin notes that the trading documents and
cargo lists of the eighteenth century show that 'negroes' and
'slaves' were listed as commodities alongside gold, elephants
teeth, redwood, etc. (1973, p. 38). This denial in practice of
human status was emphasised by the generation of an image of
the African as a beast of burden in the same period (Walvin,
1973, p. 39).

From this evidence, I argue that economic relations, by their
particular and phenomenal nature, dehumanised the African,
a material process that was expressed in thought in the notion
that the African was not a 'real' human being. Thereby, the
African became in thought and in production relations a slave.
Put in other words, the African came to be conceived of during
the eighteenth century as inherently possessing (qua slave)
an economic and political status which, in reality, was an
expression of a particular set of forces and relations of production. The synonymous categorisation, both in reality and
in thought, of African with slave, such that one stood for or
expressed the other, meant in turn the creation of an ideological
dualism (which was directly and materially based) between
human beings and slaves. This process encouraged the reproduction of previously formed imagery of the African (now slave),
as a consequence of which this dualism was developed and given
new content. This was therefore a crucial stage in the generation of racism.

I must elaborate (or qualify) this argument briefly. I specifically refer to the generation and reproduction of an imagery
and not a theory or explicit argument because, as already
argued, in the century and a half that passed between the

English colonisation of the Caribbean and the mid- to late eighteenth century, there is little or no evidence of systematic attempt on the part of merchant capitalists (or anyone else) to justify their trade and mode of production by reference to the supposed inherent biological inferiority of the 'Negro'. Certainly, there is no evidence of the explicit doctrine or theory alleging that the culture and 'condition' of the 'Negro' is a determined product of 'race'. Indeed, in this period, 'race', in so far as it was used, was not explicitly used to refer to biological variation or difference (Banton, 1977a, pp. 18, 27). In so far as there was intellectual reflection upon the enslavement of the 'Negro', it continued within a framework established by Christianity and the Bible, e.g. the biblical story of the curse on Ham as the 'servant of servants' (Jordan, 1968, pp. 17-20, 54, 56; also Davis, 1966, pp. 451-2). Nevertheless, this imagery warrants description as racism because it does identify another population by reference to a phenotypical characteristic (skin colour) and it does attribute the population with the possession of other negatively evaluated characteristics (sexuality, slavery) in an apparently deterministic manner.

The shift from imagery to 'theory' occurs from and after the 1770s and coincides with reduced significance and legitimacy being accorded to traditional, especially biblical, explanations for not only social and political affairs, but also the physical characteristics and variation in homo sapiens (e.g. Davis, 1966, pp. 446; also Curtin, 1960). Interest in biological classification grew after Linnaeus's taxonomy of the 1730s (Jordan, 1968, pp. 216-22) and the resulting intellectual writing and argument was to take on new significance as a consequence of political developments, specifically, the anti-slavery agitation and its complex relationship with the struggle for independence on the part of the North American colonists. The anti-slavery agitation necessitated the development of an argument in defence of slavery which was to take the form of systematisation and elaboration of the existing imagery (Curtin, 1965, p. 36; Walvin, 1973, p. 161; Bolt, 1971, p. 9; Lorimer, 1978, p. 24). Moreover, even those who were advancing the case against slavery were, in the process, linking the 'Negro', defined in terms of blackness, with the idea of the archetypal savage, of 'man' in his most primitive and yet pure and unspoilt state, untainted by the ways of the 'modern world'. This image of the 'noble savage' was no less racist than the arguments constructed and articulated by those defending slavery and the slave trade (Curtin, 1965, pp. 48-52; Walvin, 1973, pp. 183-6; Lorimer, 1978). But it was as a result of the efforts of those defending slavery and the slave trade that attention began to be drawn to arguments about the significance of the phenotypical differences between Europeans and 'Negroes'. Clearly, these political developments did not 'cause' the articulation of these theories because their intellectual foundations were being laid prior to this political debate about slavery. But the debate did give a new impetus and meaning to on-going intellectual activity, and served to focus the attention of the literate population on the relevant literature.

This argument is subject to two qualifications. First, one must not over-emphasise the resort to 'science' by defenders of the slave trade. A number of writers have emphasised that the first ideological source for such persons was the writings of travel writers of the previous three centuries (Curtin, 1965, pp. 34-6, 222; Walvin, 1973, pp. 28, 159-60). Again, then, the notion of ideological reproduction is relevant because the implication of this argument is that ideas whose origin lies in the sixteenth century and even earlier were re-articulated in the late eighteenth century. They were thereby given new significance and meaning in what was a quite different economic and political context. Second, one must not confuse this developing interest in and debate about slavery with interest in Africa. The focus of the former remained primarily in the Caribbean and North America in the eighteenth and very early nineteenth centuries. War with the American colonists who claimed to be defending the ideals of liberty, justice and freedom could not help but lead to a questioning of the liberty of those enslaved. MacLeod concludes (1974, p. 184): 'the first great onslaught on slavery in America was impelled by egalitarianism and by a belief in universal and natural rights: but it helped to produce a positive racism and an explicit denial of those rights'. Interest in and knowledge about the war, the ideals expressed in the course of it and its consequences were paralleled by a general ignorance about Africa. However, with the loss of the American colonies, the British government began to tighten its control elsewhere in the world and Africa and its population began to figure more seriously in connection with imperial policy. At this time, only very limited sources of information were available, namely travel writers, biologists, 'men of letters' (who were principally responsible for the 'noble savage' image) and anti-slavery writers (Curtin, 1965, pp. 30-56). Only amongst the second of these groups was there any serious attention being given to the idea that there might be a causal relationship between the African's physical appearance and cultural characteristics.

Such persons, particularly the biological writers, were to have a significant impact during the course of the nineteenth century. These we may describe as intellectuals in the Gramscian sense. That is to say, they occupied a socio-economic position in the world as a result of which they could formulate and articulate a more systematic conception of the world compared with those directly involved in production, distribution and exchange (Gramsci, 1971, pp. 8-10, 323, 334, 344, 347). But Gramsci warns (1971, p. 12):

The relationship between the intellectuals and the world of production is not as direct as it is with the fundamental social groups but is, in varying degrees, 'mediated' by the whole fabric of society and by the complex of superstructures, of which the intellectuals are, precisely, the 'functionaries'.

One facet of this process of mediation is of particular significance because in so far as the intellectual product takes a written form, then its effect is determined by both the nature and cost of its reproduction and the extent of literacy. The nineteenth century witnessed a slow but gradual growth of literacy and the gradual appearance of cheaper forms of published literature and this was a necessary condition for the spread of racism in Victorian Britain. But this does not account for the further development of racism that was to occur in the nineteenth century. It is to that process that I now turn my attention.

THE EFFECTS OF CHRISTIANITY

Here I am concerned with the way in which the Christian religion, conceived of as an ideology, had its own particular and independent effects upon the development of racism. In other words, I am suggesting that the generation of racism was influenced in certain respects by ideological relations. This was particularly important in the nineteenth century, but let us first briefly recapitulate to see how this was also true prior to this period. We have already noted the slow developing contradiction between the biblical account of the origins of the human species and the growth of secular (scientific) knowledge which produced a 'theoretical' crisis, the solution to which opened the door for the development of scientific racism. Hence, although the Bible seemed initially to have the ideological capacity (the practical adequacy) through its implied support for monogenetic explanations for human origins, to provide a bulwark against the development of polygenesis, it became increasingly unable to provide a valid explanation for the ever-increasing evidence about the range of human physical variation. The contradiction was resolved by denying that the Bible could provide an adequate explanation for this perceived phenotypical variation. A solution was therefore sought in the realms of biological science (Poliakov, 1974, pp. 224-6, 255; also Davis, 1966, p. 446) and the only remaining religious constraint upon the subsequent development of racist theories remained in the notion that all human beings were equal before God. Of course, as we have seen, material factors (the need to supply labour for plantation production) had played a major role in denying a common humanity to persons from Africa (by enslaving them), thereby weakening the religious appeal. Moreover, Christian humanitarianism was a significant motivating force in the anti-slavery movement (e.g. Curtin, 1965, p. 52) but, as we have again seen, this movement had the effect of encouraging the systematisation of racism. Finally, in the late nineteenth century, opinion within the Christian tradition shifted towards the view that some people were more equal before God than others and, ultimately, to the view that the 'black race' could only find God if guided and directed by the 'white race' (Cairns, 1965, pp. 235, 242; Eldridge, 1973, pp. 253-4).

The so far unmentioned independent impact of the Christian religion in the nineteenth century arose from the work of missionary societies in Africa. These reports commonly advanced an image of the African which, although not directly reproducing the ideas and theories referred to by the notion of scientific racism, was nevertheless an echo or refraction of these ideas and arguments. In the 1830s and 1840s there was little general or political interest in Africa, but humanitarian and missionary interest was growing and this was to be an important factor in stimulating wider interest as the century proceeded. The development of the missionary intervention was premised on the perceived responsibility to spread the Christian message, a responsibility that was viewed as a specific aspect of the broader role of taking 'civilisation' to the 'backward' and 'primitive' areas of the world. It was believed that the 'British way of life', central to which was the Christian religion, had a universal application. The perceived need to preach the gospel to the heathen was combined with the more secular notions of progress and hope for the improvement of the human condition to bring into existence a missionary movement motivated by a strong moral force (Curtin, 1965, pp. 259-60). Often, this strong moral motivation was strengthened by the notion that the missionaries were members of a divinely ordained, superior 'white race' (Cairns, 1965, p. 154).

Missionary societies were partly dependent upon financial support from 'the public' to maintain and extend their activity. To this end, they made a substantial effort to publicise their activities and 'success' in Britain, primarily through different sorts of publication, but also through public meetings. Ironically, it was partly for this reason that the tone and emphasis of the reports took the form that they did. By portraying Africa and the African as backward, savage, degraded and immoral, the missionary societies were able to justify the maintenance and extension of their activities. A composite picture of the African emerged from these contemporary reports which was no more accurate than the travellers' reports of the past. For somewhat different reasons, all these reports focused on those aspects of African cultures which were most likely to shock their British readers, the consequence being an image of the African as an immoral, over-sexed barbarian (Curtin, 1965, p. 326; Cairns, 1965, p. 99; Walvin, 1973, p. 160). It was also argued that the African was immature, emotional, excitable and impulsive and this gave rise to the child analogy, reflecting by inversion the self-image of the British as mature and responsible (Cairns, 1965, p. 93). In the 1830s, it was generally believed that the African was capable of growing out of the condition of barbarism and savagery if guided by the correct hand (Curtin, 1965, p. 243) but the child analogy was constructed later in the century as a permanent characteristic, vesting in the British the role of protector and guardian.

Although this imagery was encouraged by the desire to justify and extend missionary activity, it would be a mistake to assume that it was simply 'made up'. As with all ideology, these ideas were a partial refraction of the experienced reality of the missionaries. As we shall see shortly, they were motivated not only by the abstract notion of spreading Christianity, but also by the real and very obvious supremacy and material achievements of British capitalism. Hence, to the missionary who was a direct observer of both the material condition of the African and of the 'success' of British capitalism, and yet generally ignorant of African history, it must have been difficult not to conclude that the African was materially backward and, by comparison with British (upper class) moral standards, degenerate. There is, therefore, a sense in which one can conceive of the missionary reports as sincerely constructed and published. But if they were not specifically motivated to generate and reproduce a racist image of the African, this was certainly the effect and it was an image that was to attain wide circulation.

THE EFFECTS OF SCIENTIFIC RACISM

Another ideological factor of significance was clearly the theories of those scientists concerned with explaining human physical variation. However, some writers (e.g. Banton, 1977a) place undue explanatory importance on this factor in so far as they suggest that racism was primarily the product of scientific investigation. Such arguments have two main limitations as we have already seen. First, they ignore the extent to which scientific investigation is shaped by the economic, political and ideological context in which it is conducted (cf. Lorimer, 1978, p. 131). In this instance, the character and condition of the 'Negro' had become a matter of attention as a consequence of the activity and reflections (both verbal and written) of merchants, colonists, travellers and missionaries, amongst others. In other words, the 'intellectual agenda' had been shaped by the real activity of men and women, and questions such as 'What is the origin of the human species and how did the wide range of physical variation develop?' had real, practical implications. Given the growing challenge to biblical explanations and the development of the scientific mode of inquiry, it followed that this new mode of reasoning and explanation would attempt to provide an answer to this and related

questions. But it was not just that past events had defined an
agenda. Scientific investigation developed in the context of an
already formed image of the 'Negro', an image which was largely
negative and which had a long pedigree. There are, then, good
reasons for arguing that the course and conclusion of nineteenth-
century scientific investigation were, if not pre-determined,
at least structured by the material circumstances and ideological
trends of Victorian Britain which themselves had a longer history than did scientific investigation.

Such structuring was not solely historical. Political debate
in the mid-nineteenth century was partly structured by international events and affairs, particularly in the USA and the
Caribbean, with interest shifting towards Africa after the
1870s (Lorimer, 1978, pp. 11-12, 123). This debate provided
a context for the scientific work and active intervention of
scientists. Much of the focus of scientific debate in the 1840s
and 1850s was slavery in America (Curtin, 1965, p. 370), an
issue that was to become entangled in the American Civil War
which, in turn, had a substantial impact upon opinion in
Britain (Bolt, 1971, pp. 29-74; Lorimer, 1978, p. 162). The
Caribbean became a focus of interest in the light of the violent
suppression of a revolt in Jamaica in 1865. The predominant
political reaction within Britain was that the uprising confirmed
the inherent savagery of the African and that this could only
be contained by the imposition of strong rule by the 'white
race'. But the scientists of the day also intervened in the political debate, claiming that the uprising was excellent confirma-
tion of their theories (Bolt, 1971, pp. 76, 93, 99; Lorimer,
1978, p. 150).

Second, it is important to inquire into the circulation and
readership of the books and pamphlets written by the scientists
of the period: there is little point in carrying out a detailed
analysis of the ideas and 'findings' of an individual or group if
almost no one read and reproduced those ideas. In this connection, Lorimer notes (1978, p. 207) that although racist beliefs
were common in the mid-nineteenth century, the writings of
scientific racists had only a limited readership amongst a well-
educated minority (the ranks of that minority overlapping with
the ranks of the ruling class). Cairns states (1965, pp. 90-1)
that travellers and explorers in Africa in the mid-nineteenth
century seemed unaware of scientific ideas about 'race', suggesting that we must explain the origin of the racist imagery
of the African that their writings contained by reference to
other factors. In sum, the analytical task is not just to demonstrate that certain ideas were available in any given period,
but to show which groups generated them and which groups
reproduced them. We shall return to this point at the end of
this chapter.

THE EFFECTS OF ECONOMIC RELATIONS

Many writers regard the possibility of identifying a relationship
between the expansion of European capitalism, the development
of imperialism and the rise of scientific racism in the nineteenth
century as a test of the validity of Marxist theory (Banton,
1977a, p. 60; Lorimer, 1978, p. 13). It is more useful to conceive of this supposed relationship as yet another issue which
indicates the inadequacy of economistic Marxism and not Marxism
per se. This is because, having located the rise of scientific
racism in the middle of the nineteenth century, a limited historical knowledge (which would date the development of imperialism to the 1880s and after) leads one to conclude that the
development of scientific racism could not have originated in
the need to justify economic, political and military expansion
for the simple reason that it appeared before the imperialist
phase of British economic and political policy. I wish to argue
that we should locate the determination of the generation and
reproduction of racism by economic relations in nineteenth-
century Britain in different terms. In order to grasp the significance of my argument, it must be recalled that I am not
analysing racism as a fixed ideological product, but as a set
of ideas which undergo changes in content and structure in
the process of reproduction. I am therefore particularly concerned with the determination of economic relations on this process of ideological reproduction in nineteenth-century Britain.

I now want to argue that economic relations had a specific
impact on the reproduction of racism in at least three interrelated aspects. First, the economic and political supremacy of
British capitalism generated a response at the ideological level
in that the British bourgeoisie sought an explanation for its
position of not only national but also international domination.
Second, the capitalist mode of production, by means of its
productive capacity and the transformation of economic relations
that it entailed, created a material standard against which to
measure those populations with whom economic and political
contact have been 'encouraged' by the preconditions for the
development of that mode of production. Third, the late nineteenth-century territorial expansion of British (and European)
capitalism did not so much bring racism into existence but
rather created a terrain on which racism could be used by at
least certain fractions of the bourgeoisie to justify their demands
for expansion, whether the specific motive was political or
economic, or some combination of both. Let us consider these
points in turn.

The first can be summarised in slightly different terms by
claiming that racism became a predominant element in the world-
view (or 'common sense') of the British bourgeoisie. Extant
evidence suggests that this was not a process that was confined
to the nineteenth century. Banton claims that 'by 1850 a significant section of the European upper classes subscribed to a

rudimentary racial philosophy of history' (1977a, p. 25) and he argues that this was derived in part from English historical writing of the eighteenth and early nineteenth centuries which was concerned with finding an explanation for what were viewed as specifically English liberties and institutions. Banton's analysis can be reinterpreted in the following manner. The historical writing was the work of intellectuals, but its theme and content was a response to questions posed by the very existence of a developing bourgeoisie and capitalist mode of production. The results of the intellectuals' mental labour were to be appropriated by this newly rising class: these were the ideas with which they could understand and interpret their emerging class position, both within Britain and internationally. The nineteenth century saw the extension of the development of this aspect of dominant class ideology in so far as the new bourgoisie was able to utilise the notion of belonging to the (superior) English 'race' in order to challenge the still important position of the old landed aristocracy, membership of which was determined by family descent (Lorimer, 1978, pp. 112-13). So, the development of capitalism brought into existence a class which, eager to locate itself ideologically, appropriated, and thereby encouraged the further development of, an ideology of racism: its belief in its growing economic and political domination was interpreted in the language of 'race', first applied to itself and its own history (the English 'race') and, a little later, in relation to other populations (the black and inferior 'races').

Second, the material achievements of British capitalism, when measured against not only the rest of Europe in the early nineteenth century but, more particularly, against the colonies and Africa provided a standard against which to evaluate these other populations. In other words, the then enforced economic underdevelopment of the colonies and parts of Africa as a necessary precondition for the development of British capitalism was subsequently refracted at the level of ideological relations in the dialectic between the defined primitiveness and backwardness of the 'Negro' and the material advancement of the British 'race'. The third and fourth decades of the nineteenth century were periods of substantial economic growth and the further development of international superiority, events which created considerable pride in British achievement. Curtin comments (1965, pp. 293-4; see also Cairns, 1965, pp. 147-8):

> No wonder also that the pride of achievement should carry with it pride of race, pride in British religion and British culture and British morality, and, in the face of African 'barbarism', a rise in arrogance and cultural chauvinism even surpassing the clear beginnings already visible during the first three decades of the century.

The development of the capitalist mode of production was accompanied by changes in culture and way of life: the formation of a proletariat entailed the creation of a class mindful of the significance of the relationship between time and wage labour, while the ongoing process of capital accumulation implied never-ending 'progress' and 'change'. Moreover, although large sections of the proletariat were not to benefit directly from this, the material productivity of capitalism affirmed the ability of 'man' to act upon nature with astounding results. When colonial and African societies were measured against this very material yardstick, they were not surprisingly found wanting. Thus, the African could be despised for an apparent inability to 'work' and to dominate the environment, for maintaining 'only' a subsistence economy, for being lazy and unconcerned about rigidly measured units of time (see Cairns, 1965, pp. 76-88). Hence, the African was defined as backward because African social formations were not structured by the capitalist mode of production. Reversing that backwardness was to become defined as just one aspect of the bourgeoisie's self-appointed civilising mission. As Cairns puts it (1965, p. 222): 'The equation of civilization with commerce rested on the elementary assumption that civilization consisted of the material goods diffused by commercial transactions.'

This is not to say that the attributes of barbarism, backwardness and lack of civilisation had not been applied to the 'Negro' before the nineteenth century. Indeed, the preceding analysis has suggested that they were. But the very real and substantial material achievements of early nineteenth-century capitalism provided, for the bourgeoisie, an equally real and more substantial 'living proof' of their own capacity for advancement and the backwardness of the 'Negro'. This idea was combined with the historical associations with blackness and slavery, such that phenotypical variation (in particular, skin colour) was defined as being related in a deterministic manner with economic and cultural 'failings'. By the middle of the century, science had apparently 'discovered' (more accurately, 'constructed') an explanation for this association in the theory of 'race'.

To summarise, racism became a central element in the bourgeois ideology of the nineteenth century partly because it provided a phenomenally apparent or 'real' explanation for the material gap created by the uneven development of capitalism. In this sense, the racism of the nineteenth century was materially grounded and determined, but only because of, inter alia, the pre-existence (or historical legacy) of an imagery of the 'Negro' and because of the partly independent, intellectual construction of a theory which purported to explain that 'race' determined both history and culture. Thus, racism was a lived ideology, having a certain political adequacy for the bourgeoisie. It cannot, therefore, be construed simply as having been constructed solely and purposely to justify colonial exploitation and to divide the working class.

But, and third, once having become a central element in the world-view of the bourgeoisie, the ideology of racism could

potentially have real material effects (i.e. it could become a
'material force' as Marx put it) and this it was to have in the
late nineteenth century. It is of little consequence here
whether the imperialism of the late nineteenth century is interpreted as a scramble by the capitalist European states for direct
material benefit or was rather a more defensive initiative, aiming to consolidate and protect existing economic and political
advantages on a global scale (e.g. Gallagher and Robinson,
1953; Barrett Brown, 1974, pp. 170-200). What is significant
in this context is that racism is not accorded a determinate
role in either explanation; that is to say, the imperialism of
the late nineteenth century was not 'caused' by racism. The
motive force of imperialism lay in economic and political relations (Eldridge, 1973, p. 252) and racism was to be used by
those advancing the policy of expansion as a further justification of intervention in Africa. Hence, Cairns claims (1965,
p. 235): 'Of essential importance as a rationale for imperialism
was the almost universal British belief in the inferiority,
whether racial, cultural, or both, of Africans, the group
which imperialism was to deprive of control of its own future
development.'

So, for a Marxist analysis, it is of little relevance that late
nineteenth-century imperialism pre-dated the development of
scientific racism. What is significant is that the ideology was
reproduced to justify and, indeed, to give direction to a
specific policy of capitalist expansion. And in the process of
reproduction, certain facets of the ideology took on new and
greater significance. The most important were the notion of
trusteeship and the child analogy both of which had been in
existence before the 1870s but were to be given much greater
emphasis in the process of justifying imperial expansion (Curtin,
1965, p. 415; Cairns, 1965, p. 235; Eldridge, 1973, pp. 238-9,
242, 254). Thus, the 'white man's burden' was still to civilise
the inferior 'black races', but now the childishness of these
'races' was firmly defined as inherent and permanent, with
the consequence that the 'burden' became defined as one of
exercising strong government over 'the blacks' and finding
for them an economic and political role to play in the new
colonial societies that were commensurate with their alleged
inferiority. These notions were to come to play a major role
in structuring these new colonial social formations in Africa.
The development of mining and agriculture in these colonies
required substantial supplies of cheap labour and so the ideology could continue to be reproduced by and to the advantage
of capital if it could be used to justify forced labour (e.g.
Magubane, 1979).

But the relationship between the idea of a civilising mission
and actual capitalist expansion was not a deterministic one.
The idea was articulated from within the bourgeoisie throughout much if not all of the Victorian period, including that period
in mid-century when the interest of government and sections

of the bourgeoisie was focused on the settlement colonies (Canada, Australia and New Zealand) rather than Africa (Curtin, 1965, p. 292). Their attention came to focus on Africa after 1870 and even in that decade, all active intervention was conceived of as limited and with a specific objective in mind (Eldridge, 1973, pp. 142-4, 169). Yet not only was there an argument articulated in favour of a missionary and civilising mission in West and Central Africa in the early and mid-nineteenth century but it was also acted upon. There was not only a missionary intervention in Africa, but also an economic intervention in the form of individualistic trading, hunting and prospecting ventures. But these areas of Africa were not attractive locations for such ventures. Moreover, neither did the tropical climate, tribal warfare and the difficulties of travel make Central Africa an attractive prospect for missionary work. Thus, although the notion of the civilising mission was sufficient in itself to motivate and justify some intervention in Africa, especially when combined with petit-capitalist aspirations, the material circumstances of the area militated against any large-scale intervention supported by larger-scale capital and the government (Cairns, 1965, pp. 7-34; also Curtin, 1965, pp. 259-60, 292-4). As we have seen, economic and political conditions had to take on a very different character for the idea of civilisation to play its role in integrating sections of Africa into the world capitalist economy.

RACISM AND CLASS IDEOLOGY

As a means of summarising the main strands of the argument of this chapter, I want to make more explicit and explore one implication of the argument that racism, although not the specific, purposive creation of the bourgeoisie, was generated on a terrain structured by the development of the capitalist mode of production and appropriated by at least certain fractions of that bourgeoisie so that the ideology became a central element of its world-view by the nineteenth century. The notion of appropriation has been used to take note of the specific role of intellectuals in the generation of a systematised and scientific racist ideology. But, as I have stressed, the intellectual generation of scientific racism occurred in a context already structured not only by negative associations of blackness but also by the ongoing (although, by the end of the eighteenth century, declining) dependence of the development of capitalism upon plantation production in the Caribbean which enslaved the African, a process that was refracted in the imagery of the African as slave. We may conceive of this imagery, a historical product with a lengthy genesis, as part of the common sense of at least that fraction of the rising bourgeoisie that owed its position to active involvement in colonialism.

One must emphasise again, however, that it was not crudely

'made up' to justify a process of exploitation: there were other additional sources and influences. This imagery was systematised and developed by the scientists of the late eighteenth and nineteenth centuries. As a result of this intellectual activity, racism was reproduced in a new form and now also given the status of scientific truth. The development of British capitalism and the growing pressures of international capitalist competition were among the most important (although not the only) factors which encouraged the British bourgeoisie and its government to appropriate these notions during the course of the nineteenth century in order to both comprehend its own position in the world and justify a new phase of capitalist expansion.

Most writers are agreed that the 'upper' or 'educated classes' of the mid-nineteenth century were aware of, and themselves articulated, racist ideas and arguments (e.g. Curtin, 1965, pp. 383-4; Walvin, 1973, p. 173; Banton, 1977a, p. 25). Certainly up to the end of the first half of the nineteenth century, formal education, literacy and the ability to purchase books was limited largely to the ruling class (Williams, 1965, pp. 152-65, 187-91). These same factors probably inhibited the reproduction of the earlier imagery of the African which had been available in graphic and literary form before the nineteenth century, especially in the political debate over slavery and the slave trade (Walvin, 1973, pp. 159-60). Let us also recall that the growing working class was not regarded as a political force to which to appeal for political support at least before the mid-nineteenth century and one can see little reason why that class should have become widely conversant with racist imagery, or, indeed, interested in the African. There was a black population in Britain, concentrated in a number of cities, mainly seaports in England and especially London, but Walvin has claimed that there was little or no antagonism between white and black sailors and domestic servants in the eighteenth century. Moreover, it was the merchant fraction of the growing bourgeoisie, and not the working class, which was faced with the task of justifying slavery and the slave trade.

My suggestion is, therefore, that the articulation of racism was probably the prerogative of the dominant class up to and including the middle of the nineteenth century. I acknowledge that the evidence is not extensive and that there are many problems in attempting to assess the extent to which any ideology was articulated amongst the 'lower orders' before this period. We can be a little more certain for the period after the 1830s and 1840s. Missionary publications and travel books were published on an increasing scale from this time on (along with a parallel increase in the production and sale of political pamphlets and books specifically written to argue contemporary political issues). In much of this former literature, the older racist imagery, dating back to the travellers' reports of the sixteenth and seventeenth centuries, was combined with the more recent imagery of missionaries and travellers of the early nineteenth

century and reproduced on a much wider scale, but with little
regard for accuracy and the limitations of data sources. Curtin
has argued that it was during this period that a popular image
of the African emerged and the errors, previously confined
to a few books, now became 'common knowledge' (1965, p. 342).
The extent to which they became common knowledge is difficult
to gauge without further research, but it is undeniable that
such publications were reproducing racism to an audience of
more than the bourgeoisie.

Perhaps of greater significance and influence was the introduction of cheap fiction, novels being published in penny parts
from the 1840s and, slightly later, in a single volume in cheap
reprint form. Their market was the mental and manual working
class. By the 1870s, writers of these novels were turning away
from domestic themes and characters to imperial themes and
characters. Street claims (1975, p. 4): 'For the first time
information on other cultures, expressed in vivid, exciting
tales, was available to the mass public of England. Such
romances, with their large circulation and appeal to a recently
literate general public, are appropriately termed "popular
fiction".' These novels became the vehicle for the reproduction
of those racist notions of the bourgeois world-view, some of
which were, in turn, derived or developed from scientific racism,
to an audience of the working class (Street, 1975, p. 55):
'Popular literature, with its tradition of oversimplification of
characters and interpreting internal qualities from physical
appearance, adopted the principles of nineteenth-century racism
and gave them life in terms of the characterisation of members
of other races.' Their appearance coincided not only with the
popularisation of Social Darwinism (with its obsession with the
survival of the fittest), first in newspapers and later in these
same novels, but also with the political debate over the expansion of the empire from the 1880s onwards (Eldridge, 1973,
pp. 242-4).

All this evidence suggests that as racism was being reproduced in the late nineteenth century within the dominant class
in the manner and with the effects discussed above, it was also
being reproduced within the working class. This is a factual
claim which makes no necessary causal connection between the
two processes for that is a matter which requires separate
analysis. My point here is a simple one, that the reproduction
of racism in Britain was, by the end of the nineteenth century,
occurring not only within the 'educated classes', but also within
the working class, now permitted limited access to the 'benefits'
of education. Clearly, one such 'benefit' was to be presented
with the ideology of racism.

CONCLUSION

First, let me draw attention to the emphasis upon analysing the
generation and reproduction of racism as a process: thus, if
racism had become an element of the ideology of the dominant
class, it was as a consequence of a complex interaction of
economic, political and ideological relations, in the course of
which the 'economic' was only determinate in specific circumstances. Moreover, as an element of bourgeois class ideology,
racism was not a direct and conscious production of the bourgeoisie, although, at least at certain stages in its generation,
it was the result of an attempt to represent and understand
the social consequences of real, material problems of production.
Hence, I have emphasised ideology as a world-view which must
have a 'practical adequacy' for its advocates. It is here that
we may locate the ideological legacy of the relationship between
capitalism and colonialism, but not in an economistic manner.

Second, we can claim that by the end of the nineteenth century, this process, which can be labelled racialisation, had as
its product an explicit set of ideas and arguments (i.e. racism)
which had a circulation throughout the class structure of
Britain. These ideas, however loosely articulated, postulated
the existence of 'races' by reference to phenotypical characteristics and had their prime focus upon persons who were the
victims of British colonialism. The idea of 'race' was therefore
materially grounded in the production relations of British
capitalism and 'demonstrated' simultaneously the inferiority of
the colonial subjects and the superiority of the British 'race'
by reference to colonial exploitation. Racism was thereby available to be used by sections of all classes to interpret subsequent developments and relationships as they occurred.

6 LABOUR MIGRATION AND RACISM: THE CASE OF THE IRISH

INTRODUCTION

The previous chapter has explained the formation and reproduction of racism both historically and with direct reference to
the development of capitalism. The empirical focus has been
upon the development of racism within British capitalism
although, given the interdependence of capital accumulation in
Britain and the development of a world capitalist economy, it
would be misconceived to type this racism as a domestic 'product' with only domestic influences and effects. The histories
of Zimbabwe and South Africa are formidable testimonies to
the importance of this point. It would also be misconceived to
identify this racism, which had the colonised populations
of the Caribbean and the Indian sub-continent as its object,
as the sole manifestation of racism in capitalist Britain.
If we focus our attention a little more narrowly upon and
within Britain in the nineteenth century, we can identify the
articulation of a racist ideology which had as its object the
then growing Irish population in both England and Scotland.
It is this racism which forms part of the subject matter of this
chapter.

The racialisation of the Irish is of interest not simply because
it suggests that we must not restrict the application of the concept of racism to situations where persons distinguish one
another by reference to skin colour. Rather, what is of prime
importance in this chapter is that, by reference to the empirical example of the experience of the Irish in Britain, I want to
show that we should structure our analysis of situations involving relations between persons and groups who identify themselves and others as 'races' by reference to political economy.
This will provide us with an analytical starting point which is
logically independent of the common sense terms which are
used in everyday social interaction to construct and interpret
the social world. By refusing to begin by accepting the everyday designation of a situation as one of relations between
'races', we therefore avoid designating the problem as one of
'race relations', and thereby pursuing a theory of 'race relations'. By claiming that the analytical starting point should be
with political economy, I mean that we should ask a different
set of questions. To appreciate this claim, one must recall my
earlier argument that to label a group as a 'race' or as part of
a 'race' is an ideological process: it is to categorise a group

falsely by reference to phenotypical or genetic (real or imagined) criteria. This process of labelling has not only ideological, but also economic and political motives and effects. But,
and this is the central point, both those labelled and those
applying the label have independent and prior positions in class
relations and we must first establish the parameters of these
positions. That is to say, we must first establish how their
position in class relations is attained, maintained and/or changed (cf. Phizacklea and Miles, 1980, pp. 1-25). This is a matter
of political economy because it necessitates consideration of the
nature of the mode of production, both structurally and conjunc-
turally. This involves, respectively, establishing the general
features of the forces and relations of production and their
particular characteristics for the period and social formation
in question. Hence, the analysis is simultaneously theoretical
and historical.

But why focus on the historical instance of the experience of
the Irish in Britain? For this, there are a number of reasons
in addition to the claim that such a focus allows me to make the
case outlined above. First, such a focus challenges the common
contemporary political assumption that 'immigration' to Britain
is a recent 'problem' and that 'immigrants' are people who have
black or brown skins. Second, it allows us to give some attention to what has been, numerically, the largest immigration to
Britain. Third, it makes possible a preliminary exposition of
the argument that our analytical attention should not primarily
be with phenotypical variation but with migrant labour (of
which much more will be said in Chapter 7). Fourth, it raises
a concrete instance of the way in which racism can interrelate
with other ideologies which have a similar effect of economic
and political exclusion. In the case of the Irish, economic and
political exclusion was justified by reference to the idea of
'race' and to religious adherence. Fifth, it encourages an empirical focus upon not only England, but also Scotland. Because
the vast majority of recent migrants from the Caribbean and
Indian sub-continent have settled in the major urban centres
of England, most of the recent political and academic debate
has been limited to England. However, because there are parallels between the Irish migration of the nineteenth century and
the New Commonwealth migration of the twentieth century, we
can usefully focus upon Scotland not only as a means of establishing the limits of the specificity of the recent English experience but also because the reasons for and effects of the migration of labour to Scotland are worthy of attention in their own
right (Miles, 1981, 1982).

Let it be stated at the outset that I am not the first to argue
for a comparative approach to history and effects of migration
to Britain. Both Foot (1965) and Allen (1971) have written books
which aim to establish a case for such a focus and both stress
the historical continuities in the reaction of the 'indigenous'
population to the arrival of different groups of migrants. How-

ever, both set their analyses within some form of 'race relations' framework and neither of them breaks with the consequent convention of using analytical categories which fail to anchor the respective migrant groups within the class structure. In the case of Allen's text, the comparative analysis promised by the title is poorly developed. More recently, Jones (1977) has compared the reactions to the Irish, Jewish and New Commonwealth migrations to Britain with the specific intention of examining the development of British welfare legislation. Other writers have provided straightforward accounts of other migrations to Britain (e.g. Tannahill, 1968; Garrard, 1971; Gartner, 1973). As already stated, my intentions are of a rather different order.

BRITISH CAPITALISM AND IRISH LABOUR

It is significant that those who have written about the Irish in Britain have been, in the main, economic historians, with a more recent increasing level of interest amongst persons who would probably identify themselves as social geographers. The only substantial self-consciously sociological contribution is that of Jackson (1963). Moreover, a large proportion of these writers have been concerned less with the Irish per se and more with the pattern of and reasons for economic development in Britain since the late eighteenth century. Such writers, whether or not they have adhered to Marxist categories of analysis, have been forced to devote attention to Irish migration to Britain because, as we shall see, Irish labour was a crucial component of capitalist development. Indeed, in the case of the west of Scotland, it is difficult to see how capitalist industrialisation could have occurred at the scale and speed that it did without Irish labour. This is less true for England, although in certain regions Irish labour was of crucial significance for the development of certain capitalist enterprises. My point is not that sociologists pursuing a theory of 'race relations' should now, belatedly, give thought to the Irish in Britain. Rather, by reference to the example of the Irish migration to Britain, I want to argue that the political and ideological reaction to the Irish from within the British population can only be understood if we have first examined the nature of and reasons for the migration. Redford testifies to the significance of this migration (1976, p. 131):

> The flood of Irish pauperism which swept over England during the great potato famine no longer appears as an isolated disaster, but is seen in its true character as the culminating wave of a rising tide of Irish immigration which had been steadily creeping further over England for many years previously. This persistent exodus from Ireland was by far the most significant feature of British migration

during the nineteenth century, and merits very full investigation.

This 'persistent exodus' was neither a simple nor a single movement of persons from Ireland to Britain. It neither began nor terminated with what English historians call the Great Famine (a great misnomer, given the continued export of food from Ireland to Britain throughout the period 1845-50 - see Handley, n.d., pp. 157-68) and it did not consist of a one-way, permanent movement from Ireland to Britain. I shall therefore break down this exodus into analytical parts for the purpose of clarity of presentation, but before I can do that it is first necessary to outline the nature and condition of the Irish economy in the late eighteenth and early nineteenth centuries.

(i) The circumstances and conditions of the Irish economy
Most studies of migration, when searching for the factors which 'push' people to leave the area and/or country of their birth, usually conclude that some combination of overpopulation and poverty are the crucial factors. In other words, it is suggested that it is the economic and social condition of the migrants that is the determinant cause. Such claims are, at best, only a half-truth because they obscure the nature of (and often changes of) the forces and relations of production (cf. Portes, 1978, pp. 5-10), a point that is well demonstrated in the case of Ireland.
   The nineteenth century witnessed important changes in the relationship between both different regions within Ireland and the Irish and British economies. Lees argues that as the century opened, the Irish economy fell into two parts. On the one hand, large sections of the north and east were increasingly dominated by large farms producing grain and cattle, mainly for export to England. In addition, in Ulster, potatoes, grain and flax were grown, the latter to supply the growing textile industry in and around Belfast. On the other hand, the west and south-west were dominated by peasant subsistence production. These were the most densely populated regions of Ireland, and it was here that potato cultivation had had its greatest effect. Potato cultivation made it possible for the peasants (who were either tenants paying a cash rent to the landowner or small landowners) to subsist on a much smaller area of land, the consequence being extensive sub-division of landholdings. The major dynamic of the nineteenth century was an increasing demand from England for agricultural goods, combined with the flooding of the nascent Irish market with British goods produced by developing, capitalist industries. The effect in Ireland was the collapse of domestic industry, an increased rate of farm consolidation and changes in agricultural production (primarily the decline of corn production and an increase in cattle and related dairy production), the latter resulting in a lowered demand for farm labour and the withdrawal of leases

(Lees, 1979, pp. 22-31).

The decline of the textile industry was of particular significance in affecting regional variation in emigration from Ireland
before the famine (Cousens, 1965). Linen was the most important product of the textile industry, but mechanisation in Britain ensured British domination of this product as the century
proceeded. The Irish textile industry also had to contend with
the competition of cheaper cotton goods made in Britain. Union
with Britain in 1801 was followed by the lowering and then the
abolition in 1824 of protective tariffs, the result being the
immiseration and, ultimately, the elimination of the handloom
weaver, first in the whole of the south and later in the north-
east of Ireland where the weaving of cotton had lingered around
Belfast with the support of Scottish capital (Green, 1944;
Cousens, 1965). After 1863, arrangements were made for
organised emigration (Green, 1944, p. 40), and Cousens makes
the point that where a family's livelihood was completely or
predominantly dependent upon textile production, emigration
was almost inevitable if no other employment was available and
if there was no land upon which to rely for some means of
support (1965, pp. 26-8).

In sum, changing forces of production in Britain threatened
directly the basis of the existence of the domestic handloom
weaver and, indirectly, the peasant tenant farmer, especially
in the east where farm consolidation was occurring on the
initiative of the landowning class, anxious to supply the agricultural produce demanded by the rapidly industrialising
British economy. In this context, the famine which followed
the appearance of potato blight in 1845 served to speed up
suddenly and dramatically a process that was already under
way. However, the threat of starvation was not always in itself
a, or the only, factor enforcing emigration. During the period
of the famine, population loss was much lower in the west where
extreme pauperism prevented movement while it was greatest
in north and central Ireland and parts of the south. In some of
the latter areas, the eviction policies of landowners forced
peasants off the land, a process that was to continue after the
famine was over and which was motivated by the economic
benefits of amalgamation and rationalisation. This process was
much less common in the west where the land was, generally,
of poorer quality and was more efficiently utilised as small
rented holdings (Cousens, 1960, 1961-2). This economic fact
had its cultural correlate, a long-established way of life, the
implications of which are made clear by Cousens (1961-2,
p. 288): 'Neither famine nor eviction loosed the hold of the
peasantry in much of the west.' The consequence of what
might also be seen as the uneven penetration of capitalist forces
of production was an accentuation of the uneven economic and
social development of the Irish economy as a whole. It was not
only that the cultural tradition of the peasant militated against
emigration, but also that capitalist development in Britain did

not require or have as one of its effects the destruction of
the economic basis of subsistence production in the west.

(ii) Seasonal migration and agricultural labour
By the time of the famine of the late 1840s, there was already
well established a pattern of seasonal migration from Ireland
to Britain, the migrants arriving in mid-summer to assist in
harvesting. When harvesting was complete and/or when the
migrant had earned a desired sum of money, he (and most
migrants were male) would return to Ireland to finish the year's
work on the land. There is a record of this seasonal migration
which goes back to the early eighteenth century, but it was on
a small and limited scale until the 1790s, from when the numbers
involved began to increase fast, especially in the second and
third decades of the nineteenth century. Irvine (1960, p. 239)
has estimated that some 60,000 harvesters came for the season
in 1841. A peak was reached during and immediately after the
famine, after which there was a dramatic decline (Johnson,
1967, p. 97; Collins, 1976, p. 49).

In order to explain the genesis of this seasonal labour migration, it is necessary to consider the nature of and the relationship between the agricultural productive forces in both Ireland
and Britain. In the case of Ireland, agricultural productivity
on the very small farms in the west was low and subsistence
was the norm. Where the population was growing, where there
was a low marginal productivity of labour and where there were
few or no alternative forms of employment which could produce
a cash wage, seasonal labour migration offered a solution to the
very pressing material problem of paying the rent (Collins,
1976, p. 45; Johnson, 1967, p. 99). The nature of the productive cycle on these small, family farms made it possible for the
father and/or sons to leave for much of the summer and the
initial destination was the east of Ireland to bring in the wheat
harvest. However, the demand for labour was soon outstripped
by the supply. Moreover, the provision of a regular steamboat
service to English and Scottish ports in the early nineteenth
century (Irvine, 1960), along with an increasing demand for
agricultural labour in Britain, served to attract these seasonal
migrant labourers across the Irish Sea.

In Britain in the early nineteenth century, an agricultural
revolution was well under way, involving the introduction of
labour-intensive crops but only limited mechanisation. The
consequence was both an increased yield and an increased
demand for labour but only at certain periods in the productive
cycle; in other words, the agricultural revolution increased
land but not labour productivity (Timmer, 1969). In the case
of grain crops, the most significant increase in demand for
labour came at harvest time: the introduction of threshing
machines ensured that this task could be done quickly soon
after the harvest, but there was no parallel mechanisation
of harvesting (Kerr, 1942-3, p. 366; Collins, 1976, pp. 38-9).

These changes were occurring simultaneously with the depopulation of rural areas because industrial capital required labour in the fast-developing towns and cities: the most rapid rate of population growth in the industrial towns was in the first half of the nineteenth century (Saville, 1957, p. 3). Most of the fast-developing manufacturing towns were in the west Midlands and north-west of England (and in west, lowland Scotland) and most of the labour they required came from the surrounding rural areas (Redford, 1976, pp. 62-7, 183). So, certainly after 1800, industrialisation ensured the loss to agricultural production of a labour surplus in the rural areas which could have met the increasing seasonal demand for harvesters. Additionally, and for the same underlying reason, there was also occurring a decline of rural industry. This also deprived farmers of a source of seasonal labour because handloom weavers and rural craftsmen would turn their hands to harvesting in the late summer (Collins, 1976, p. 40).

It is of significance that the demand for seasonal labour in agriculture was not in itself new: the uneven spread of farm workloads and an inadequate distribution of labour relative to demand at the seasonal peaks had for a long time necessitated seasonal migration. What was new in the early nineteenth century was an increased demand for seasonal labour at a time when pre-existing sources of supply were in decline. For example, in the late eighteenth century harvesting in Lincolnshire, Nottinghamshire and the Vale of York had been carried out with the assistance of handloom weavers from the West Riding (Mason, 1972, p. 131; Collins, 1969, p. 439; 1976, p. 42). In lowland Scotland, the Highlands were an important source of seasonal labour, as also were the handloom weavers in the villages around Glasgow (Handley, n.d., p. 7; Kerr, 1942-3, p. 366). The decline of handloom weaving and the general movement into the towns in the early nineteenth century, by coinciding with the developments already mentioned in Ireland, ensured that English and Scottish farmers would happily welcome the arrival of Irish seasonal migrants (e.g. Handley, 1970, p. 268).

But this source of seasonal labour was not a permanent one. In Britain in the 1850s an upturn in the trade cycle, the Crimean war and heavy emigration further reduced the amount of indigenous labour available, the consequence of which was strikes and increased wages. Moreover, urban employment opportunities were continuing to increase and the gap between farm and non-farm incomes continued to widen, further encouraging the movement of population, and so labour, from rural to urban areas. It was in this context that there occurred after the famine in Ireland a decline in seasonal migration. Why this happened is not completely clear from the literature but it is no doubt of significance that from 1850 the predominant destination of migration became America (Redford, 1976, p. 158). Given the divergence in the level of income that could be earned in

America compared with post-famine Ireland, it is obvious why
potential migrants would opt for permanent emigration to
America rather than remain in Ireland but supplement an inadequate income with seasonal wage labour in Britain. As for those
migrants who were not willing to migrate to America, but pre-
ferred to come to Britain, they could earn a larger wage by
moving into the industrial areas. Whatever the reason, there
were severe labour shortages in the 1860s (Collins, 1969,
pp. 469, 472; 1976, p. 50). The ultimate consequence of this
declining supply of labour was the encouragement of the mechanisation of harvesting (Collins, 1976, p. 50).

Clearly, seasonal migration of Irish labour was of considerable
importance in ensuring a supply of labour to agriculture at a
time when industrial capital was directing labour away from
rural areas and into the growing industrial towns. From the
perspective of British agriculture, seasonal migration represented, in the words of Collins (1976, p. 59): 'an efficient
allocation of resources at a stage of economic development when
mechanization was neither technically possible nor always
socially desirable and when labour, properly distributed, was
a cheap and flexible factor of production'. Put in other words,
the development of British capitalism in the nineteenth century
was partly dependent upon the labour of the Irish seasonal
migrant.

(iii) Irish labour and English industrial capitalism
The fact and experience of seasonal migration had its own effect
upon the Irish migrants themselves. It brought them into contact with a radically different sort of society which, despite
the often appalling working and living conditions, offered what
would seem to be an escape from subsistence agricultural production by means of high wages. Such knowledge, when fed
back to the farms and villages of Ireland, ensured the development of a steady stream of migrants (cf. MacDonald and
MacDonald, 1964; Watson, 1977a). It also encouraged the seasonal migrant to become a permanent settler in the industrial
towns (Johnson, 1967, p. 110; Redford, 1976, p. 149). Such
individual motivation was the converse of the increasing demand
for unskilled and semi-skilled labour. This demand was, in
certain sectors (e.g. railway construction, building) and at
certain times, also a demand for seasonal labour (Kerr, 1942-3,
p. 374; Redford, 1976, p. 150; Collins, 1976, p. 48), but the
vast majority of Irish migrants who entered the industrial economy did so as permanent immigrants.

Precise terminology is important here. Capital's demand for
labour is the crucial factor, but this should not blind us to the
fact that labour migrates and is sold not solely to satisfy capital.
Indeed, to be exact, it is not labour that migrates, but people,
and what they sell is their labour power. The needs of such
people vary according to material and other circumstances and
this affects the terms of their movement. Thus, we have a

threefold distinction between seasonal migrant labour, long-term migrant labour and immigrant labour. The former two categories have in common a continued economic and political commitment to the social formation from whence they migrate while the latter refers to a movement which is viewed as permanent, with no intention, at the point of departure, of return. Such a distinction must be made bearing in mind the fact that the migrant may later decide not to return, i.e. 'become' an immigrant. Such a transition I conceptualise as the permanent settlement of migrant labour.

The predominant areas of immigrant (and migrant) settlement of the Irish in England were London and Lancashire with less substantial settlements in south Wales and the west Midlands (Lawton, 1959, p. 40). These areas of settlement were areas of high labour demand. The extant evidence shows that the vast majority of these permanent settlers were employed in semi- and unskilled manual work, engaged in bricklaying, roadmaking, canal-cutting, railway construction, harbour construction and dock labour (Redford, 1976, pp. 150-1; Treble, 1973, p. 234; Jackson, 1963, pp. 78-87; Lovell, 1977; Kirk, 1980). The Irish also entered the cotton mills in Lancashire as handloom weavers, a job that was rapidly becoming obsolete given the transition to power looms (Werly, 1973, p. 352; Kirk, 1980, pp. 84-5). In Bradford, the Irish were heavily concentrated in the low skill and poorly paid jobs in the town's growing textile industry (Richardson, 1968). In London, which had a different labour market to that which existed in the north-east, the Irish in mid-century were predominantly employed in clothing, transport, food and construction. They were also represented in certain skilled trades (e.g. shoemaking, tailoring), but these were already showing signs of being trades in decline and conditions were deteriorating (Lees, 1979, pp. 88-92). In Newcastle in the mid-nineteenth century, the Irish provided much of the unskilled labour in the growing shipbuilding yards (Dougan, 1968, p. 36). But it was not only that the jobs of the Irish were semi- and unskilled for, as Redford points out (1976, p. 154):

A less attractive class of work in which the Irish were largely engaged consisted of jobs which Englishmen disliked because the work was dirty, disreputable, or otherwise undesirable. Much of this was petty trading and huckstering, keeping lodging houses and beer houses....Many of the Liverpool Irish were employed in soap-boiling; while in Bermondsey the Irish were chiefly employed in fellmongers' and tanners' yards, or in glue factories.

In the light of this, one is not surprised that the Irish tended to live in the cheapest and poorest accommodation. Moreover, and significantly, there is clear evidence that there were, in the growing industrial towns, areas where the Irish tended to be concentrated. Pooley has shown that in Liverpool the Irish tended to live in high-density, multiple-occupied, sub-standard housing and that this was because of their limited ability to pay rent, this in turn reflecting their employment in semi- and unskilled jobs (1977, pp. 371-3). Evidence for Bradford shows an almost identical picture (Richardson, 1968, pp. 47-51, 54). Redford states more categorically (1976, p. 159): 'The Irish in Great Britain always lived in the cheapest houses; families were often to be found sharing house with several other families, and they retained their native practice of keeping pigs in the house.' Such an emphatic claim is misleading in so far as there was a small proportion of Irish who did enter the expanding skilled trades and who, if the example of Liverpool was repeated elsewhere, lived in the more comfortable suburbs (Pooley, 1977, p. 373; see also Richardson, 1968, p. 52). The semi- and unskilled Irish were not only living in the cheapest and poorest quality accommodation, but they also tended to be segregated in such accommodation. Werly claims that, in Manchester, Irish Town and Little Ireland existed as physical 'ghettoes' which were both geographically and culturally segregated (1973, pp. 346-7; see also Engels, 1969, pp. 122-5; Lowe, 1977, p. 15; Kirk, 1980, p. 87). In Bradford, eight separate zones of Irish settlement have been identified, each having a distinct social and cultural homogeneity (Richardson, 1968, p. 47). Pooley notes the geographical segregation of the Irish in Liverpool, but claims that there exists little evidence of cultural cohesion (1977, pp. 377-8; see Lovell, 1977, for contrary evidence for London).

All this evidence overwhelmingly supports the contention that the Irish immigrants of the nineteenth century and their descendants constituted an important part of the semi- and unskilled fraction of the growing working class. With the help of their labour power was built the vital capital infrastructure of English industry, in particular the railways, canals, roads and docks. But much of this work was heavy, dangerous, seasonal and prone to sudden termination if capital was not forthcoming to continue with construction. Neither was it highly paid, although the income was greater than that which could be earned in Ireland. For the Irish, this meant that a wage was not guaranteed. For capital, this meant something different for, as Jackson puts it (1963, p. 82): 'The existence of a large pool of cheap labour at a time of national expansion proved an essential ingredient to the rapid industrial advance.'

(iv) Irish labour and Scottish industrial capitalism
Much the same case can be made for Scotland. However, the place of Irish labour in the development of Scottish capitalism requires separate consideration for three reasons. First, the scale of Irish migration to Scotland was much greater than in the case of England. Second, the development of capitalism in Scotland has some historically specific characteristics (see

Hechter, 1975; Dickson, 1980) which may be significantly
related to the role and position of Irish labour in Scotland.
Third, the peculiar character of the Scottish state (or proto-
state) has a particular relevance to an appreciation of the
nature and strength of the reaction towards the arrival and
employment of Irish labour in Scotland. For these reasons, I
cannot agree with those writers who make no distinction
between the place of Irish labour in England and in Scotland
(e.g. Jackson, 1963; Redford, 1976). The significance of
these points will be discussed in the following sections of this
chapter.

Given the scale of the Irish immigration, the growing concentration of Scottish population in the central lowland belt and
the increasing demand for labour in the nineteenth century,
the Irish came to constitute a much larger proportion of the
Scottish population than in England. According to the 1841
census, nearly 5 per cent of Scotland's population was Irish-
born, but this figure excludes the children born of parents
born in Ireland and Handley estimated that the proportion of
the Scottish population of Irish descent was probably 10 per
cent in 1841 (n.d., p. 45). Given the concentration of the
Irish in the west of Scotland, and particularly around Glasgow,
the proportion of the population which was of Irish descent was
obviously higher in this area. In the period preceding the
famine migration, it was estimated that more than a quarter of
Glasgow's population was of Irish descent (Handley, n.d.,
p. 55).

The development of Scottish capitalism in the later nineteenth
century was dependent upon both the prior development of
coal-mining and the textile industries (Dickson, 1980, pp. 140,
187), as well as the creation of a transport infrastructure. Of
course, this was true in a general sense for England too, but
in Scotland there was initially a much greater problem of labour
supply because, in part, there was a much smaller agricultural
hinterland upon which to draw. Thus, while in England the
development of industrial capitalism was dependent upon the
migration of labour from the rural hinterland, in Scotland it
was much more dependent upon the migration of labour from
outside the 'national' boundary (see Redford, 1976; Saville,
1975). It was in the first half of the nineteenth century that
Irish labour played such an important role in the development
of industrial capitalism, although one cannot ignore the fact
that labour was also drawn from the Scottish Highlands (e.g.
Handley, 1970, pp. 1-41; Campbell, 1980, pp. 14-16). Treble
records that the Irish were a vital part of the labour force
building the railways in Scotland in the period 1828 to 1850:
Irish navvies, having completed work in the north of England,
often travelled to Scotland if work was available, while others
came directly to Scotland from Ireland (1972, pp. 43-4; see
also Handley, 1970). The fast expansion of the coal-mining and
related iron-mining industries was also very dependent upon

the supply of Irish labour (Handley, n.d., pp. 46-59; Duckham, 1970, p. 309; Campbell, 1980, p. 15). A study of mining in Lanarkshire makes this very clear: between 1841 and 1851, the proportion of Irish in Coatbridge rose from 13.3 per cent to 49.1 per cent and this coincided with the intensive develop- ment of collieries and ironworks in the area. The result of this movement of Irish into Coatbridge was that almost 60 per cent of the unskilled metal workers and just over 44 per cent of the mineworkers in the area were Irish. Considering the general category of unskilled jobs, almost 36 per cent of these were occupied by the Irish (Campbell, 1979, pp. 178-80). Whether these proportions of Irish in the coal-mines and ironworks were repeated throughout the west of Scotland is difficult to ascer- tain. However, the fact that Handley refers specifically to the employment of Irish immigrants in the coalfields of Ayrshire, Lanarkshire, Dumbartonshire and West Lothian (n.d., pp. 46- 65) in the period before the famine migration suggests that the Irish did constitute a significant and notable proportion of the mine workforce throughout the west of Scotland.

Mention should be made of the role of Irish labour in the textile industry. The manufacture and export of linen under- went expansion after, and partly because of, the Act of Union and bequeathed both capital and skill to the subsequent development of what was to become the more important cotton industry (Dickson, 1980, pp. 100-1). Also of prior significance was silk manufacture in Paisley, but that too was to become less important than cotton manufacture after the 1790s. The development of cotton manufacture was rapid and large-scale and by the 1820s, the vast majority of the industrial labour force in Scotland was employed either in cotton or in one of the comparatively declining sectors (Handley, n.d., p. 44; Murray, 1978, p. 1).

The bulk of the expansion took the form of cotton domestic handloom weaving (although the early nineteenth century also saw the beginning of the evolution of factory production) and the expansion was paralleled by an increase in immigration from Ireland, many of the immigrants having been handloom weavers in the declining Irish linen industry. Murray has estimated that by 1820, the proportion of handloom weavers who were Irish was less than 25 per cent and this had risen to around 30 per cent by 1838 (1978, p. 33). The importance of Irish labour to the development of the industry is further emphasised by the fact that the settlement pattern of Irish immigrants coincided very closely with the principal weaving areas. Moreover, a large proportion of Irish immigrants entered the industry at a time when the wages and living standards of weavers were falling (that is, between 1812 and 1840). When declining wages eventually had the effect of discouraging further entry into handloom weaving after 1840, it tended to be Scots who with- drew or who did not enter the industry, with the consequence that the Irish constituted an increasing proportion of the

workforce for at least part of the period of the decline of the
industry (Murray, 1978, pp. 33-4, 62; see also Handley, n.d.,
pp. 122-3).

The other industries in which Irish labour was prominent in
the period up to the famine immigration, if not in such large
proportions, were building, sugar refining and bleaching
(Handley, n.d., pp. 50, 65; Lobban, 1961, p. 271). Indeed,
the distribution of Irish labour after 1850 remained much the
same, the concentration being greatest in textiles and coal and
iron industries as well as in navvying and labouring on railway
and urban construction (Handley, n.d., pp. 263-73; Walker,
1979).

There are two points of special importance which should be
made about this pattern of employment. First, Irish labour
was engaged in predominantly semi- and unskilled manual tasks.
As in the case of England, there are references to a small number of Irish constituting a part of a petite-bourgeoisie through
letting rooms, running pubs and pawnbroker's shops (e.g.
Walker, 1979, p. 120), but all writers are agreed that the vast
majority of Irish were wage labourers engaged in semi- and
unskilled work (e.g. Handley, n.d., p. 273; Lobban, 1961,
p. 271). In the textile industry in the early nineteenth century,
Glasgow was the centre for the production of plain (and cheap)
cotton weaving while Paisley retained a specialisation in more
skilled production (fine muslins and silk). The greater concentration of Irish labour in and around Glasgow is explained by
the concentration of Irish labour within the less skilled and
specialised sector of textile production (Murray, 1978, pp. 32-
3). In Lanarkshire, Campbell argues that the Irish formed a
higher proportion of ironstone miners than coal-miners because
the former was much more arduous (1979, pp. 178-9). This
bears out the earlier and more general claim made by Handley
that the Irish tended to be employed in jobs which, because
of the physical effort required or because of limited prospects,
were not attractive to a large proportion of 'native' labour.
Indeed, Handley continues (n.d., p. 74):

> It was not a case of Scots abandoning types of unskilled
> labour to the strangers in favour of the skilled branches,
> because both the unskilled and skilled forms of labour
> were new ones, created and being created by the require-
> ments of the industrial revolution that was under way. The
> Irish in Scotland made that revolution in part possible and
> by their labour established jobs for Scottish workers.

More recent historical writing suggests that there were important exceptions to this argument (see below), but the evidence
that I have so far cited does support the view that by a concentration in those sectors of the Scottish economy which constituted the basis of the development of industrial capitalism,
the migration of labour from Ireland was a crucial factor making

possible the ascendancy of capitalist relations of production
in Scotland. Second, it would seem that this concentration of
Irish labour in semi- and unskilled jobs was true for not only
the immigrants from Ireland, but also for their Scottish-born
children. Handley claims this to be so (n.d., p. 272) and
Lobban provides evidence which directly supports this view
(1961, pp. 276-7). None of the evidence cited by those who
have written in more detail on particular industries contradicts
it. The implication is that immigrant status was not in or by
itself sufficient to explain the concentration of Irish labour in
semi- and unskilled wage labour.

Given the role of Irish wage labour in the developing Scottish
capitalist economy, it is, again, not surprising that the available evidence suggests that the Irish tended to live in the
poorest housing and to experience the worst living conditions.
Of course, the housing of the growing working class throughout Britain was generally of appalling quality in this period,
and especially so in Glasgow, but the condition of at least a
significant, if not large, proportion of the Irish was generally
worse than indigenous labour. Handley reports that in the
period up to 1845, the Irish were the least able to afford
accommodation and were the worst housed. Their accommodation
was even more likely to be overcrowded due to the necessity
of newly arrived immigrants having to lodge with previously
arrived immigrants. This seems to have remained the case for
most of the nineteenth century. Given the housing standards
of the time, epidemics of typhus, cholera and relapsing fever
were common and the Irish seem to have been particularly
prone to their effects (Handley, n.d., pp. 105-8, 277). Murray
records that with the increasing entry of Irish and Highland
immigrant labour into handloom weaving after 1815, there was
increased competition for the limited available accommodation,
so forcing up rents in the main weaving centres. The result
was not only that weavers were forced to make their homes in
older and poorly constructed property, but also that families
were forced to live in a single room. He notes that in the case
of Irish weavers, overcrowding was intensified by the necessity
to take in lodgers to supplement the family income (1978,
pp. 153-4). Campbell, in his study of miners in Lanarkshire,
reports that the Irish tended to be spatially segregated but
he provides no evidence on comparative housing conditions
(1979, p. 188). In Greenock, the Irish in mid-nineteenth century were much more likely to be living in houses with a small
number of rooms and to be residentially segregated (Lobban,
1961, pp. 275-8).

So, we may conclude from this accumulation of evidence that
Irish labour was predominantly semi- or unskilled wage labour,
employed in those sectors of capitalist production which created
the skills, knowledge and a further accumulation of capital
which were vital factors in encouraging the development of
heavy industry in the second half of the nineteenth century.

In addition, Irish labour was well represented in the construction industry which built the transport and urban infrastructure of Scottish capitalism. It seems unlikely that Scottish capitalism would have developed so fast or in the same manner without the addition of Irish labour to the growing proletariat during the nineteenth century.

IRISH LABOUR AND RACISM

To this point I have suggested that it is by means of political economy that we can explain the migration of labour and the position in class relations that migrant and immigrant labour comes to occupy. But to close the analysis at this point is to duck both the crucial issue of whether the political and ideological reaction towards the Irish migrants can be characterised as racist and to segregate the influence of political and ideological relations from production relations. Although political and ideological factors seem not to have obstructed the flow of immigration from Ireland to Britain (a flow that is therefore to be explained primarily in terms of the changing economic relations between the two), the class position of the migrants in Britain was not determined solely by production relations. As I have argued elsewhere (Phizacklea and Miles, 1980), racism should be conceived of as an important ideological dimension of class fractionalisation and it is to the historical record of agitation against Irish labour that I now wish to turn.

(i) The historical record
There is no doubt that both the Irish seasonal migrants and the Irish immigrants became the focus of not only an ideological offensive but also discrimination and physical violence during the nineteenth century in Britain. What is problematic is how we might conceptualise the nature, extent and origin of the opposition to their presence.

Jackson has concluded that there was 'remarkably little widespread trouble' and that the Irish, during the nineteenth century, 'achieved a status and respect in many areas which allowed them to ignore the latent hostility' (1963, p. 156). It is difficult to quantify what is to count as 'little widespread trouble', while to state that the 'little' is 'remarkable' is to imply that there is good reason to expect that there should have been 'more'. Jackson's conclusion is therefore problematic by reason of raising more questions than it answers. I want to argue by way of contrast that the historical record can be interpreted to suggest that not only should we analyse the reaction in Scotland separately from that in England, but also that at certain times in certain areas of England and Scotland during the nineteenth century, anti-Irish agitation led to civil disorder on a scale which required the state to utilise the police and army to restore 'law and order'. Moreover, and particularly in

Scotland, civil disorder occurred against the background of
persistent ideological campaign against the presence of the
Irish. Granted that this disorder and campaign did not occur
throughout Britain throughout the nineteenth century (and in
that sense was not widespread), but in certain decades and in
certain areas the agitation and violence was persistent and
involved large numbers of people. Moreover, for at least the
period 1865-71, anti-Catholic agitation occurred in several
towns throughout England and Irish Catholics were prominent
in the riots that ensued.

In England in the 1820s and 1830s, the appearance of Irish seasonal labourers in the south, Midlands and Yorkshire was followed
by physical disturbances and campaigns against their employment
The opposition came from English rural labourers while the
landowning class continued to welcome the arrival of Irish
labour. Indeed, when seasonal labour began to decline after
1850, farmers complained about the absence of Irish labour
(Kerr, 1942-3, p. 375; Collins, 1969, 1976). Collins has suggested, however, that the tension and conflict was much greater
in the growing urban areas than in the countryside (1976,
p. 56; see also Lowe, 1977), and the evidence certainly bears
him out. This conflict, not surprisingly given the pattern of
setttlement of Irish immigrants, occurred in the north-east of
England and seems to have centred on railway construction
and the fast-growing textile area of Manchester/Liverpool
(e.g. Kirk, 1980, p. 72). Treble refers to conflict and a riot
between English and Irish navvies between late 1845 and early
1846 during the construction of the railway line between Carlisle
and Penrith and again at Cleckheaton and around Barnsley in
1848-9. But these were far from being the only incidents involving English navvies and the Irish because Treble records the
former attacking the Irish no matter what their occupation.
Moreover, the fact that contractors are reported to have adopted
a policy of keeping English and Irish navvies employed on different sections of the line suggests at least that there had been
sufficient real conflict to persuade them that there was great
potential for further conflict and, so, disruption of production
(1973, pp. 234, 238-40). Brooke's study of the Pennine region
suggests that conflict did not occur during the construction of
all railway lines but, then, as he himself notes, only a very
small number of Irish were employed on the construction of the
Pennine lines (1975-6, p. 45).

Lancashire seems to have been the location for the most prominent violence and agitation after 1850. The presence of a
substantial Irish population in Liverpool became the focus of
much political agitation (Hanham, 1959, p. 285), while for
Manchester there are reports of the Irish experiencing job
discrimination (Werly, 1973, p. 353) and working separately
from the English in the cotton mills (Redford, 1976, p. 163).
Riots involving English and Irish are reported to have occurred
in Stockport (1852), Oldham (1861) and Stockton (1872) (see

Foster, 1974; Steele, 1976; Kirk, 1980). Moreover, a number
of the riots that occurred following the agitation of William
Murphy took place in Lancashire. However, Murphy's activities
were not limited to Lancashire for he appeared and spoke
publicly in Wolverhampton (1867), Walsall (1867), Birmingham
(1867), Tynemouth (1869), Woolwich (1869), Whitehaven (1871)
as well as Rochdale, Stalybridge, Ashton-under-Lyne, Oldham,
Bolton and Manchester (all in 1868). Murphy lectured on the
supposed iniquities of Catholicism, but he was also concerned
to encourage anti-Irish sentiment and in this he seems to have
been successful. His lectures came to be well-attended, particularly by Irish Catholics, and they tended to challenge
Murphy's propaganda with violence, and on a considerable
scale. In Wolverhampton, 10,000 Irish were reported to have
prevented Murphy from speaking while in Birmingham, houses
were badly damaged, crowds grew to between 50,000 and
100,000, dozens of casualties required hospital treatment and
'law and order' was only restored by the intervention of troops.
A riot in Ashton-under-Lyne began with an attack by an Irish
crowd upon a gathering of Murphy's supporters and was
followed by damage to a Catholic chapel and the complete destruction of furniture in twenty Irish houses; in the course of
this, one Irishman died (Hanham, 1959, pp. 303-8; Arnstein,
1975). Hanham has argued that the anti-Irish sentiment stirred
up by, amongst other things, the activities of Murphy, was
sufficiently strong to help bring about the defeat of the Liberals
in the area in the 1868 general election (1959, p. 303; see also
Kirk, 1980, pp. 91-5). Unfortunately, no sustained attempt has
been made to investigate the incidence of anti-Irish sentiment
and violence in England and so we have no way of knowing
whether this list of events and incidents is exhaustive but,
whatever the answer to that question, this evidence does suggest that the Irish were the object of considerable political
agitation and violence in the 1820s and 1830s and again in the
1840s and 1860s, particularly, but not exclusively, in the north-
east.

In Scotland, the agitation and violence seems to have been
more sustained and its effects have been more widespread and
long-lasting. There is some evidence of disturbances in the
rural areas in the 1830s which expressed opposition to the
presence of Irish seasonal labourers (Collins, 1969; Handley,
n.d., pp. 19-20), but, with the exception of a major clash
between Irish and Highland labour engaged in canal-building
in 1818, most of the reported incidents took place in the Glasgow
area and its agricultural/industrial hinterland. That this spatial
concentration of agitation and violence cannot be simply
explained by reference to the large proportion of Irish in the
west of lowland Scotland relative to elsewhere is made clear
by the fact that in Dundee, which had a similar proportion of
Irish in its population, there seems to have been a much lower
level of conflict. This is explained by Walker to be the con-

sequence of certain political characteristics of the town (1979, pp. 114-22; also, 1972).

The Irish seem to have become the focus of critical attention soon after immigration increased. Literate contemporaries of the handloom weavers between 1790 and 1850 claimed that the weavers were becoming increasingly immoral and many attributed this to the movement of Irish labour into the trade. It was argued that the Irish were dishonest, indolent and improvident and that they consequently had a pernicious effect on the morals of the native Scots. The weavers also gained a reputation for drunkenness, violence and petty theft and, again, these characteristics were said to be particularly typical of the Irish (Murray, 1978, pp. 175-8). But, at least up until mid-century, most of the violence and agitation centred around railway construction and coal-mining. Concerning the former Handley (n.d., pp. 38-41; also 1970, pp. 267-320) refers to several incidents involving Highland and Irish labour in large numbers (often in excess of 1000 persons), as a result of which the military had to be called in to stop the conflict. In Dunfermline in this early period, all the Irish were forcibly expelled from the town on one occasion. Within the mining industry, there was considerable and continuous conflict (Campbell, 1979, p. 181): 'For decades, the antagonism between Scots and Irish miners found frequent expression in violence.' Campbell has compiled a list of outbreaks of violence involving Irish and Scottish workers, totalling 55 incidents for the period 1831-83 (1979, pp. 316-19). A considerable proportion of these involved miners in the Coatbridge area. In 1835, Airdrie became the focus of disturbances which went on for several days and culminated in the following way (Handley, n.d., pp. 145-6):

A crowd of four or five thousand from the town and the surrounding district paraded up and down the streets throughout the night. By morning they were ripe for mischief. They wrecked the Catholic chapel, which was also the school and the houses of two Catholics.

Anti-Irish agitation and violence continued after the famine immigration. Greenock and Gourock became the centre of much of this in the early 1850s. For example (Handley, n.d., p. 235):

Throughout the year 1852 anti-Catholic disturbances were continual. Armed mobs paraded the streets. Catholic shops were broken into and the offenders fined a paltry twenty shillings, subscribed by their friends. A man who attempted to take the life of a Catholic policeman with pistol and dagger received a sentence of only thirty days from the local bailie. The mockery of justice displayed by the local bench encouraged the rabble. At last in January 1853 the government had to step in, suspend the magistrates, the fiscal and the town clerk and appoint in their place a stipendiary magistrate.

Dumbarton was also a centre of periodic violence and in 1855 one shipyard dismissed all the Irish employees following an incident in which two of their number had been victims of physical assault (Handley, n.d., p. 254). Again, industrial towns in Lanarkshire also experienced unrest and violence in the 1850s (Handley, n.d., pp. 255-6). There was a major riot lasting several days in Partick in Glasgow in August 1875 and another in Coatbridge in 1883: on both occasions hundreds of people were involved, fighting was widespread and the Riot Act had to be read (Handley, n.d., pp. 257-9).

These outbreaks of violence, of which there were many more, were paralleled by anti-Irish sentiment expressed in newspapers, pamphlets and Royal Commission reports as well as from the church pulpit and in letters written by church ministers to newspapers (Handley, n.d., pp. 73, 138, 141). Anti-Catholic periodicals were published and certain newspapers gained a particular notoriety for their anti-Catholic bias (Handley, n.d., pp. 239-48).

(ii) Was the response racist?
So, having demonstrated the existence of opposition to Irish immigration and the Irish presence in England and Scotland, it is now necessary to consider its nature and foundation. It is important to note at the outset that many of those whose evidence I have drawn upon have no doubt that they are analysing 'racial prejudice' and 'racial conflict' (e.g. Treble, 1973; Brooke, 1975-6; Redford, 1976; Handley, n.d.). Indeed, some of these writers write of the Irish as a 'race' in the sense of nineteenth-century scientific racism. For example, Brooke writes (1975-6, p. 46): 'It is immediately apparent that relations between the races must have been reasonably satisfactory since the Irish on these lines at the time of the censuses were heavily outnumbered and, because of their dispersal over many miles of track, acutely vulnerable to molestation.' The examples could be multiplied several times over. The use of such terminology may, in the manner of the sociology of 'race relations', be refracting the language of the everyday world, but this we must not take for granted. It is necessary to demonstrate that the Irish were conceived of by contemporaries in the nineteenth century as a 'race' and that, identified as such, they were then accorded certain (real or ascribed) negative (cultural) characteristics. In other words, was the agitation and violence against the Irish accompanied by the ideology of racism (see Phizacklea and Miles, 1980, pp. 20-3)?

It would seem that those who wrote about the Irish presence and the supposed effects of that presence certainly conceptualised the Irish as a 'race'. A 'Times' editorial of 3 July 1852 included the claim:

The series of riots at Stockport is about one of the most awkward incidents that could possibly occur at this juncture.

The ill blood which has been gradually nourished in that town is only a sample of the feeling which recent events have produced between the two races and the two religions that chiefly divide these islands.

Moreover, having noted that it was the houses and property of Irish Catholics which were damaged in the riots, the editorial offers the following evaluation: 'The Protestant English were as superior in the result as they were in their cause, and for once truth was great and prevailed, without any of the qualifications or delays which usually mar that blessed consummation.'

As for Scotland, the writer of the introduction to the results of the 1871 census claimed that (quoted in Handley, n.d., pp. 321-3): 'This very high proportion of the Irish race in Scotland has undoubtedly produced deleterious results, lowered greatly the moral tone of the lower classes, and greatly increased the necessity for the enforcement of sanitary and police precautions wherever they are settled in numbers.' Whether this terminology was used or, indeed, widespread in the working class is difficult to say. The analysis of historians of the working class has always been bedevilled by the consequence of a barely literate working class, the absence of an adequate written record. However, if the testimony of Engels is anything to go by, even if the actual language of 'race' was not employed in Manchester in the 1840s by the working class, it would seem that the Irish were identified by not only their language and/or accent, their culture and their often shabby appearance, but also by their (supposed) physical characteristics (1969, p. 123):

Whenever a district is distinguished for especial filth and especial ruinousness, the explorer may safely count upon meeting chiefly those Celtic faces which one recognises at the first glance as different from the Saxon physiognomy of the native, and the singing, aspirate brogue which the true Irishman never loses.

So, conceived of as a 'race', as a separate physical type, the Irish were also attributed with a range of negative social and cultural characteristics. As has already been implied, these included the claims that the Irish were particularly prone to violence, drunkenness and theft. Particularly in the period after the famine, Irish immigrants were held responsible for overcrowding, inadequate sanitation and the spread of disease (Handley, n.d., pp. 177-98). These particular claims came to be generalised into the argument that the Irish were directly responsible for both the material and moral deterioration of the Scottish working class. A medical officer, writing in 1847, claimed (quoted in Handley, n.d., pp. 193-4):

the low Irish emigrants who are now settled in great numbers in Edinburgh, and in fact constitute nine-tenths of our pau-

pers, were the original and immediate cause of the deterioration of the lower classes....Old byres, stables and
out-houses, never previously considered habitable, were
used by them as places of abode perhaps for the greater
facilities such places afforded for raising a pig, which
many of them continued to do in their new abodes. In
proportion as these Irish increased, the Scottish artisans
and labourers were driven from their neighbourhood, as
they found it impossible to live with any comfort in the
midst of filth, vermin, quarrelling and fighting which
constantly attended the abodes inhabited by these immigrants.

Similar arguments and claims were articulated throughout
Britain (Jackson, 1963, pp. 40-42; Kirk, 1980, pp. 68-9,
87-9).
    Moreover, and significantly, these arguments and claims
were articulated coincidentally with the increasing publicity
being given to the work of scientific racists: the mid-nineteenth
century was not only the high-spot of scientific racism (see
Chapter 5) but also of Irish immigration. Curtis has argued
that these theories of scientific racism played an important part
in the formulation of the stereotype of the Irish that developed
in Victorian England (1968, p. 5; see also Curtis, 1971 and
Lebow, 1976). This stereotype, he argues, attributed the Irish
with the characteristics of ignorance, laziness, primitiveness,
childishness and emotional instability (1968, p. 54): 'Irishmen
thus shared with virtually all the nonwhite peoples of the empire
the label of childish, and the remedy for unruly children in
most Victorian households was a proper "licking".' Curtis's
argument has not gone unchallenged and Gilley has argued that
English attitudes to the Irish were more complex and less based
on a 'racial distinction' than the former asserts (1978). The
second claim is mistakenly formulated: Gilley argues that there
is no objective criterion of 'race' upon which the English could
focus their negative evaluation of the Irish but, as I have
argued at length, differences of 'race' do not exist. Rather, in
certain situations and conjunctures, certain physical features
are attributed with social significance. As I have just shown,
the Irish were explicitly defined as a separate 'race' and it was
believed that the Irish could be identified by physical criteria.
Gilley's former claim has more substance, but the fact that the
stereotype of the Irish was complex and contained both negative
and positive aspects does not destroy Curtis's argument if it is
modified to allow for the fact that it is a characteristic of ideologies that they are inchoate and even contradictory (see
Phizacklea and Miles, 1980, pp. 131-2).
    Despite these criticisms of Gilley's critique, it does serve
to remind us in relation to Curtis's argument that the hostility
and violence experienced by the Irish in England and Scotland
were not solely motivated by or expressed in terms of scientific

racism. As far as Handley is concerned (n.d., p. 134): 'The chief reason for native animosity against the immigrants was the fact that the vast majority of them were Catholics.' Stated without reservation in this way, this claim is not easily sustained and Handley's own text contains contradictory evidence, as we shall see. But it is incontestable that anti-Catholicism was a significant strand to the hostility towards the Irish.

In England, there is a tradition of anti-Catholicism which predates the Reformation and there are records of incidents initiated by anti-Catholic sentiment from the seventeenth century onwards. Such incidents were motivated by the belief that Catholicism was to be equated with superstition, idolatry and moral corruption and, given the allegiance to the Pope and Rome, was likely to be supportive of subversion against the state. During the nineteenth century, two events in particular (the Maynooth Grant of 1845 and the restoration of the Catholic hierarchy in Britain in 1850) served to stimulate anti-Catholic agitation within all classes on a wide scale, although in neither case did the opposition cohere into a national and sustained political movement (Norman, 1968). More generally, the 'Irish question' provided a platform for Protestant opinion throughout the nineteenth century. Much of the agitation was carried out by the clergy, although there were also a number of itinerant preachers who successfully encouraged not only anti-Catholic sentiment but also violence (as we have already seen). This evidence makes it difficult to accept Handley's claim that 'the relationship between the English and Irish navvy was not complicated by religious prejudice' (1970, p. 271).

However, it would seem that the anti-Catholic agitation in Scotland (at least in the west lowlands) was more sustained and extreme. Handley's text suggests that anti-Irish sentiment was less easily disentangled from anti-Catholic sentiment, to the extent that one became almost synonymous with the other (e.g. n.d., p. 141). It might be thought that this is to be explained by the fact that the number and proportion of the Irish was much greater in the west of Scotland than in England, with the possible exception of Lancashire. Moreover, the English exception seems to prove the rule: the focus of the most serious anti-Irish agitation in England was Lancashire. There is a good reason to be suspicious of this argument if it is understood to mean that numbers are an active 'cause' although the Irish presence is a sine qua non. If numbers were the active, determinant cause, then one would expect anti-Irish agitation to have been continuous and to have coincided with the peak period of immigration. This was certainly not so in England (e.g. Foster, 1974, p. 244; see also Kirk, 1980, p. 83) while, for Scotland, Handley's account suggests a cyclical rise and decline of agitation and disturbances which can be related to the occurrence of specific events (n.d., pp. 77-8, 234ff).

The extremity of the conflict in Scotland compared with England might also be measured by reference to its apparently greater degree of institutionalisation. Although, as in England, much of the anti-Catholic agitation originated from the church (Handley, n.d., pp. 131, 136, 141), other institutions played a role too. In some cases, their very existence was indicative of the depth of opposition. For example, the Protestant Association, formed in 1835, organised lectures on what it identified as the political and religious evils of Ireland, while the Scottish Reformation Society, formed in 1850, organised anti-Catholic lectures (Handley, n.d., pp. 137, 233). In addition, at least two specifically anti-Catholic periodicals began publication in 1851 and two newspapers were particularly notable for their anti-Catholic bias in mid-century (Handley, n.d., pp. 239-48; Norman, 1968, p. 65). Finally, one must note the significance of the Orange Order. Although it had an institutional existence in both England and Scotland (e.g. Senior, 1966, pp. 151-76, 230-1, 260), its political significance has been greater and longer lasting in Scotland, its parades constituting 'proof' of Protestant ascendancy (e.g. Handley, n.d., pp. 142-6, 257). Although the formation of the Orange Lodges was a measure of the existence of anti-Catholic sentiment (Senior, 1966, p. 156), their continued existence and activity independently contributed to the continued articulation of anti-Catholic sentiment (Campbell, 1979, pp. 182, 185).

How, then, might we account for this apparently more vehement and sustained reaction against the Irish in Scotland in terms of their Catholicism? No doubt, the fact that Scottish migrants played a significant part in the colonial exploitation of Ireland has to be considered because they took their Presbyterianism with them and so assisted the process by which religious adherence became a matter of political and economic significance in both Ireland and Scotland. But, in addition, I want to suggest that particular attention should be paid to the history and character of the Scottish Kirk. The Scottish Reformation was not only a reaction against and rejection of Catholicism, but also of the presence of French Catholics in Scotland. Thus, Smout has argued (1972, p. 54; see also Donaldson, 1972, pp. 52-3): 'there was a general identification in the popular mind of ecclesiastical corruption with the hierarchy, of the hierarchy with the regent, of the regent with the resented satellite status of Scotland to France, of France with Catholicism and militant Papacy'. Moreover, the Scottish Reformation was not actively assisted by the ruling class and the form of church government that eventually came to predominate reflects this (Reid, 1960, pp. 37-8):

It was a system of self-governing congregation held together by a hierarchy of councils culminating in a national synod. It refused to imitate the Roman Church either in its organisation or in its services. Church government by presbyters (ministers and elders) was, the Reformers of France, Geneva and Scotland believed, in accordance with the New Testament pattern: this indeed was the one sort of Protestant Church which could properly call itself reformed.

Further evidence for the claim that opposition to Catholicism actively structured the Scottish Kirk is found in Smout's claim that the presbyterian form of church government was a means by which the laity could ensure that the previous abuses and corruptions of Catholic priests would not reappear (1972, p. 58). By contrast, the English Reformation was more uncertain in its outcome and the form and practice of the Anglican church continued to give rise to suspicions in Scotland of the possibility of a return to Catholicism. Later, this same fear, but with its focus being Scotland and not England, ultimately determined the Kirk's decision not to oppose the Act of Union of 1707 (Reid, 1960, pp. 106-7).

The Act of Union, or rather its consequences, accorded the Kirk with much greater power and influence. The Union emasculated the Scottish state, leaving it without direct political power or control over the monopoly of legitimate physical force. But the state was not completely dismantled. As a result of Union, the Kirk was guaranteed a permanent existence as the Church of Scotland, and came to serve as a focus of national sentiment. Yet, there was no means by which that sentiment could be expressed politically within Scotland. Consequently, so Harvie argues (1977, p. 28; see also Donaldson, 1972, p. 112): 'during the great age of European nationalism, formal Scottish nationalism was a marginal component of a Scottish politics which was fundamentally religious'. The continued and separate existence of the Kirk (as well as legal, educational and banking systems) provided the institutional location for an indigenous ruling-class fraction, lacking direct political power, but exercising nevertheless a form of political power through religion. The power of the Kirk was particularly significant in the control of moral conduct, but its influence did not stop there (Reid, 1960, p. 188; see also Harvie, 1977, p. 128):

> The chief 'managers' of Scottish affairs in the eighteenth century were themselves Presbyterians - the Dukes of Argyll till 1761, then Henry Dundas (Viscount Melville), the son of a great legal family. They used every means they could to influence Scotsmen towards support of the Government. The most powerful body in the country was the Kirk, and patronage was a useful means of getting the Government's supporters into parish pulpits.

If political power was exercised through the institution and ideology of the Kirk, then the religious predominance of the Kirk had to be maintained for both political and religious reasons. Although Catholicism made some limited advances in the Highlands after 1690, throughout the eighteenth century there were no more than between 20,000 and 30,000 Catholics in the whole

of Scotland (Donaldson, 1972, p. 108). Consequently, until
the nineteenth century, there was no serious religious challenge
to this position of political prominence held by the Kirk.

Given this context, church ministers (as proto-state functionaries) were more than likely to regard the immigration of
the Irish, the majority of whom adhered to the Catholic faith,
as a religious threat to themselves and their church and,
because of the role of the latter, a threat to the state. A similar reaction was likely from the laity in so far as their religious
commitment was significant to them or, at least, could be made
to be so. But this is only to say that there was in existence an
already sympathetic audience for anti-Catholicism: the active,
agitational role of the minister, itinerant preacher and Orange
Lodge should not be played down. But, in turn, there was a
tradition of popular anti-Catholic protest to serve as a reminder
of the potential for effective agitation. Put in other words, the
anti-Catholicism of the Kirk was over-determined by the peculiar character of the Scottish proto-state, itself a product of,
inter alia, the anti-Catholicism of a previous era.

In sum, anti-Irish sentiment and political activity in England
and Scotland in the nineteenth century were not unidimensional.
Certainly, one strand was racism, but anti-Catholicism constituted another, and the two strands seem to have become inex-
tricably intertwined. Indeed, one should expect this to have
been so because the essence of scientific racism was that
phenotypical variation determined cultural difference. Consequently, the 'degeneracy' of the Irish 'race' could be measured
by the adherence to Catholicism: Handley notes a court report
in the 'Scottish Guardian' which identified an Irish defendant
as having a wide mouth and low, 'villainous' forehead and which
added a reference to 'the proverbially belligerent disposition
of the half-civilized, and wholly Romanized savages' (n.d.,
pp. 245-6). However, this should not be read to mean that
racism and anti-Catholicism are synonymous. Both ideologies
have separate and distinct parameters, such that anti-Catholicism could be and was articulated quite independently of any
racist claim (and vice versa). My point is simply that the historical record shows that racist sentiment and argument regard-
ing the Irish incorporated anti-Catholicism as its cultural component and that this is to be expected given the nature of
racism. This is not to deny that anti-Irish agitation was not also
primarily motivated by anti-Catholicism. The precise importance
of this distinction awaits a more detailed historical analysis
which is beyond the scope of this text.

RACISM AND PRODUCTION RELATIONS

I have shown that both the seasonal migrant and the permanent
immigrant from Ireland to Britain were the focus of ideological
and political agitation in Britain and that that agitation was

articulated partially in a racist form. Moreover, that agitation
was clearly not the prerogative of the ruling class: most of
those who participated in the disturbances were from the working class. The latter were not, however, reacting in political
and ideological isolation. Church ministers, itinerant preachers
and Conservative Party politicians (not to mention the activities
of Orange Lodges in Scotland) were active in encouraging anti-
Irish sentiment (e.g. Kirk, 1980, pp. 91-5), but this does not
complete the explanation. We also have to take account of the
fact that British capital derived advantages from the existence
of a supply of semi- and unskilled labour in such a quantity
as to ensure both low wages and a reserve army of labour and
this had implications for the terms on which the English and
Scottish working classes could sell their labour power for
capital's wage. I want to demonstrate the significance of this
point against the background of my critique of the Marxist
argument that defines and explains racism in terms of its function for capital. My critique of this argument has, to this point,
focused on its application to the question of the historical origin
of racism. I now want to begin to consider its application to
the problem of explaining the articulation of racism by the
working class. This will be pursued further in Chapter 7.

It is possible to treat the historical evidence with greater
respect if, following the line of argument developed in Chapter
5, we explain the development and articulation of racism not so
much in terms of a strategy of capital (although this cannot be
dismissed as irrelevant), but more in terms of the various
ideological possibilities open to different fractions of different
classes to understand and explain their position within, and
direct experience of, production relations. Capitalist production
relations do not 'cause' racism but they constitute the terrain
upon which racism (along with other ideologies) is articulated
by real people, not simply and solely to justify certain courses
of action, but also to interpret their experience of production
relations and of the effects of those relations at the various
levels of a social formation. Such a perspective creates the theoretical space for the possibility that the articulation of racism
within the working class may refract at least partially its own
experience of the world and that other experiences may challenge that ideology.

I have found no evidence which supports the view that the
English and Scottish ruling classes encouraged labour migration
from Ireland and/or the articulation of racism as part of a
preconceived strategy to blunt the solidarity of their respective
working classes. Indeed, as already indicated, there is clear
evidence that industrial employers in Scotland were opposed in
the early nineteenth century to the placing of any check on
migration from Ireland while Scottish farmers remained in
favour of seasonal migration from Ireland throughout the nineteenth century (Handley, n.d., pp. 19, 81, 287; 1970, p. 268).
In England, there is clear evidence of there being opposition

from at least the public authorities towards the anti-Irish riots
in Lancashire, if only on the grounds of their desire to maintain
'law and order' (Foster, 1974, p. 246; Arnstein, 1975). What
the dominant sections of capital collectively and primarily
required was labour for the sake of production and if that
labour could not be obtained from within the geographical
boundaries of the nation state, then there was no obvious reason why it should not be obtained from Ireland.

Yet the employment of labour from Ireland had economic and
political consequences for both the industrial bourgeoisie and
the indigenous working class. Concerning England, Kirk has
argued that the employment of Irish labour in the cotton industry of Lancashire led to acute competition in the labour market
and that complaints to this effect were widely voiced during
the riots (1980, p. 85). It has been argued, also, that Irish
labour was employed at a lower wage in agriculture, railway
construction and handloom weaving and was often first introduced to break a strike (Treble, 1973, p. 240; Redford, 1976,
p. 160). Redford suggests that this was possible primarily
because Irish labour was used to a lower standard of living
when compared with English labour. In other words, the
socially defined necessary living wage was lower for Irish
labour. This led to hostility on the part of English labour, a
response that was countered within railway construction by an
attempt by employers to employ Irish labour on separate sections
of a line (Treble, 1973, p. 240).

For Scotland one can construct a similar argument. Handley,
although arguing elsewhere in the same work that the main
impetus for anti-Irish agitation was religious antagonism, nevertheless notes that Irish labourers were often first employed
in coal-mining as strike-breakers and that the industrial working class was opposed to Irish migration because the migrants
increased competition for work and so reduced wages (n.d.,
pp. 75, 131; 1970, pp. 275-6). More recent evidence for Lanarkshire shows that direct competition for work in coal-mining was
a direct stimulus to conflict (Campbell, 1979, p. 181). A recent
Marxist account of the development of Scottish capitalism reports
that Irish labour was often first employed to break strikes and
its presence in Scotland ensured the existence of a permanent
reserve army and a downward pressure on wages (Dickson,
1980, pp. 139, 161-5, 189).

If these were real consequences of Irish migration, then it
would appear that British working-class hostility to Irish
migration can be explained as being economically grounded.
Moreover, in so far as one can argue that an unregulated labour
market and the determination of wage levels by supply and
demand are integral to the capitalist mode of production, then
it may appear that there are grounds for claiming that capitalism 'causes' racism (assuming that the opposition to Irish labour
is expressed in terms of attributed 'racial' characteristics). But
it is at this point that the real analytical problems arise.

If sections of the indigenous working class had a real, material reason to express hostility toward the Irish, their subsequent articulation of hostility in terms of 'race' and religion cannot be explained simply as the product of ideological indoctrination by the ruling class. If the reality of competition for jobs and reduced wages is a prime motivation for the articulation of racism, there is no need to posit a capitalist conspiracy to divide the working class. Rather, racism can become the means by which sections of the working class actively make sense of their experience of some of the effects of capitalist relations of production. The fractionalisation of the working class consequent upon this process may have consequences which are advantageous to the bourgeoisie, but it does not follow that one can then explain the fractionalisation as the result of a conscious strategy to 'divide and rule', as the functionalist explanation suggests. Moreover, it does not follow from this that the expression of racism is, by definition, functional to capital. As already indicated, the expression of hostility towards the Irish in Scotland in the 1830s and 1840s in newspapers, pamphlets and official government reports does not seem to have been generally supported or legitimated by agricultural and industrial capital. This is not surprising because one must expect at least an ambiguous reaction from capital which derives advantages from the migration of labour that is also the very stimulus to hostility. In such circumstances, an attempt by labour to increase its own return on the sale of labour power by demanding an end to migration and the employment of Irish labour is likely to be opposed by capital because it would probably lead to an increase in wage costs. Moreover, in Scotland it may have been that the existence of a reserve army of labour kept wages down and provided the basis for conflict within the working class, but it also served to ensure the survival of a domestic form of production within the textile industry, the ultimate consequence of which was the decline of the industry in the face of English capitalism (Dickson, 1980, pp. 142, 186, 198; Slaven, 1975, pp. 104, 165). In these circumstances, one cannot seriously claim that the conditions which supported the expression of hostility towards Irish labour in Scotland were absolutely functional to Scottish capital. Rather, one should recognise that any ruling class has to take account of a series of economic and political interests and that there is no inevitable congruence between those interests which dictate the pursuit of a single, unambiguous strategy.

CONCLUSION

A political economy of labour migration should therefore be the starting point for an analysis of political and ideological conflict which is expressed in terms of 'race' (and religion) and which occurs between and within classes. Indeed, the very develop-

ment of such conflict marks the development of lines of division
within classes. The question of how we might conceptualise that
process of division is considered in the following chapter with
respect to a more recent migration to Britain, that from the
New Commonwealth (a term which refers to those colonial countries which received political independence from Britain after
1945). This is to suggest that the conclusion of that analysis
(which focuses upon the notion of the fractionalisation of classes) applies also to the case of the migration of Irish labour to
Britain and so, more generally, that there is value in a comparative analysis of labour migrations, both in terms of their
conditions of occurrence and in terms of their effects on economic, political and ideological relations.

But in making such a suggestion, we should recognise that
although there is a broad similarity between the Irish and New
Commonwealth migrations in so far as both were directly stimulated by a demand for labour by sections of British capital,
there are also important differences between them. Notably,
the Irish migration occurred during (indeed, was necessitated
by) the dynamic and initial expansion of the capitalist mode of
production while the New Commonwealth migration, although
stimulated by the post-1945 economic expansion, occurred in
the wider context of a different phase of capitalist production.
Capitalist forces of production have become increasingly capital-
intensive such that the most dynamic sectors require propor-
tionately less labour power. These sectors of production contrast sharply (both in terms of being highly capital intensive
and paying high wages) with those undergoing cyclical decline
(e.g. textiles, metal manufacture) and with certain sectors
of service industry, particularly those under direct state control (e.g. public health and transport) which, because of low
wages, inter alia, have experienced a severe shortage of labour.
Thus, whereas both Irish and New Commonwealth labour became
concentrated in the semi- and unskilled sectors of manual production, these sectors have played a different structural role
relative to the general dynamic of capitalist expansion in the
different historical periods under review. To make the point
concrete, while a proportion of Irish labour in the nineteenth
century did enter less dynamic sectors of production (e.g.
handloom weaving in Scotland), the larger proportion was concentrated in sectors which were integral to capitalist expansion
and accumulation (e.g. construction, railway development,
coal-mining, etc.). The same cannot be said for the large proportion of New Commonwealth migrants. The fact that the latter
are often selling their labour power in sectors of production
which are visibly in decline and that the conditions which stimulated labour migration have been reversed has implications for
the repercussions of the migration upon political and ideological
relations as we shall see in the next chapter.

But a final comment is required here about those repercussions. Very generally, one can claim that both migrations were

followed by a hostile reaction from sections of both main classes which was articulated in terms of 'race'. However, the racialisation of New Commonwealth migrants was more extensive than the racialisation of Irish migrants. This is evident in the fact that the hostility towards Irish labour was articulated not solely in terms of 'race' but also, and significantly, in terms of religion: thus, certain of the migrant's phenotypical and cultural (e.g. religion) characteristics were attributed with political and ideological significance as a means of justifying a negative, hostile reaction. Although phenotypical and cultural characteristics of New Commonwealth migrants have been, similarly, the focus of negative evaluation, there has been a much greater emphasis upon the former. This is reflected in the fact that a predominant element in the political and ideological reaction to New Commonwealth migration has been the claim that the migration has produced a 'race relations' situation in Britain, a claim (or, rather, a construction) that was not made in the case of the Irish migration. This cannot be explained by the fact that New Commonwealth migrants were 'coloured': both Irish and New Commonwealth migrants had the potential to be identified as distinctive by reference to phenotypical characteristics (and, indeed, the Irish were so identified) and so what requires explanation is the greater significance attributed to phenotypical variation in the case of New Commonwealth migration. Accordingly, our analytical focus is not the 'colour' of New Commonwealth migrants because in itself that explains nothing, but rather the nature of and the reasons for the reaction which attributed that phenotypical feature with such overriding significance. Part of the explanation for that, to be pursued in the following chapter, will focus upon the particular way in which racism was constructed as an ideological legacy of British colonialism.

7 RACISM AND CLASS STRUCTURE: MIGRANT LABOUR IN CONTEMPORARY CAPITALISM

INTRODUCTION

In this final chapter, I wish to pursue my argument to establish the significance of political economy by confronting directly the issue of the position of migrant labour within class relations. It will be structured around a critical review of the major theoretical positions as they have been concerned with New Commonwealth migrants, to be followed by an elaboration of the alternative concept of racialised fraction of the working class which pays due regard to the significance of racism as an element in the process of racialisation.

In considering the New Commonwealth migration to Britain, there are two introductory empirical points to be made to clarify formally the relevance of this migration to the analytical project in hand. The first is that we are dealing with what was at the outset a labour migration and not a permanent immigration. The stimulus to the movement of population was a shortage of labour in the British economy of the 1950s and the intentions of those leaving the Caribbean and the Indian sub-continent were to return at some future point in time. Accordingly, the migrants maintained a wide range of economic, political and ideological links with their countries of origin (e.g. Watson, 1977a). Second, by that token, I am not directly concerned with the arrival of 'Asians' in Britain from Kenya in 1968 and Uganda in 1972 (Hiro, 1973, pp. 206-11; Humphry and Ward, 1974), a migration which was stimulated primarily by economic and political factors in these countries against the background of their colonial origins. These count formally as migrations of political refugees, although the political and ideological reaction to them was very similar to that which followed the earlier labour migration.

MIGRATION AND CLASS STRUCTURE: SOME THEORIES

Within both sociological and Marxist literature concerned with the class structure of Britain, recognition is given to the fact of migration to Britain from the New Commonwealth. Within this literature, the following distinct theses can be distinguished. The first and third of these arguments can be described as Marxist, while the second is sociological and is based upon Weberian premises and assumptions.

(i) Unitary working class thesis
This claims that 'coloured immigrants' to Britain share with the
indigenous working class the dependent conditions of exploited
wage labour and that the practice of racial discrimination only
serves to increase the impact upon these 'immigrants' of those
otherwise common disadvantages. From this perspective, 'immigrants' are an integral part of the working class (Westergaard
and Resler, 1976, pp. 356-60).

(ii) Underclass thesis
This claims that the impact of discrimination is crucial in allocating 'immigrants' to a specific class position apart from the working class. It is argued that 'immigrants' do not share the same
experience as the working class because of the impact of discrimination upon their position in the employment, education
and housing markets. Discrimination ensures that they occupy
an inferior position in these three markets, with the consequence
that they are not and cannot be assimilated into the working
class. They therefore constitute a class beneath the working
class by virtue of their inferior circumstances and life chances,
an interpretation which is captured in the concept of 'underclass' (Rex and Tomlinson, 1979, pp. 275-6).

(iii) Divided working class thesis
This claims that class position is determined by the position in
the relations of production and that in Britain, this leads to
the identification of two main classes, the bourgeoisie and the
working class. Both 'immigrant' and indigenous workers, it is
claimed, constitute the working class by virtue of their identical
position in production relations. To this point in the argument,
there is agreement with the unitary working class thesis. However, it is then argued that, because of their lower incomes
and inferior social conditions, 'immigrants' occupy a distinct
economic position within the working class and that this is
paralleled by a subjective division within the same class. Consequently, the working class is conceived of as being divided
into two distinct strata (Castles and Kosack, 1973, p. 477;
cf. Moore, 1977).
   These three theses are mutually exclusive by virtue of their
different interpretations of the impact of racial discrimination
upon the class structure. They are, therefore, unsatisfactory
for different reasons. The unitary working class thesis is partly
founded upon empirical claims which are contradicted by the
available evidence (see Phizacklea and Miles, 1980, pp. 17-20)
and is mistaken in claiming that discrimination creates no
'special disabilities' for 'immigrants'. For example, immigration
law has placed New Commonwealth migrants in a quite distinct
and disadvantaged position in political and legal relations (with
the result, for example, that they are often required to produce their passports to demonstrate their right to live in Britain: see the 'Guardian', 30 May 1980; the 'Sunday Times',

17 August 1980), while racial discrimination places specific
economic constraints upon migrants which are not placed upon
indigenous labour (for example, by limiting promotion opportunities: Smith, 1977, pp. 182-90). The underclass thesis
mistakenly assumes that discrimination is the sole factor determining the position of migrants in what are defined as the three
different markets which come to constitute the determinants of
class position. It attributes no explanatory significance to the
status of being migrants (Phizacklea and Miles, 1980, p. 227).
Additionally, by defining class in subjectivist terms at the
level of distribution of resources via markets, it rules out
consideration of the significance of relations of production.
Finally, the divided working class thesis makes the unwarranted assumption of there being a homogenous working class
which is 'divided' only by 'immigration'. In fact, the working
class is fractured by many political and ideological divisions,
and these divisions existed prior to migration from the New
Commonwealth. Moreover, it operates with an economistic
definition of class, a position that is now largely rejected within
Marxist analysis.

By rejecting the available theoretical positions, including
those which would claim a Marxist parentage, it might seem that
I am expressing sympathy with the arguments of Parkin who
has claimed that traditional sociological theorising and, even
more particularly, Marxist theory, have proved themselves
incapable of conceptualising the class structure of contemporary
capitalist societies because of their inability to take account of
'racial, ethnic and religious conflicts' (1979, pp. 4, 9, 29-31,
37). This is not so, and I want to examine critically Parkin's
claim in order to outline and develop further the argument that
migrant labour in Britain should be conceived of as constituting a racialised fraction of the working class (Phizacklea and
Miles, 1980, pp. 1-25).

MARXISM, MIGRATION AND CLASS THEORY

Parkin has developed a critique of Marxist theories of class
primarily on the basis of an assertion that these theories cannot adequately take account of (1979, p. 4): 'those complexities
that arise when racial, religious, ethnic, and sexual divisions
run at a tangent to formal class divisions'. This assertion is
supported by the claim that Marxist theories place their emphasis upon structural factors, that is, upon the position occupied
by persons in production relations. Parkin claims that these
theories, because of this emphasis, are unable to take account
of the significance of the social and cultural characteristics of
the persons who occupy those positions in productions relations (1979, pp. 37, 42). Parkin thereby locates the major
analytical problem as being the need to specify the connection
between class divisions and 'ethnic/communal' relations (1979,

pp. 33, 42).

Parkin's solution to the problem originates in the notion of social closure, which refers to the process by which social groups attempt to maximise their rewards by restricting the access of other groups to resources and opportunities. He identifies two main forms of social closure (exclusion and usurpation), only the former being significant in this context. Exclusionary social closure, he continues, can operate by reference to individualist and to collectivist criteria, and the precise character and combination of these criteria determines the type and range of subordinate social collectivities. The use of individualist criteria excludes individuals from access to rewards and opportunities by reference to their ability to meet certain standards or qualities, while the use of collectivist criteria excludes individuals by reference to characteristics that are integral to their identification as a member of a group ('race, religion, ethnicity and so on ...'; 1979, p. 68) and that are negatively defined. From these premises, Parkin argues that three main types of subordinate group can be identified (see Figure 7.1). This serves to illustrate clearly his claim that (1979, p. 4; my emphasis): 'Societies marked by conflict between religious or racial communities do not exhibit *the same type of class structure* as societies lacking such conflict, notwithstanding similaries in their occupational systems and property relations.'

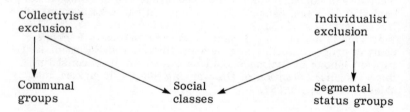

Figure 7.1 Social closure and class structure
Source: Parkin (1979, p. 68)

The position is consolidated by arguing that exclusionary social closure can be used by one part of a class against another part but because that process occurs within the subordinate class, this is secondary to their primary strategy of responding to the exclusionary strategy of the dominant class. Hence (1979, pp. 112-13):

one of the attractions of the closure model is that it highlights the fact of communal cleavage and its relationship to class, and seeks to analyze both within the same conceptual framework. More generally, it proposes that intra-class relations be treated as conflict phenomena of the same general order as inter-class relations, and not as mere disturbances or complications within a 'pure' class model.

Parkin's thesis shares a number of characteristics with that offered by Rex and Tomlinson, and described above as the underclass thesis. Rex and Tomlinson also place great analytical significance upon exclusionary processes within what are conceived of as employment, education and housing markets. Moreover, by asserting the existence of an underclass, Rex and Tomlinson are implicitly assent to the idea that 'racial conflict' gives rise to a quite distinct class structure. There is, therefore, a common rejection of structural analyses located in production relations in favour of an emphasis upon the social process of distributing resources and opportunities. Rex and Tomlinson and Parkin share an absolute silence on the question of the origin of the resources and opportunities that are distributed and, thereby, determine the class structure. I shall return to this silence as an aspect of my critique of Parkin. There are four points to be made.

First, by operating analytically only at the level of phenomenal relations, Parkin necessarily operates with a reified notion of 'race'. 'Race', 'racial divisions' and 'racial conflict' are all posited as real phenomena which are either produced by other processes or are factors/influences in their own right. For example (1979, p. 89): 'exclusion strategies ... are frequently employed by one segment of the subordinate class against another, most usually on the basis of race, sex, ethnicity, or some other collectivist attribute'. My objection to this reification is argued in Part I of this text.

Second, no attempt is made to specify and separate out theoretically the supposedly different types of communal group conflict. We are not provided with any criteria by which we can identify a 'racial' conflict from an 'ethnic' conflict or a religious conflict. Rather, 'common sense' is the order of the day because, it is assumed, the conflict in Northern Ireland is between Protestants and Catholics and the conflict in South Africa is between 'black' and 'white'! Conceptual confusion is further intensified by the existence of a chapter entitled 'Internal class cleavages and the ethnic factor' which suggests the existence of some undefined general attribute (i.e. ethnic/ethnicity) which perhaps takes different specific forms, as when it is claimed that (1979, p. 31): 'there has been little if any attempt to incorporate within the framework of analysis those forms of internal cleavage that arise on the basis of religious, linguistic, racial, and cultural differentiation'. Yet elsewhere Parkin refers to 'exploiting racial group' and 'dominant ethnic group' (e.g. 1979, p. 35), suggesting that the 'ethnic factor' is a specific phenomenon of the same order as the 'racial factor'. Parkin has, in fact, inherited the same problem faced by Lyon (see Chapter 3) although, unlike Lyon, he does not attempt to blow any empirical life into these categories. My critique of this conceptual confusion is again elaborated in Part I of the text.

Third, it is not clear whether the different communal groups identified by Parkin are 'allowed' to occupy a class position. The dualistic typology of types of exclusion clearly concludes that there are different types of subordinate group which are presented as being mutually exclusive (see Figure 7.1). One is forced to conclude from this that the identification of a communal group excludes its members from having a class position. Yet, elsewhere in the text there are clear references to a subordinate class having distinct segments, with one segment using exclusion strategies based upon collectivist criteria against another (e.g. 1979, pp. 89, 93).

Fourth, in the midst of this analysis of exclusion strategies concerned with the distribution of resources, Parkin's argument becomes dependent upon references to labour migration, territorial conquest and state activity. For example, it is argued that the emergence of 'ethnic conflict' is the partial result of labour migration from the perimeter of Western Europe and from ex-colonial territories (1979, p. 33). Elsewhere, we are told (1979, p. 95): 'In all known instances where racial, religious, linguistic, or sex characteristics have been seized upon for closure purposes the group in question has already at some time been defined as legally inferior by the state.' For Parkin, these are no more than secondary facts which fill in some gaps in his conceptual model. Accordingly, they warrant neither explanation nor incorporation into the conceptual model. In effect, there is a great silence about colonialism and the internationalisation of the labour market, a silence that results from Parkin's refusal to consider production relations. I wish to argue not only that this is the key omission in Parkin's argument, but also that it is by beginning with these factors that we create the foundation upon which to analyse within a Marxist framework the relationship between migration and class structure. In the process of so doing, it is necessary to reject the notion of racial/ethnic conflict/divisions as being equivalent to class conflict/divisions.

'RACE' AND CLASS STRUCTURE

Elsewhere, I have argued that one cannot utilise the concept of class and construct the notion of 'race' as equivalents; that is, they do not refer to two specific types of the same general phenomena (1980, p. 184). I now want to enlarge on that claim in order to pursue the argument initiated above. The primary emphasis of that analysis was that within Marxist theory, the concept of class is anchored in production relations, a structural feature of social formations. With reference to any particular social formation, one proceeds by first identifying its dominant mode of production because this constitutes the foundation for the subsequent identification of the primary classes. The existence of dependent modes of production entails the

existence of additional classes. This structural identification
of the primary antagonistic classes is but a first step in the
direction of a specific, historical analysis of the social formation.

Accordingly, this first step tells us nothing per se about
the particular economic, political and ideological character of
the classes, e.g. the content of class struggles and the way
in which the classes are fractionalised. All that is established
by this first analytical intervention is the sites or structure
of class positions. Thereafter, historical analysis of the economic, political and ideological relations of that social formation
entails consideration of the persons who occupy those positions,
their political consciousness and the strategies that they actively
pursue (that is, the class struggle) within the structural constraints established at the outset.

When Parkin claims that Marxist theories of class analyse only
class sites or positions, he is ignoring the claim, clearly stated
by Marx, that men make history but not 'freely'. Rather, that
history (which is simultaneously a history of class struggle)
is made within clear material constraints which derive from the
interests of the classes mapped out by the mode of production
(Marx, 1963, pp. 180-1; 1968, pp. 80-1). One can agree that the
structural determination of class is a meaningless abstraction
in the absence of considering the persons who occupy those
positions and their practices, but historical analysis of those
persons and the class positions they occupy is a hallmark of
Marxist analysis (cf. Sayer, 1979, p. 149).

This first analytical step, the mapping of class positions,
contains no space for a notion of 'race': this is simultaneously
because this step is analytically prior to all other considerations
and because there is no phenomenon which one can signify as
'race' (see Chapters 1 and 2). I have, however, accepted that
phenotypical difference exists and that social significance and
meaning has been and is attributed to certain aspects of such
difference. I have suggested that this process can be grasped
by the concept of racial categorisation. This concept now
requires some further elaboration. It is used to refer to a
process of delineation of group boundaries and of allocation
of persons within those boundaries by primary reference to
(supposedly) inherent and/or biological (usually phenotypical)
characteristics. It is therefore an ideological process, but it
has effects at all three levels of a social formation: economic,
political and ideological. These effects can, in combination,
cohere to lead to the formation of fractions within classes. The
process of categorisation occurs at two analytically distinct
but usually related levels: at the level of thought and at the
level of action. The process can have as its object the indenti-
fication and reproduction of groups which are self- or other-
defined, while the criteria used to define the groups can be
positively or negatively evaluated.

As an ideological process, racial categorisation must arise

upon and within the context of a material process of production (Marx, 1971b, pp. 20-1). Hence, it is a process which occurs within the parameters established by the previously determined mode of production, parameters which include the mapping out of class positions. In other words, the process of racial categorisation is secondary to the essential process of class formation, unless the boundaries established by the process of racial categorisation are coincidental with class boundaries. This exception, which is an instance of the over-determination of class boundaries, is a significant and major one, and it opens the door to the analytical consideration of the case of South Africa (see Wolpe, 1972, 1975, 1976) and of the slave mode of production (e.g. Genovese, 1969; Hindess and Hirst, 1975).

The process of racial categorisation, and its effects, should therefore always be analysed as occurring within a particular historical and material context. Assumptions should not be made about the existence and character of the process of racial categorisation apart from the dual dimensions of the context. One can illustrate the significance of this point by reference to the ideology of racism which, I have argued, has undergone a lengthy historical process of articulation and reproduction. But the process has occurred within a certain context and conditions (including the growth to world predominance of the capitalist mode of production and the location of the centre of that growth in certain formations in Western Europe and, later, in the USA) which has ensured that the ideology has had a specific object, the populations of the social formations which were forced into dependence upon these Western European economies. Thus, racism as an ideology must always be analysed as a particular historical construction, one form of which has had as its primary object the populations of those economically dominant formations, whose phenotypical features have been negatively evaluated. Another form developed on the mainland of Europe and had as its object the Jewish population. But one cannot therefore use the concept of racism to refer to other ideologies which are articulated by those groups first defined by racial categorisation; which positively evaluate by way of reaction the phenotypical criteria used to identify the group boundary; and which have as one of their objects the rebuttal of racism (e.g. the ideology of Black Power, the ideology of Ras Tafari). Such ideologies nevertheless remain to be analysed as instances in the process of racial categorisation in so far as they continue to attribute political and ideological significance to phenotypical variation.

In order to conceive of the prime effect of racial categorisation upon class structure, a further concept has to be introduced, that of class fraction (Poulantzas, 1973, pp. 77-84; 1978, pp. 14-24; Phizacklea and Miles, 1980, pp. 6-7, 24-5), which permits the conceptualisation of the main lines of division within class boundaries. These lines of division result from the coincidence of different positions in economic, political and ideological relations within previously identified class relations. By virtue of these different positions, there develop different interests within classes which can be expressed in explicit struggles between class fractions. The process of racial categorisation can then be viewed as affecting the allocation of persons to different positions in the production process and the allocation of material and other rewards and disadvantages to groups so categorised within the class boundaries established by the dominant mode of production. Such effects cannot and do not alter the ultimate structure of production relations because the resulting fractionalisation occurs at the level of relations between persons occupying positions which share the same structural relationship with the other main class(es). But they do ensure that the structure of production relations takes a distinct form because of the real effect of racialisation at all levels of the social formation: this entails recognising that capital has specific interests deriving from the use of migrant labour and its racialisation and that a new dimension is added to class struggle as a result of a creation of a racialised fraction within the working class.

In order to understand the impact of racial categorisation upon class fractionalisation within Western Europe since 1945, it is necessary to identify the primary dynamic within the capitalist mode of production which created the terrain for racial categorisation, that is, labour migration. Labour migration is therefore a major dimension of the material and historical context for racial categorisation in Britain (and much of the rest of Western Europe) since the Second World War.

LABOUR MIGRATION AND CLASS FRACTIONS

Now let me summarise the argument to this point. Parkin, in common with the sociology of 'race relations', begins his analysis with what appear as the 'facts' of 'race difference' and then attempts to analyse the 'effects' of this difference upon the distribution of resources and rewards (e.g. jobs, housing, education). The error is to ignore the processes by which 'race difference' is socially constructed and the processes by which 'resources and rewards' are first produced before they can be distributed. I now want to argue that it is by beginning the analysis with the production process and by simultaneously acknowledging racial categorisation as an ideological process with its own determinate effects that one can identify one important dimension of class fractionalisation in Britain. However, this dimension is not a specifically British phenomenon, as the political economy of labour migration since 1945 in Western Europe reveals (e.g. Nikolinakos, 1975; also Salt and Clout, 1976).

Material production requires labour power and labour power itself has to be produced and distributed. With the development

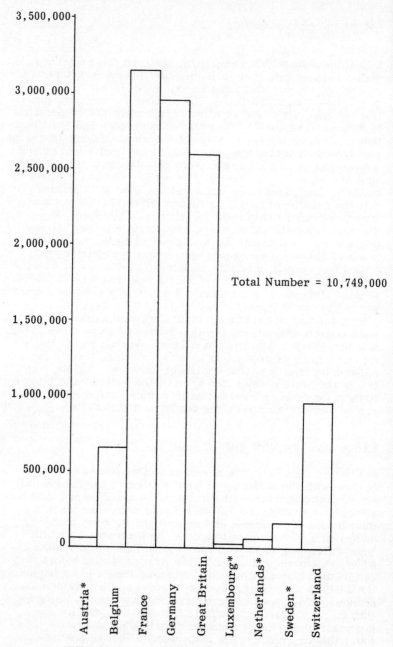

Total Number = 10,749,000

*Indicates economically active migrants only

Figure 7.2 Number of migrants in Western Europe by country
(c. 1970)
Source: Castles and Kosack (1973, p. 4).

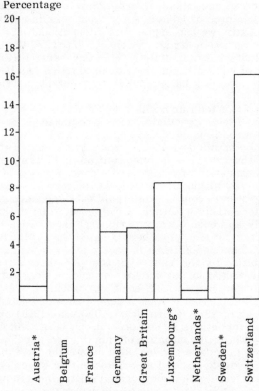

Percentage

*Includes economically active migrants only

Figure 7.3 Migrants as percentage of total population of
countries of Western Europe (c. 1970)
Source: Castles and Kosack (1973, p. 4)

of the capitalist mode of production, the geographical migration
of people both within and across national boundaries has become
integral to its continued existence (Portes, 1978). The scale of
such migrations has been enormous: for example, some 36 million
persons (of which 87 per cent came from Europe) migrated to
the United States in the period 1820 to 1924, this period being
marked by the shift to the predominance of capitalist production relations (Rosenblum, 1973, pp. 45–51). In a general sense,
then, there was nothing new about the massive labour migration
into Western Europe in the 1950s and 1960s (see Figures 7.2
and 7.3): the dominant capitalist economies experienced a major
shortage of labour and were unwilling or unable to resolve that
shortage by creating a new reserve army of labour from amongst
sections of the population within the national boundary and not

then involved in wage labour. A solution was to encourage the migration of a source of labour power from outside national boundaries. Thus, we can argue that international labour migration has become a structural characteristic of the capitalist mode of production (cf. Castells, 1975; Carchedi, 1979): the reproduction of capitalist relations of production has become dependent on obtaining labour power from outside national boundaries.

But this in itself tells us nothing about the source of that labour power. The intermediate concept required to locate and explain the source is uneven development (itself a structural tendency of the capitalist mode of production). This refers to the fact that the historical development of capitalism has led to a massive accumulation of capital and a concentration of productive resources within the boundaries of certain social formations and a growing economic (and political) dependence on those social formations by others which come to be defined as geographically and economically peripheral (and hence the language of 'centre' and 'periphery': Langholm, 1971; Seers et al., 1979). This dependence is partly the product of the direct exploitation by the 'centre' of the 'periphery's' resources, classically illustrated in the instance of colonialism. But it is also clearly evident both within social formations in Western Europe (e.g. the claimed economic dependence of Scotland upon England: Hechter, 1975; Nairn, 1977; Dickson, 1980) and between social formations in Western Europe (e.g. Nikolinakos, 1975; Paine, 1974). One measure of this uneven development within Western Europe is the inability of certain 'peripheral' formations to provide either full employment or wages comparable to those offered elsewhere, or to initiate 'indigenous' capitalist development on a scale to challenge the 'centre' economies. These dependent formations include Turkey, Greece, Italy, Spain and Portugal, and they therefore contain a potential migrant labour force. In this respect, their position is similar to that of a number of colonies and ex-colonies of Britain and France, which also contain within them a potential, mobile labour force. In sum, uneven capitalist development is both precondition and cause of the internationalisation of the labour market. The crucial stimulus for the actual migration of labour from these peripheries was the demand for labour in the 1950s and 1960s by capital in the metropolitan centres (Castles and Kosack, 1973).

This major labour migration did, however, have some specific characteristics which must be noted. First, in the majority of cases, the migration was not initiated and determined solely by the 'free play' of market forces (as in the cases of Irish migration to Britain and European migration to the USA in the nineteenth century), but involved the direct intervention of the state on behalf of capital (Carchedi, 1979). Labour is recruited by state agencies set up in the peripheral formations by means of a contract which mediates the wage labour/capital

relationship (Corrigan, 1977): the individual is recruited to
sell his or her labour power for a particular period of time,
usually to a particular employer and under certain political/
legal constraints (such as no right of permanent settlement,
either as an individual or with a family) (e.g. Berger and
Mohr, 1975). Second, this method of procuring labour power
and bringing it into contact with capital by means of a time-
specific contract was itself the result of a decision to obtain the
greatest possible degree of control over the use of that labour
power (although without appearing to break the ideological
sanctity of the wage-labour relationship to capital) so that
its utilisation could be related to the cyclical nature of capitalist
production. Thus, when the demand for labour at the 'centre'
fell, the persons providing that labour power could be
'returned' to the 'periphery'. Third, the use of contract migrant labour ensured that capital at the 'centre' did not have to
meet the cost of its original production (the source of labour
power, a human being, has to be fed, sheltered and educated),
nor the cost of its reproduction when wage labour was not
available at the 'centre'. This offsets the structural tendency
for the rate of profit under capitalism to fall (Castells, 1975;
Carchedi, 1979). Fourth, because it constituted a solution to
a particular problem at a particular point in time, one cannot
assume that the migrant labour system will constitute a permanent characteristic, or at least not in terms of its earlier size
and form (Paine, 1977, 1979).

It is at this point that we much acknowledge that the instance
of Britain is historically distinct from that of Germany, France
and Switzerland. I have argued this elsewhere (Phizacklea and
Miles, 1980, pp. 10-23) and need only point out here that it was
not until 1971 that British capital had made available to it the
political/legal framework for a migrant labour system determined by contract (Sivanandan, 1976; Freeman and Spencer,
1979). Since 1971, British capital has not faced a major structural shortage of labour (but rather the opposite) and so has
not had reason to utilise widely the framework established by
the 1971 Immigration Act.

Prior to 1971, the demand for labour in Britain was met, not
from the peripheral formations of Western Europe, but from
certain peripheral formations in the wider world economy,
colonies and ex-colonies. The entry of migrants from these
formations into Britain was initially structured by a political/
legal legacy of empire, the notion (enshrined in the 1948
British Nationality Act) that all persons living in the empire
were British citizens and, accordingly, had the right to enter,
live and work in Britain alongside Britain's indigenous population. The immigration control legislation of 1962, 1965, 1968,
1969 and 1971 (see Runnymede Trust, 1980, ch. 2) is no more
than the story of the eradication of that notion and right. However, up until 1962, and in response to the demand for labour,
people migrated from the Caribbean and Indian sub-continent

freely and often with their families. Thereafter, restrictions
were increasingly placed upon both the migration of persons
who wished to enter Britain for the specific purpose of selling
their labour power and upon the migration of persons who
were dependents of people who had become sellers of wage
labour before 1962 (and also in the period 1962-71, although
the numbers were very small after 1965). Because of these
circumstances, British capital and the British state did not
have direct economic and political control over migrant labour
by means of a contract, did not have the power to expel labour
power at a cyclical downturn of the economy and so became
directly responsible for at least the costs of reproduction of
not only the migrants themselves but also their families and
children. With all this in mind, we can now return to the question of class fractionalisation.

There are three major characteristics of the labour migration
from the Caribbean and the Indian sub-continent which are
relevant to the consequent class fractionalisation. First, the
demand was for wage labour, with the result that the majority
of persons who migrated to Britain in the 1950s and 1960s
were destined to enter production relations in a proletarian
class position. It is therefore a nonsense to argue that 'immigrants' were prevented from 'entering' the working class by
racial discrimination practiced by employers and workers (e.g.
Rex and Tomlinson, 1979): an analysis which determines class
position by reference to the sphere of distribution alone makes
the error of confusing human practice with the constraints set
upon that practice by the need to reproduce production relations in a particular, historically determined form. In this case,
our concern is with capitalist relations of production in Britain
in the period after 1945. Rather, because the majority of
migrants entered Britain to sell their labour power for a wage,
they automatically became part of the working class.

Second, the demand for labour was not spread equally across
all sections of the economy but was limited to certain sectors of
production and distribution (e.g. Unit for Manpower Services,
1977). One of these was a group of industries which had been
integral to the early domination of British capitalism but which
had subsequently become less competitive on the world market
and were consequently undergoing decline, e.g. textiles,
metal manufacture. Faced with tight profit margins and out-
dated technology (e.g. Cohen and Jenner, 1968), production
could be maintained by low wages and this led to an outflow of
'indigenous' labour in a period of full employment. In these
circumstances, migrant labour became replacement labour. In
the case of metal foundries, the employment of migrant labour
coincided with a process of de-skilling in combination with
mechanisation (cf. Braverman, 1974), reducing the number of
skilled jobs and increasing the number of, comparatively,
semi-skilled jobs (Unit for Manpower Services, 1977, p. 47).
Another group consisted of more advanced, capital-intensive

industries whose conditions of work also made labour supply
problematic in a period of full employment, e.g. food and car
manufacture. And finally there were those service industries
which were also characterised by low wages and unsocial hours
(e.g. hospitals, public transport). Hence, it is clear that
within the structural position of wage labour, migrants were
recruited to a particular position in production, that is, to
manual labour, often (but not solely) semi- and unskilled,
with low wages and poor working conditions (Smith, 1977).

The third factor was that migrant labour was recruited from
colonial and ex-colonial social formations, and at a time when
the retreat from empire and its repercussions was a matter
underlying the political agenda (Nairn, 1977, ch. 5). As was
shown in Chapter 5, the interdependence of capitalist development and colonial exploitation were at least partly responsible
for the articulation and reproduction of racism as an ideology
within Britain. Racist images and beliefs were therefore an
element of British national culture, shaped as it was by the
need to explain and rationalise colonialism (cf. Lawrence,
1974, pp. 46-68). Consequently, migrants from the colonies
and ex-colonies were not entering a neutral ideological context
when they came to Britain to sell their labour power. There
are two dimensions to this. The fact of the decline of British
capitalism as an imperialist power is partly grasped by sections
of all classes in Britain, and this fact can come to be measured
and symbolised by the very presence of 'colonial subjects' in
Britain (e.g. Pearson, 1976). In addition, the negative imagery
of those 'colonial subjects', which is signified in the meaning
attributed to phenotypical difference, was available for reinter-
pretation if the stimulus existed. The subsequent racial categorisation of migrant labour will be discussed further below.

The result of these three characteristics, when combined
with the previously mentioned political initiative to change the
legal status of the migrants from one of Commonwealth and
British citizen to that of alien, is that the migrants occupy a
structurally distinct position in the economic, political and
ideological relations of British capitalism, but within the
boundary of the working class. They therefore constitute a
fraction of the working class, one that can be identified as a
racialised fraction (see Phizacklea and Miles, 1980, esp. pp. 20-
5). This claim serves to locate my theoretical argument as a
development of the divided working class thesis which I outlined at the beginning of this chapter.

At that earlier stage, I criticised the formulation of the
divided working class thesis by Castles and Kosack (1973),
partly on the grounds that they operated with an economistic
definition of class. I want to emphasise that point here by
further reference to the specificity of the British situation in
comparison with the other labour-importing countries of Western
Europe. Castles and Kosack's argument was directed against
what they viewed as the failure of 'race relations' research to

grasp the common political economy underlying both labour
migration and the expression of racism throughout Western
Europe. Their object of critical inquiry was correctly chosen,
but their theoretical solution was shaped to too great an extent
by their economistic Marxism. Their failure to take account of
the impact of political and ideological relations upon class formation ensured not only that they ignored the extent to which
the British working class was fractionalised prior to the post-
1945 labour migration, but also that they failed to appreciate
the significance of the impact of the political/legal framework
for labour migration into Britain. That framework remained
distinct from that in the rest of Western Europe until 1971,
with the consequence that the process of migration more closely
approximated the pattern and sequence identified as chain
migration (MacDonald and MacDonald, 1964; see also Chapter 3).
The fact that such a large proportion of migrants from the
New Commonwealth to Britain have not only established families
in Britain, but have also appeared to take up the right of
settlement (despite the maintenance of the ideology of return
to the 'home') has meant that British capital and the state has
had to face the cost of the reproduction of those families to a
much greater extent than other countries in Western Europe.
Finally, they overstate the homogeneity of racism as an ideology
in Western Europe by ignoring the specific impact of the colonial
legacy in the case of Britain, a legacy which arguably means
that there is much greater significance attached to phenotypical
difference. It is a common error of much 'classic' Marxist
analysis that it fails to appreciate that racist ideologies take
different forms (cf. Hall, 1978, p. 26; 1980, pp. 336-7) and
Western Europe is an important arena for demonstrating that
(see Chapters 4 and 5).

Despite these points of disagreement, there is value in their
work in so far as they establish the importance of political
economy for an analysis of those situations which are defined
as 'race relations'. Through the political economy of migration
one is able to establish both the material dynamic for the
geographical movement of people across national boundaries
and the terms on which those people enter production relations
in the country to which they migrate. It is misleading to view
them solely as 'self-motivated immigrants' because their migration is only possible by virtue of the process of capital accumulation and this provides us with the thread by which we can
then go on to conceptualise their position in class relations in
the capitalist economies of the 'centre' (Carchedi, 1979), taking
full account of the importance of political and ideological relations. It is using such a perspective that we can proceed to
reject the claims of Parkin and of Rex and Tomlinson concerning
what they define as the failings of Marxist analysis.

In advancing this counter-assertion, I am not ignoring the
fact that the sociology of 'race relations' has much to say about
the history of New Commonwealth migration to Britain (e.g.

Deakin, 1970) and emphasises that this migration was stimulated by a shortage of labour in the British economy of the
1950s (e.g. Peach, 1965, 1968, 1979; Robinson, 1980). But
these analyses are essentially empiricist: they identify a number of empirical correlations without locating those correlations
within a wider explanatory framework which takes full historical
account of the preconditions for labour demand and for, in
the case of Britain, the colonies and ex-colonies becoming the
source of labour migration. There is a world of difference
between observing that certain industries in Britain were facing a labour shortage in the 1950s and arguing that the process
of capital accumulation and the uneven development of the
capitalist mode of production created the need for labour migration and the means by which that need could be met.

RACIAL CATEGORISATION OF MIGRANT LABOUR: THE BRITISH CASE

Although the material demands of British capital was the determinate factor in stimulating the labour migration from the New
Commonwealth in the 1950s and 1960s, we cannot establish an
equally clear and singularly determinate economic motive for
the subsequent political and ideological reaction to the migration. It is important to try to establish by reference to historical analysis the sense in which this reaction (which I
typify as racial categorisation) was independent of directly
economic pressures and the sense in which it was grounded in
(but even then not necessarily directly determined by) such
material factors.

As already indicated, the migrants from the Caribbean and
the Indian sub-continent did not enter a neutral political and
ideological context when they came to Britain. On the one hand,
they entered a politico-legal context which defined them as
British citizens while, on the other, they entered an ideological
context shaped in part by the need to justify and rationalise
the colonial exploitation of the previous three centuries. As
we have seen, the ideology of racism was crucially structured
(but not solely determined) by these processes. Herein lies
one instance of the relative autonomy of racism as an element
of the ideological process of racialisation. Racist imagery was
therefore available as an element of British national culture,
available to be reproduced to categorise these migrants whose
labour power was so urgently required on London Transport
and in the textile mills of Lancashire. The interesting and
decisive question concerns who it was who articulated that
racist ideology, and for what reason. The former question is
perhaps more easily answered than the second.

Sections of the working class in certain of the major English
conurbations became active in anti-immigration organisations
(Foot, 1965), but they were not without direct support amongst

the dominant class in the late 1950s. A small number of Conservative politicians were very vocal in their opposition to
New Commonwealth migration, but the role of employers is not
clear for, as Freeman and Spencer have pointed out (1979,
p. 65): 'The evidence is ambiguous. There was high black
(and white) unemployment in 1961-2, but there were also
specific labour shortages, particularly in the public service
industries.' What is not questionable is that by the early 1960s
there was in existence within both the working class and the
ruling class a political movement of opposition to New Commonwealth migration and that that movement gave expression to
racist sentiment and belief. Its most obvious and immediate
effect was the introduction of racist immigration control in
1962. There is little point in outlining the subsequent development and success of this movement here because it only involves repeating what others have clearly established (e.g. Foot,
1965; Deakin, 1970; Hiro, 1973; Moore, 1975; Sivanandan,
1976; Rex and Tomlinson, 1979). What is worth dwelling on is
the nature and significance of this political and ideological
reaction to labour migration from the New Commonwealth and
the terms with which we should attempt to analyse it.

Much of the reaction does not seem to have been expressed
in the form of the articulation of an explicitly racist ideology
like that formulated by the amateur scientists of the nineteenth
century, although the activities of the various fascist groups
constitute a significant exception (e.g. Billig, 1978). Rather,
racist images and beliefs are expressed in a piecemeal and often
inconsistent form (Rex, 1970, p. 154; Phizacklea and Miles,
1980, pp. 131-2; Miles and Phizacklea, 1981). Nevertheless,
the language of 'race' was and is used to refer to and describe
these migrants, the object of much of the political agitation
is to ensure that they are less favourably treated (or even
'repatriated') than the rest of the working class, and the
practice of racial discrimination is widespread in the allocation
of jobs and housing. The result has been a racialisation of
migrant labour (see Figure 7.4). Migrants came to Britain to
sell their labour power. They were met with an increasingly
negative political and ideological reaction, particularly in the
1960s and 1970s, which succeeded in applying the label of
'race' to the migrants. Consequently, they were negatively
racialised and were thereby assigned a special position in
ideological relations (as well as simultaneously being assigned
to a specific position in economic and political relations).

This specific position is signalled in the 'everyday world'
by the notion of 'race relations'. What is at issue here is not
so much that 'race relations' are defined as problematic by
the state and by sections of both the ruling and the working
class, but more the fact that the notion is employed at all.
One can easily demonstrate the specificity of the employment
of the notion by pointing out that neither the Irish nor the
Jewish migrations of the nineteenth century were defined as

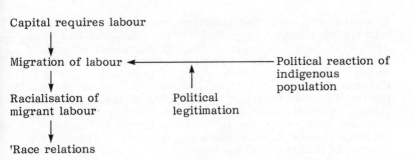

Figure 7.4 Racialisation of migrant labour

creating 'race relations' situations in Britain (although they
were racialised to a significant degree). Moreover, one can
point to the fact that entry of Vietnamese in the late 1970s did
not come to be defined as likely to 'worsen race relations', but
they rather were defined as political refugees, a significant contrast to the reaction to the Kenyan and Ugandan 'Asians' in 1968
and 1972 who were also, in fact, political refugees. The
notion of 'race relations' is a phenomenal, social construction,
a way not so much of interpreting social relations, but of
constructing social relations in a particular ideological form.
The reproduction of the notion ensures that social significance
continues to be attributed to phenotypical variation such as
to have an ongoing determinate effect on political and economic
relations both within and between classes. That the persons
so labelled were and are migrants, locked into the demands of
the capitalist mode of production, is therefore obscured by
their being constructed as distinct 'races' by the majority of
the British population at all levels of the class structure.

This ideological process of racialisation is not to be understood as an illusory process. As a social process, it is real
not only in the sense that the label of 'race' is constructed
and applied in the social world but also in the sense that its
application has its own determinate effects. Those effects can
decisively shape the form and direction of class struggles. The
process of class fractionalisation is paralleled by the production and reproduction of particular political interests which
are expressed in a specific ideological form. The imposition of
racist immigration controls stimulates resistance from those
affected by them. Discrimination in employment, racist police
practice and political attacks inspired by fascist political
parties all similarly and necessarily bring about a distinct political consciousness and political practice from those subject to
these processes. For Caribbean, Indian and Pakistani migrants, this constitutes the substance and reinforcement of
fractionalisation within the British working class. And, indeed,
sections of the working class have had their own, independent
effect on establishing and reinforcing this fractionalisation

because of the racial discrimination practised by trade union officials and members (e.g. Radin, 1966; Miles and Phizacklea, 1977, 1978) and because of working-class support for and membership of the National Front and British Movement (e.g. Walker, 1977; Miles and Phizacklea, 1979; Husbands, 1979; Fielding, 1981), etc. This economic and political division within the working class therefore spawns a set of distinct political interests and strategies which can take a multitude of forms, including everything from self-defence groups to English-language classes, from revolutionary sects to community associations (although the formation of many of these can also be encouraged by distinct cultural interests).

The emergence of these particular interests and the necessity for a distinct political practice by the class fraction so created mirrors the racial categorisation. Indeed, the political and ideological boundary can be actively reinforced by the explicit utilisation and re-evaluation of the notion of 'race', as illustrated in the formation of political organisations which have as one aim the developing of a positive identity for the 'black race' (e.g. Midgett, 1975; Miles, 1978). In this way, the language of 'race' (once having been positively re-defined), can come to be utilised as a solidaristic and unifying force (cf. Banton, 1977a, pp. 136-55). But equally, if not more, likely is a decision not to become involved in the political organisations of the working class, or, if they are joined for pragmatic reasons, not to participate actively within them (cf. Lawrence, 1974, pp. 130-60; Phizacklea and Miles, 1980, pp. 189-223). Whichever strategy is 'chosen', it must always be analysed not in isolation, but in relation to the original expression of racism and the accompanying exclusionary activities. And although particular political interests are constructed which are specifically those of a racialised class fraction because of racism and racial discrimination, they are also general class interests because the fractionalisation constitutes another obstruction to the emergence of that class as a more unitary political force.

To this point in this section, I have argued that those who migrated to Britain in the 1950s and 1960s were faced with a negative response which can be described as racialisation because sections of all classes focused their ideological and political reaction upon the migrant's phenotypical characteristics. But this process occurred within certain material parameters and cannot be explained solely in terms of the simple reproduction of a racist ideology constructed in an earlier period as some have done (e.g. Sivanandan, 1973; Lawrence, 1974).

There are two senses in which racialisation is anchored in material relations which I wish to mention here. The first is that the object of the process of racialisation is not a group of people in the abstract, but a group of people who occupy a specific position in production relations. The migrants of the

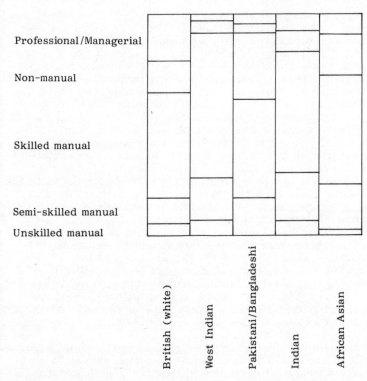

Figure 7.5 Male job level analysed by country of origin
Source: Smith (1977, p. 73)

1950s and early 1960s were, as we have seen, a replacement labour force, coming to Britain to occupy positions vacated by individuals who had moved into other sectors of wage-labour employment (e.g. Bohning, 1972, pp. 55-8). In this period, racial discrimination could not have been the major factor in allocating migrants to a position in production relations. Rather, employers were recruiting migrants primarily because there was no other source of labour available to them (e.g. Wright, 1968, pp. 41-7). But it soon became obvious that racial discrimination by employers served as a constraint when those migrants sought promotion or employment in sectors where there was no such shortage of labour (e.g. Daniel, 1967; Smith, 1977). Thus, racialisation (in the form of direct discrimination) has served to reinforce and maintain the economic stratification of wage labour: the racialisation of the migrants is simultaneously their confinement to certain ranks of wage labour, namely manual labour and often predominantly in semi- or unskilled jobs (see Figure 7.5).
Indeed, the extent of this confinement has encouraged some

interest in the applicability or otherwise of the concept of dual
labour market to describe this situation in Britain. The concept
derives from research in the USA and refers to the existence
of two distinct labour markets, one characterised by low wages,
poor working conditions, unstable employment and few opportunities for advancement and the other by precisely the opposite
characteristics. Moreover, the persons who occupy these two
distinct markets tend to be distinguished by other characteristics; for example, those occupying the former labour market
tend to be female and/or 'black' (Doeringer and Piore, 1971;
Piore, 1979, pp. 35ff.). Bosanquet and Doeringer (1973) concluded from British data that there was a close similarity with
the situation in the USA.

Although it is unlikely that migrants constitute the sole source
of labour in the 'disadvantaged market' in Britain, the fact that
they are rarely employed outside it is testimony to the significance of racial discrimination. Moreover, the fact of this
concentration has its own ideological effect in that it appears
(i.e. can be interpreted) to demonstrate the 'suitability' of
'racialised' labour for only low skilled, low paid manual jobs.
Thereby, phenotypical appearance can be equated with a disadvantaged position in production relations: the negative connotations of 'blackness' come to overlap with and reinforce
the negative connotations of much semi- and unskilled manual
work and so adds another level of meaning to the already existing fractionalisation of wage labour.

The second concerns the ideological significance of the struggle over the distribution of scarce resources within the working class in the urban context, particularly in those areas
undergoing material decline. With Annie Phizacklea, I have
argued elsewhere that material decline constitutes an important
underlying dynamic to the articulation of racism within the
working class (Phizacklea and Miles, 1979, 1980; Miles and
Phizacklea, 1981). In most of the major English conurbations
there are areas of declining capitalist production which are
also characterised by poor housing conditions, inadequate provision of social and other services and other measures of depri-
vation. These are also areas which for various reasons have
often been chosen by migrant labourers and their families as
areas of residential settlement. The coincidence of their settlement with material decline, combined with their demand for
access to resources (especially housing) which are in short
supply has, in the context of the racist legacy of colonialism,
served as a direct stimulus to the articulation and reproduction
of racism within the working-class resident in such areas. Such
racism, born of the direct experience of material decline via
'common sense' reasoning (the coincidence of decline and residential settlement being interpreted causally, leading to the
conclusion that 'the blacks cause decline') is arguably that
which served as the initial current from within the working
class in the late 1950s and early 1960s which resulted in the

formation of immigration control associations (cf. Lee, 1980).
This was a crucial stage in the racialisation of British politics
because British governments interpreted their appearance
with electoral significance and so set about appeasing this
racism. Moreover, it is probably upon this form of racism
that fascist political organisations subsequently developed in
English urban areas in the 1970s when Labour and Conservative
governments failed to solve the 'inner city crisis' and baulked
at following the racist policy of immigration control to the
logical conclusion of compulsory 'repatriation'.

In both of these instances cited, the process of racialisation
is locked into and has its own effects upon the reproduction
of material inequality and disadvantage within the working
class. This process is simultaneously the reproduction of
inequality per se and of the allocation of persons to different
positions in the structure of inequality, with ideological and
political significance coming to be attached to phenotypical
differences. A consequence is that the material disadvantage
of the migrant appears as disadvantage caused by 'race'. This
appearance is as misleading as the image in the desert of the
palm trees and water which was referred to in Chapter 2. The
disadvantage results from the combination of positions of
material inequality structured by capital (low wages result from
an attempt to maintain profitability) with a particular process
of allocation of persons to those positions, the process con-
sisting in part of the reproduction of racism as an ideology and
the practice of discrimination. The disadvantage and the ideological form in which it appears must therefore always be
analysed and presented as a social (i.e. human) construction
and not as a biological determinant.

To give more substance to these arguments, an analytical
emphasis which is distinct from that previously employed is
required. Rather than begin (and end) by searching for
empirical evidence of discrimination or the expression of racism,
it is necessary to begin by analysing the material processes
themselves. Discrimination is an important dimension of the process by which migrants were allocated to a position within
class relations, but it is not the sole dimension. We need to
know much more about the demands of capital and the operation
of labour markets since 1945. This applies in particular to
the labour markets for those sectors of production and distribution which actively recruited migrant labour in the 1950s and
1960s, i.e. the foundry industry, textiles, public transport,
hospitals, and so on. We require a much more extensive examination of the ownership and structure of capital, the pattern
of labour demand and the conditions of work for each of these
(and other) sectors, both individually and in relation to each
other, and historically up to the present period. Similarly, we
need to know more about the historical process of material
decline in English cities before we can locate the reasons for
and effects of the settlement of migrant labour in those cities

(see Paris, 1978; Phizacklea and Miles, 1980, esp. pp. 42-68).

And what of the significance of this process of racialisation for British capital? Did British capital require or even actively promulgate this process as some seem to suggest (e.g. Sivanandan, 1976, p. 358)? The question is posed falsely in this simplistic form, not least because it invites a tautologous answer (with 'effects' being interpreted as active causes: see Chapter 4). Moreover, such a question makes a series of unwarranted assumptions. First, one cannot assume the existence of a single demand by British capital because it is not a homogeneous entity. Rather, what I have referred to above as British capital is in fact a collection of different economic and political interests: capital is fractionalised in the same manner as labour. Thus, one can anticipate (in the absence of clear evidence) that those employers facing an acute labour shortage in the early 1960s could have been less than happy about the possibility of controls over immigration, whereas others may have been simply disinterested because they could not identify any implications for themselves. Castells concedes this same general point when he argues for a distinction between, on the one hand, big capital and, on the other, medium and small capital when considering the economic significance of migrant labour (1975, pp. 57-8).

Second, as I have consistently argued in different ways in preceding chapters, there is no inevitable logic which supports the claim that racism is functional to capital. One can accept that neither the British state nor British capital have made any major, sustained effort to reduce the articulation of racism and the practice of discrimination (e.g. Moore, 1975; Sivanandan, 1976; Lea, 1980). Moreover, one can also accept that the British state has probably devoted more effort and resources to implementing racist immigration controls than it has to ensuring 'racial equality'. Indeed, we can go so far as to claim that the state has played an important role in legitimating racism in Britain by virtue of its implementation of racist immigration control. But none of these empirical claims necessarily add up to the conclusion that British capital and the state have consciously pursued a policy of actively encouraging the articulation of racism in order either to better exploit black labour and/or to divide politically the working class. If that is so, then the proponents of such a thesis should produce the empirical evidence. The extant evidence is, however, consistent with the claim that these latter consequences are the product of a complex of processes operating within the constraints of British capitalism, some of which I have outlined above. Moreover, one must take account of the fact that racism and discrimination give rise ultimately to political conflict and violence as is now clearly evident in the events of the 1970s. And, as Freeman and Spencer have argued (1979, p. 63):

not only does overt conflict threaten the State (though
conflict may also be used as a pretext for strengthening
it), but its legitimacy is threatened when the liberal ideology upon which it rests is made transparent. For, as
liberalism is inherently opposed to racism, the liberal
state must project itself as anti-racist ... State action is
called for to ensure the liberal façade persists. Meanwhile,
it must take action to modify the worst excesses of racism.

Following from this point, and finally, we cannot assume that
the British state serves as an automatic vehicle for the expression and implementation of the demands of the different fractions of capital. The nature and role of the state in contemporary capitalism has been the focus of much debate recently and
the direction of the debate has been influenced by the need to
avoid economistic/deterministic explanations and to identify the
nature and extent of state autonomy (e.g. Poulantzas, 1973;
Miliband, 1969; Holloway and Picciotto, 1978; Gough, 1979).
Once having accepted this 'relative autonomy' of the state, it
becomes necessary to demonstrate empirically the relationship
between the role of the state in the process of racialisation and
the perhaps conflicting demands of the different fractions of
capital. The former has been extensively documented and analysed, but the relationship with the conflicting demands of capital
has not and there the matter must rest at present, unresolved.

THE REPRODUCTION OF A RACIALISED CLASS FRACTION

To this point, the discussion has focused specifically upon
migrants from the New Commonwealth. But these migrants are
producing what is commonly (and misleadingly) called a 'second
generation', some of whom were born before their parents migrated but who experienced most of their education in Britain,
and others who were born in Britain. There is much academic
and political interest in this 'second generation', not least
because sections of it seem to have been more active in their
opposition to racism and discrimination than their parents.
Here, I am not explicitly concerned with the political consciousness and practice of the 'second generation' per se (but see
Ballard and Ballard, 1977; Bhatti, 1978; Brah, 1978; Miles,
1978; Cashmore, 1979; Peggie, 1979; Pryce, 1979), but more
with the general question of its position (potential or actual) in
class relations. An attempt to delineate this position will provide us with an alternative terminology to that of 'second
generation', which implies a simple historical and structural
continuity between parents and children. There are a number
of reasons why the analysis developed above does not automatically apply to the 'second generation'. These require speci-
fication in order to avoid assuming that the prime and sole focus
of analytical interest is their shared 'blackness' with their

parents. Consistent with my earlier arguments, I want to suggest that the focus should not be their 'race' but the position the persons occupy in economic, political and ideological relations.

The starting point for delineating this position is the fact that the 'second generation' are not migrants: they did not leave their country of birth to simultaneously meet a demand for labour and aim ultimately to advance their own economic interests in the country of birth. For a large proportion of the second generation, Britain is the country of birth, and even for those born in the Caribbean and the Indian sub-continent, they did not themselves 'choose' to migrate to satisfy the demands of British capital. But, because of their parents' presence and class position in Britain, they constitute a poten-tial addition to wage labour. Certain political and ideological implications derive from this structural determinant as we shall see. It is within this context that we can go on to assess the significance of racial categorisation for the 'second generation', particularly for their destined position in British class rela-tions.

Hall et al. (1978) are perhaps alone in having redefined the question of the 'second generation' in terms of the process of class reproduction, although they address their argument almost exclusively to migrants from the Caribbean and their children. Their analysis shares certain core assumptions and concepts with that offered here but differs in one fundamental respect, its reification of 'race'. Hall et al. claim that their focus is not to catalogue racial discrimination but to analyse the manner in which capitalism reproduces a divided working class (1978, p. 346): 'Race is one of the main mechanisms by which, inside and outside the workplace itself, this reproduction of an inter-nally divided labour force has been accomplished.' Similarly, (1978, p. 394):

> The structures through which black labour is reproduced ... are not just coloured by race; they work by means of race. We can think of the relations of production of capitalism articulating the classes in distinct ways at each of the levels or instances of the social formation - economic, political, ideological....Race is intrinsic to the manner in which the black labouring classes are *complexly constituted* at each of those levels.

Hall et al. here construct 'race' as an active force which has its own, real effects, in this instance, at the level of the reproduction of classes. Yet no attempt is made to define what precisely 'race' is or refers to. The authors seem to be trading on 'common sense' because these and other claims imply that the concept is being used to refer to biological difference, as when they claim (1978, p. 355): 'The second generation simply *is* a black generation, knows it is black and is not going to be

anything else but black.' Such a claim, taken in the context
of the reification of 'race', indicates that Hall et al. have
created a biological deus ex machina (i.e. blackness) which
obscures what is, in fact, an ideological construction which,
by being reproduced in the context of a certain form of production relations, has an important impact upon both intra- and
inter-class relations. I have used the concept of racialisation
to explicitly indicate the existence of a social process in which
human subjects articulate and reproduce the ideology of racism
and engage in the practice of racial discrimination, but always
in a context which they themselves have not determined. The
outcome of the process of racialisation, when seen in the context of the reproduction of capitalist relations of production,
is the reproduction of classes and their fractions.

Moreover, Hall et al. confuse structural realities with what is
taken as the actual political consciousness of West Indian youth:
for example, they write of youth collectivity experiencing
English society as racist (1978, p. 354). It is undeniable that
one of the central structural characteristics of British capitalism in the 1970s was the shift away from full employment, the
very characteristic that led to labour migration in the 1950s
and 1960s. This has meant, almost certainly, not only that there
are few opportunities for the children to enter wage labour at
a higher skill and wage level than their parents, but also that
there were fewer opportunities to enter wage labour at all. It is
important to stress that we are here discussing not a matter
of human choice, but the fact that the British capitalist economy
could not provide paid employment for all those available for
wage labour and hence Hall et al.'s claim that a large proportion of black youth is now confined to the role of a reconstituted
reserve army of labour (1978, pp. 380-1). The crisis of profitability and the attempt by governments to reconstitute the
process of capital accumulation has meant, inter alia, the
disappearance of jobs for which West Indian (and other) youth
were previously destined, with the result that the option of
wage labour at the subordinate level within the working class
of their parents is increasingly being withdrawn. This process
is analytically distinct from two others which, when taken with
the first, work towards the same outcome, the reconstitution
of a reserve army of labour within the national boundary (as
there is, as yet, no political/legal mechanism by which to
'expel' this category of persons as is the case elsewhere in
Western Europe). The additional processes are the political
decision on the part of some West Indian youth to refuse wage
labour at the subordinate level of their parents (e.g. Howe,
1973; for a critique see Cambridge and Gutzmore, 1974-5; Hall
et al., 1978, pp. 370-89) and the role of discrimination in pre-
venting West Indian (and 'Asian') youth from access to wage
labour at higher levels of skill and wages when they are as well
qualified as those with whom they are in competition (e.g.
Ballard and Holden, 1975).

The combined outcome is that a substantial proportion (although the precise proportion is a matter which requires empirical clarification) of the 'second generation' is outside wage labour and is therefore formally (i.e. economically) outside the working class. This has served to revive interest in the Marxist concepts of reserve army of labour, lumpen-proletariat and a range of derivatives (see e.g. Obregon, 1974, esp. pp. 415-26; Hall et al., 1978, pp. 378-81). How this structural position is experienced is another, although related, matter. Most certainly, a large proportion interpret (and usually correctly) their position as the outcome of racism and discrimination as Hall et al. show, particularly those who consciously refuse 'shit work'. But there are other possible interpretations, some of which follow from the fact that this outcome is not the basis of the collective experience of the totality of the 'second generation'. A proportion (again, we do not know how great or small) has been drawn into wage labour, and 'willingly' so, and this provides the firmest ground for the reproduction of the view that racism and discrimination are not all-determinant factors. There is now some evidence that, amongst West Indian youth, there is some sort of division of experience and ideological interpretation, that not all 'black youth' experience English society exclusively and solely as racist (e.g. Troyna, 1979; Gaskell and Smith, 1981).

These criticisms should not be interpreted in such a way as to deny the significance of the project outlined by Hall et al., but rather as a way of reconceptualising some of their claims. Their argument represents a clear break with the sociology of 'race relations' in that they do not discuss the practice of racial discrimination in isolation as an empirical fact, but rather in relation to the reproduction of class relations. The process that played a major role in the further fractionalisation of the working class following the migration of labour is ensuring that that fractionalisation is being reproduced in relation to the children of those migrants. But, first, racialisation is not the only factor determining the position of those children in economic, political and ideological relations as they leave the direct care and control of their parents. And, second, the process of reproduction cannot create the same set of circumstances as faced by their parents. Herein lies the significance of the crisis of capitalist profitability and the consequent formation of a reserve army of labour (of which racialised youth constitute a significant element). The process of reproduction is therefore a complex one. It is also currently ongoing. I want now to identify a number of the other factors that are integral to understanding this process.

First, the impact of the experience of racism and discrimination is likely to be different for the migrants' children, partly because of their different position in political/legal relations. This, in turn, seems to be giving rise to a different political practice, itself an important dimension of the reproduction of

class relations and of fractions within classes. Although the
migrants entered Britain as British citizens, it was by virtue
of their Commonwealth status under the 1948 British Nationality
Act (Runnymede Trust, 1980, pp. 30-1) and not by birth in
Britain. Yet an increasing proportion of their children are
British citizens by birth and have been brought up to believe
that that is so, carrying the implication of an equality of treatment with all other British citizens by birth. Moreover, they
do not have the experience of a 'home' elsewhere which can
serve as an alternative identity or even as a rationalisation in
the face of racial categorisation (the 'migrant ideology' and
'myth of return' so much emphasised by 'ethnic relations'
research). Consequently, there is less of an ideological buffer
to soften the impact, which leads one to expect a more hostile
ideological and political response to racism and discrimination.
This, indeed, is already evident in some of the political events
of the late 1970s and early 1980s. It also carries the implication
that the ideological and political response of the youth will be
more persistent and coherent when compared to that of their
parents, so making it more possible to cut across distinctions
between, for example, employed and unemployed and between
West Indian and 'Asian'. The response to a negative racial categorisation involves inverting the evaluative element but retain-
ing the notion of 'race' as the dimension of categorisation:
'race' will be positively appraised around a construct of blackness and common historical exploitation. But this is not an
inevitable or an even development, as the negative evaluation
of and even open antagonism towards 'Asians' evident in certain
strands of radical West Indian political philosophies demonstrates (e.g. Cashmore, 1979, pp. 181-90).

Second, we should consider the role that the education system
plays in the process of class reproduction as a result of the
task of equipping those who proceed through it with the skills
and qualifications to enter wage labour at different levels.
There is a growing body of evidence which demonstrates that
the children of migrants have a lower level of examination
success and are more likely to opt out of education completely
at the age of sixteen than the children of other sections of
the manual working class, although there is no overall agreement about the explanation for these and other facts (Coard,
1971; Taylor, 1973; Milner, 1975; Driver, 1977; Giles, 1977;
Tomlinson, 1978; Edwards, 1979; Stone, 1981). To enter the
labour market with poor or no qualifications restricts access to
a wide range of forms of wage labour, leaving mainly low
skill/low wage jobs as the only ones which might be entered.
And, in the course of the late 1970s, this sector of wage
labour has been particularly badly affected by the crisis of
profitability, eliminating jobs that might otherwise have been
filled by those 'failed' by the education system. But the matter
is not solely one of passing or failing examinations. There is
also a qualitative ideological element in so far as the experience

of education can actively assist in the formation of a 'black'
identity. Integral to this process are a number of factors which
range from the direct articulation of racism by teachers to
the ideological content of education which reproduces racist
beliefs and ignores or misrepresents the historical experience
of the objects of British colonialism (e.g. Coard, 1971; Milner,
1975). Consequently, we can view education as an allocatory
system, 'awarding' (or not 'awarding') criteria which play a
significant part in determining the precise position of individuals within class relations. By both failing a disproportionate
number of the children of migrants and contributing to the
process of racialisation, the education system is not only producing semi- and unskilled labour, but also persons with a
racialised identity. It is therefore an integral aspect of the
reproduction of a racialised fraction of the working class.

Third, and underlying the previous two points, is the significance of the historical and cultural distinctions between
migrants from the Caribbean and from the Indian sub-continent.
Part of the significance of these distinctions lies in their potential for the creation and maintenance of political and ideological
divisions within the racialised fraction of the working class.
This is another complex issue in its own right, requiring more
extended discussion than is possible here. Part of the issue
concerns the extent to which the historical culture of the
migrants from the Indian sub-continent entails the possession
of certain financial, social and political advantages when
responding to the structural constraints imposed by racial
categorisation. For example, it has been argued that the Sikh,
Hindu and Moslem cultures each provide a coherent, positive
identity for migrants faced with racism and discrimination and
that traditions of petit-bourgeois enterprise make possible an
alternative economic strategy when access to or advance within
the category of wage labour is obstructed. In so far as these
circumstances do not apply to migrants from the Caribbean,
then it is argued that they are comparatively disadvantaged
(cf. Lyon, 1972). Additionally, there are questions about the
extent to which these different historical and cultural traditions
are being reproduced amongst the children of migrants (e.g.
Ballard, 1978; Brah, 1978; Wilson, 1978, pp. 103-20) and about
the extent to which the experience of racism and discrimination
over-rides and replaces these cultural distinctions and encourages the development of a common, racialised political consciousness.

In sum, the process of racialisation is operating in Britain to
assist both the reproduction of fractions of the working class
and the structuring of the formation of a new reserve army of
labour. What is therefore so often analysed as the 'problem'
of the 'second generation' or of 'youth' should be reconceptua-
lised in terms of production relations and the reproduction of
class relations. These former concepts entail an unnecessary
emphasis upon characteristics of human subjects (for instance,

their age, which means a certain period in their life-cycle) to the complete exclusion of consideration of the structural position that such persons occupy. The life period referred to by these notions is the period when the vast majority first occupy a position in production relations in their own right (or, for a minority, enter further or higher education) rather than through their parents. It is, therefore, a period when, in the process of allocation of persons to positions, the future structure of class relations is formed, both by the changing demands of capital for wage labour and by a refusal on the part of individuals to occupy the position for which they might appear destined.

THE PETITE-BOURGEOISIE

The assumption of this chapter to this point is that all the migrants from the New Commonwealth came to Britain to sell their labour power for a wage and continue to do so. This is certainly so for the vast majority, and hence the emphasis upon analysing the class position of the migrants as a fraction of the working class. But not all migrants occupy such a position in class relations. A proportion own capital and run a business, usually employing wage labour and/or utilising the labour power of members of the kin group. It would appear that the capital involved is relatively small in most cases, although casual observation suggests that some of the businesses, especially those involved in international trade and banking, are developing into more substantial concerns (cf. Nowikowski and Ward, 1978-9). But in the absence of more detailed evidence, one is left to assume that the majority of businesses are of a size and nature to define their owners as occupying a petit-bourgeois class position.

   Underlying the formal question of the existence and size of this petite-bourgeoisie is an issue which has occupied some political attention. It is commonly observed that it has been migrants from the Indian sub-continent who have developed their own businesses and not migrants from the Caribbean. Such an observation is often accompanied by a belief that a majority of these migrants are small businessmen in some form or another. These observations quickly lead to an explanation which attributes an inherent capacity for petit-bourgeois enterprise to 'Asians' or 'Asian culture', an explanation which easily leads to a racist conclusion. Some writers have referred to this supposed capacity to initiate small businesses as constituting a potential solution to the 'inner city' crisis (e.g. P. Hall, 1977). And the Conservative Party has made some efforts to mobilise 'Asian' businessmen on the assumption that their economic activity indicates a predisposition to the politics of free enterprise (Layton-Henry, 1978). What these arguments and initiatives share is an ignorance of the empirical evidence that is available and a failure to pursue a historical and materialist analysis. One can account for the development of a petite-bourgeoisie from among the New Commonwealth migrants without suggesting that it reflects some inherent characteristic of the migrants or their culture.

First, the actual proportion of migrants who occupy a petit-bourgeois class position as compared with a proletarian class position would seem to be small. Smith's data for the early 1970s shows that only 8 per cent of his 'Asian' sample and 6 per cent of his West Indian sample could be classified as self-employed (1977, pp. 92-3). Indeed, one would expect this to be so given that the stimulus for the migration was a shortage of wage labour in certain sectors of the British economy. More-over, this evidence suggests that some West Indians do occupy a petit-bourgeois class position. Smith speculates that a large proportion of self-employed West Indians are casual labourers in the building industry rather than owners of capital who also employ wage labour. This may be so, but it is also the case that the West Indian population in Britain is serviced by West Indian-owned grocers, travel agents, barber shops and so on.

Second, it is relevant to recall that those who voluntarily migrate are a self-selected group, usually personally motivated by a desire to improve personal and family social and economic circumstances. The implication is that there is potential for them to adopt any economic strategy that might assist the rea-lisation of that end. Entry into self-employment can therefore result from a simple rational calculation of predicted economic benefit, although the range of options is structurally deter-mined by the circumstances of the wider economy. Moreover, those who decide to migrate can include persons who were pre-viously involved in petit-bourgeois activity before coming to Britain. For example, of the twenty-three self-employed Pakis-tanis interviewed by Anwar, fourteen ran some form of business prior to migration (1979, p. 126; see also Nowikowski and Ward, 1978-9, pp. 5-6).

Third, the formation of a migrant community reproduces a distinctive pattern of cultural organisation which requires the provision of various services. These can only be provided by those with the relevant knowledge and contacts. This applies particularly to the supply of foodstuffs, but also to a wide range of other commodities, from records to clothes and textiles. There is, therefore, a material and culturally determined requirement for shop-keepers and traders to meet these demands from within the migrant population (e.g. Dahya, 1974, pp. 90-5). Significantly, Anwar reports that for the majority of the Pakistani businesses that he surveyed, the owners reported that over 80 per cent of their customers were Indians or Pakistanis (1979, p. 129). The important exceptions to this included those who were engaged in manufacturing in order to serve a wider market, e.g. clothing.

Fourth, petit-bourgeois enterprise can be a means of avoiding at least some of the experience and constraints or racism and discrimination, particularly when the business primarily serves fellow migrants. For those who report this as an important motivation (Anwar, 1979, p. 125), entry into the petite-bourgeoisie is clearly a means to an end.

Fifth, the establishment of a small business is an ideal which is not uncommon amongst all those who sell their labour power for a wage (e.g. Goldthorpe et al., 1968, pp. 131-6) because it appears to offer the opportunity to avoid the routine and subjection to an imposed discipline over which one has little direct control, particularly in factory production. The experience of wage labour therefore creates the desire to escape its constraints and there is no de facto reason why this should not apply to migrant labour, particularly when faced with racialisation. Significantly, Anwar reports that all the self-employed persons that he interviewed had previously been wage labourers in Britain (1979, p. 128).

Sixth, the migration can be directly prompted by the prospect of establishing a business or developing a business already established. Although the main demand for labour in the 1950s and early 1960s was for labour in certain sectors in industry and public services, Watson has pointed out that there was also occurring at this time a change in taste and demand within the restaurant trade. This was simultaneously assisted by the stimulus to further migration from Hong Kong, the result being the growth of the Chinese restaurant and 'take-away' (1977b, pp. 182-4, 191-3; see also Nowikowski and Ward, 1978-9, pp. 5-6). One can logically anticipate that the same process lay behind the development of Indian restaurants and 'take-aways'. This also helps to explain the Italian migration of the 1950s and 1960s, a migration which was a continuation from earlier in the century when Italians were able to exploit other possibilities in the catering trade (see Palmer, 1977). The involvement of these different groups of migrants in restaurant ownership suggests that we should investigate the political economy of the catering trade in Britain rather than the 'ethnicity' of the migrants.

I outline these distinct but interrelated factors in order to indicate that the explanation for the development of a petite-bourgeoisie from the ranks of migrant wage labour cannot be mono-causal. Moreover, and more importantly, I wish to question the tendency of 'ethnic relations' research to offer explanations primarily in terms of migrant culture and 'choice'. The development of a petite-bourgeoisie depends not only upon there being a group of persons willing to develop and run a small business, but also upon the existence of material conditions which ensure the profitability of small capital. Contemporary capitalism is dominated by large, national and international units of production and distribution, and this limits the 'space' for the successful operation of very small units of capital. A small and 'specialised' market is one where one can anticipate the profitable operation of small capital. Another is labour-intensive production or provision of services which can operate by means of informal controls over labour power and by low wages. A grocer providing foodstuffs from the Caribbean or the Indian sub-continent is an example of the former while the manufacture of clothes by means of home-working is an example of the latter. In sum, an investigation of the development of a petite-bourgeoisie from the ranks of New Commonwealth migrant labour is as much an investigation of the structure and operation of capital in different spheres as it is of the individuals who occupy the class position of petite-bourgeoisie.

IN CONCLUSION: A CLASS DIVIDED

The process of racial categorisation or racialisation is simultaneously the historical consequence and the site of subsequent struggles between classes and of the formation and reproduction of class fractions. The ideology of racism and the practice of racial discrimination are central components of this process of racialisation which has determinate effects on ideological, political and economic relations. These determinate effects, some of which I have mentioned in this chapter, are a measure of the relative autonomy of racialisation as an ideological process. Consequently, although it is relevant, it is not sufficient to search for and 'measure' the extent of racist belief and the practice of discrimination. These should be analysed as moments in the reproduction of the mode of production, not least because they are integral to the process of allocation of persons to positions in production relations. But 'effects' cannot be understood solely in terms of the 'economic'. In contemporary Britain, following labour migration from the New Commonwealth, racialisation has resulted in the articulation and reproduction of the idea of 'race relations'. It is important that this be recognised historically as a new ideological construction immediately within and often at the centre of British political and economic relations (although I have not denied that in the preceding centuries the racialisation of 'colonial' subjects has had effects on British political relations).

The crucial point is that 'race relations' do not exist naturally or essentially by virtue of the existence of phenotypical variation: rather, certain forms of social relations are constructed as 'race relations' and this requires specific explanation. The notion of 'race' carries for a large proportion of all classes a certain set of negative meanings which attach to certain patterns of phenotypical variation. These meanings receive expression in a wide range of socio-economic contexts as a means of description and interpretation. But the effects of the social construction of 'race' differ according to class position. For example, the racialisation of migrant labour from the New Commonwealth and its relative confinement to the position of manual wage labour in the context of scarcity of housing and social services, etc., has different implications for other fractions of the working class when compared with the ruling class for whom such scarcity is not a problem, except in so far as it becomes the focus for a political challenge to its position as a ruling class. Nevertheless, for both classes, the process of racialisation (which occurs at the level of ideological relations) has effects on, but is also structured within and by, economic relations. By this I mean that although the process of racialisation has an independent effect on production relations in so far as, for example, it directly assists in the allocation of persons to positions in those relations, it does not in itself determine the existence of the positions. The existence of the positions is determined by the mode of production.

Where racialisation is an aspect of the fractionalisation of classes, this has to be understood not only structurally but also as ongoing political and ideological struggle. Racialisation, and the material and political disadvantages that are its consequence, produce a political and ideological response from those who are its object. The response is ideological in so far as those who are the object must construct a way of conceptualising themselves and their circumstances. The response is political in so far as those who are the object negotiate a strategy by which to actively challenge their subordination. But in the instance of Britain, those responses take place within parameters set by the reproduction of a capitalist mode of production still undergoing the effects of a withdrawal from direct colonial exploitation. That sets limits not only to what can be achieved by that struggle but also to the form that the struggle can take. I purposely use the notion of 'setting limits' because I want to acknowledge that the struggle could take one of a number of different ideological and political forms (see Phizacklea and Miles, 1980, ch. 2). Hence, in the 1960s and early 1970s, the predominant response (but not the only response: see Howe, 1973; Hall et al., 1978) can be characterised as a form of political withdrawal (e.g. Lawrence, 1974; Pryce, 1979) but there are now clear indications that the response is taking a different form. Racism and racial discrimination are now more actively challenged and in a way that re-evaluates the negative connotations of racialisation but which does not and cannot reject racialisation per se because it is now expressed in a distinct set of disadvantaged, material circumstances. Hence, ideology remains the site of struggle between and within the classes.

A crucial dimension of such struggles concerns the role of ideology in cementing the political cohesion of a group identified by racialisation. Personal experience, both direct and mediated (as by one's parents and by television, for example) is an important determinant of political consciousness. The

experience of racism and discrimination is common to a large
population in Britain. This includes people who occupy different
class positions and people whose historical and cultural origins
are different. The latter should not be understood simply as
personal differences but equally as structural differences which
have a foundation in production relations as has previously
been suggested. Migrants from the Caribbean come from social
formations which underwent a different economic and political
process of colonialism from those in the Indian sub-continent
(see Mintz, 1974; Lowenthal, 1972; Barratt Brown, 1974; Blackburn, 1975). As a consequence of such differences, one cannot
assume that the experience of racialisation will automatically
lead to the development of a common political ideology in Britain
which centres on an inversion of the negative evaluation of the
idea of 'race'. This is not to deny that such a development is
possible, but rather to claim that its conditions of development
must refer to more than the common experience of racialisation.
Additionally, there is the problem of specifying the form and
object of the political practice that might follow from the development of such ideological cohesion and on this matter there is
considerable disagreement in the literature (e.g. Howe, 1973;
Cambridge and Gutzmore, 1974-5; Hall et al., 1978; Rex and
Tomlinson, 1979; Phizacklea and Miles, 1980).

A further dimension is relevant to this same general point.
I have placed considerable stress upon the category of migrant
as a means of identifying the underlying material determinants
of population movements, but its significance does not stop
there. Migrants motivated by the demand of capital for labour
usually retain some economic, political and ideological commitment to their country and region of birth, to which they intend
to return at some future point in time. In the case of contract
labour, the 'idea of return' is backed by the legally determined
necessity of return. Thus, although they occupy necessarily a
class position (albeit fractionalised) in the social formation to
which they have migrated, the migrants have the potential of
occupying a perhaps different class position upon their return
to their social formation of origin. Therefore, migrants often
retain or develop a distinct set of interests, sometimes based
directly upon land and property ownership, in the social
formation from which they migrated. This is an important 'com-
plication' for an analysis of the class position of migrant labour
in contemporary capitalism (Moore, 1977, pp. 145-8) and has
implications for the form and direction that their political consciousness might take in Britain (Phizacklea and Miles, 1980,
passim).

However, and controversially, the logic of the preceding
argument leads to the conclusion that struggles which do emerge
in reaction to racialisation cannot be analysed as 'race struggle',
and for two reasons. First, 'race' is an ideological construction
which has developed within certain historical and structural
parameters. To attribute the idea of 'race' with descriptive and

analytical value in this way is itself, therefore, ideological (as I have claimed contra the sociology of 'race relations'). It can be no more than the object of explanation. Second, the construction of 'race' occurs within the context of class boundaries which means that the participants in all struggles, whatever their form and object, have a position in class relations. Consequently, all ideological and political struggles articulate with class relations. Thus, one must always recognise that a racialised class fraction is simultaneously (and dialectically) a fraction of a class which has an antagonistic relation to other classes.

An important consequence of the latter point is that divisions within the working class should not be assumed to be absolute and universal. Class fractions are historically constituted in circumstances that must always be spelled out. In the case of Britain, it is undeniable that the institutions of the labour movement have played a major role in the racialisation of migrant labour: trade unions have actively practised and tacitly accepted racial discrimination while Labour governments have been as active as Conservative governments in enacting racist immigration controls. Nevertheless, a majority of these racialised migrants remain a working-class fraction and the institutions of the labour movement are not the sole source of class consciousness. The experience of wage labour and the fact of institutional attachment to the labour movement (by reason of trade union membership) constitute a foundation for the development of a political ideology and practice which expresses priority to class politics (Phizacklea and Miles, 1980, passim).

The emphasis of this chapter (in common with the previous two chapters) results necessarily in the impression of a single division within the working class. It is, however, a false impression because I have made no attempt to locate the development and significance of this fractionalisation in the context of additional bases of division. These include sex, level of skill, manual/non-manual labour, religious belief, country of birth, all of which can support the formation of class fractions as a consequence of their being actively constituted as objects of economic, political and ideological significance. These remain to be analysed in relation to the process of racialisation in order to identify how and why each might overlap or coexist with others. What I have attempted is an analysis which outlines the main boundaries between and within the main classes in Britain following the labour migration of the 1950s. The process of racialisation has been analysed as establishing both the further fractionalisation of the working class and the basis for subsequent conflicts and struggles, some of which will be internal to the working class (as are those which arise from working-class racism and discrimination) and some of which will have a dual character as struggles of a racialised working class fraction, but as against capital (as are the struggles against racist immigration controls and policing motivated by

racism). The continued existence of such struggles involves
the reproduction of the class divisions that they first express.
The outcome of those struggles will be determined by, inter
alia, political practice and ideological struggle, and cannot be
analysed in advance of the development of that practice and
struggle.

BIBLIOGRAPHY

Adams, P. (1979), A note on sexual division and sexual differences, 'm/f',
    no.3, pp. 51-7.
Allen, S. (1971), 'New Minorities, Old Conflicts', New York, Random House.
Althusser, L. (1969), 'For Marx', Harmondsworth, Penguin.
Althusser, L., and Balibar, E. (1970), 'Reading Capital', London, New Left
    Books.
Anwar, M. (1979), 'The Myth of Return', London, Heinemann.
Arnstein, W.L. (1975), The Murphy Riots: a Victorian dilemma, 'Victorian
    Studies', vol. 19, no. 1, pp. 51-71.
Ballard, C. (1978), Arranged marriages in the British context, 'New Com-
    munity', vol. 6, no. 3, pp. 181-96.
Ballard, R., and Ballard, C. (1977), The Sikhs: the development of South
    Asian settlements in Britain, in J.L. Watson (ed.) 'Between Two Cultures',
    Oxford, Basil Blackwell.
Ballard, R., and Holden, B. (1975), The employment of coloured graduates
    in Britain, 'New Community', vol. 4, no. 3, pp. 325-36.
Banton, M. (1970), The concept of racism, in S. Zubaida (ed.) 'Race and
    Racialism', London, Tavistock.
✷(1977a), 'The Idea of Race', London, Tavistock.
—(1977b), 'Rational Choice: A Theory of Racial and Ethnic Relations', SSRC
    Working Papers on Ethnic Relations, No. 10, London, SSRC.
—(1979), Analytical and folk concepts of race and ethnicity, 'Ethnic and Racial
    Studies', vol. 2, no. 2, pp. 127-38.
—(1980), Ethnic groups and the theory of rational choice, in UNESCO,
    'Sociological Theories: Race and Colonialism', Paris, UNESCO.
Banton, M., and Harwood, J. (1975), 'The Race Concept', Newton Abbot,
    David and Charles.
Barnicot, N.A. (1964), Taxonomy and variation in modern man, in A. Montagu
    (ed.), 'The Concept of Race', New York, Free Press.
Barratt Brown, M. (1974), 'The Economies of Imperialism', Harmondsworth,
    Penguin.
Barrett, M. (1980), 'Women's Oppression Today: Problems in Marxist
    Feminist Analysis', London, Verso.
Barth, F. (ed.) (1969), 'Ethnic Groups and Boundaries: The Social Organiza-
    tion of Culture Difference', London, George Allen & Unwin.
Bell, D. (1975), Ethnicity and social change, in N. Glazer and D.P. Moynihan
    (eds), 'Ethnicity: Theory and Experience', Cambridge (Mass.), Harvard
    University Press.
Ben-Tovim, G. (1978), The struggle against racism: theoretical and strategic
    perspectives, 'Marxism Today', July, pp. 203-13.
Berger, J. and Mohr, J. (1975), 'A Seventh Man', Harmondsworth, Penguin.
Beteille, A. (1977), 'Inequality Among Men', Oxford, Basil Blackwell.
Bhatti, F.M. (1978), Young Pakistanis in Britain, 'New Community', vol. 6,
    no. 3, pp. 243-7.
Biddiss, M. (ed.) (1979), 'Images of Race', Leicester University Press.
Billig, M. (1978), 'Fascists', London, Harcourt Brace Jovanovich.
Blackburn, R. (1967), The unequal society, in R. Blackburn (ed.), 'The
    Incompatibles', Harmondsworth, Penguin.
Blackburn, R. (ed.) (1972), 'Ideology and Social Science', London, Fontana.

Blackburn, R. (ed.) (1975), 'Explosion in a Subcontinent', Harmondsworth, Penguin.

Blauner, R. (1972), 'Racial Oppression in America', New York, Harper & Row.

Bodmer, W.F. (1972), Race and IQ: the genetic background, in K. Richardson, D. Spears, and M. Richards (eds), 'Race, Culture and Intelligence', Harmondsworth, Penguin.

Bodmer, W.F., and Cavalli-Sforza, L.L. (1976), 'Genetics, Evolution and Man', San Francisco, W.H. Freeman.

Bohning, W.R. (1972), 'The Migration of Workers in the United Kingdom and the European Community', Oxford University Press.

Bolt, C. (1971), 'Victorian Attitudes to Race', London, Routledge & Kegan Paul.

Bosanquet, N., and Doeringer, P.B. (1973), Is there a dual labour market in Great Britain? 'Economic Journal', vol. LXXXIII, pp. 421-35.

Bourne, J. (1980), Cheerleaders and ombudsmen: the sociology of race relations in Britain, 'Race and Class', vol. 21, no. 4, pp. 331-52.

Brah, A. (1978), South Asian teenagers in Southall, 'New Community', vol. 6, no. 3, pp. 197-206.

Braverman, H. (1974), 'Labor and Monopoly Capital: the Degradation of Work in the Twentieth Century', New York, Monthly Review Press.

Bristow, M., et al. (1975), Ugandan Asians in Britain, Canada, and India: some characteristics and resources, 'New Community', vol. 4, no. 2, pp. 155-66.

Brooke, D. (1975-6), Railway navvies on the Pennines, 1841-1871, 'Journal of Transport History', vol. 3, pp. 41-53.

Cairns, H.A.C. (1965), 'Prelude to Imperialism: British Reactions to Central African Society, 1840-1890', London, Routledge & Kegan Paul.

Cambridge, A.D., and Gutzmore, C. (1974-5), The industrial action of the black masses and the class struggle in Britain, 'The Black Liberator', vol. 2, no. 3, pp. 195-207, 275-7.

Campbell, A.B. (1979), 'The Lanarkshire Miners', Edinburgh, John Donald.

Campbell, R.H. (1980), 'The Rise and Fall of Scottish Industry, 1707-1939', Edinburgh, John Donald.

Carchedi, G. (1979), Authority and foreign labour: some notes on a late capitalist form of capital accumulation and state intervention, 'Studies in Political Economy', vol. 2, pp. 37-74.

Cashmore, E. (1979), 'Rastaman', London, George Allen & Unwin.

Castells, M. (1975), Immigrant workers and class struggles in advanced capitalism: the Western European experience, 'Politics and Society', vol. 5, no. 1, pp. 33-66.

Castles, S., and Kosack, G. (1972), The function of labour immigration in Western European capitalism, 'New Left Review', no. 73, pp. 3-21.

—(1973), 'Immigrant Workers and Class Struggle in Western Europe', Oxford University Press.

Centre for Contemporary Cultural Studies (1978), 'On Ideology', London, Hutchinson.

Clarke, S. (1980), 'Jah Music', London, Heinemann.

Coard, B. (1971), 'How the West Indian Child is Made Educationally Subnormal in the British School System', London, New Beacon Books.

Cohen, A. (ed.) (1974), 'Urban Ethnicity', London, Tavistock.

Cohen, B.G., and Jenner, P.J. (1968), The employment of immigrants: a case study within the wool industry, 'Race', vol. 10, no. 1, pp. 41-56.

Cohen, P. (1968), 'Modern Social Theory', London, Heinemann.

Collins, E.J.T. (1969), Harvest technology and labour supply in Britain, 1790-1870, 'Economic History Review', vol. 22.

—(1976), Migrant labour in British agriculture in the nineteenth century, 'Economic History Review', vol. 29, no. 1, pp. 38-59.

Corrigan, P. (1977), Feudal relics or capitalist monuments? Notes on the sociology of unfree labour, 'Sociology', vol. 11, no. 3, pp. 435-63.

Corrigan, P. (ed.) (1980), 'Capitalism, State Formation and Marxist Theory: historical investigations', London, Quartet.

Corrigan, P., and Sayer, D. (1981), How the law rules, in H.F. Moorhouse, R. Fryer, A. Hunt, and D. McBarnet (eds), 'Law, State and Society', London, Croom Helm.

Cousens, S.H. (1960), The regional pattern of emigration during the Great Irish Famine, 'Transactions and Papers of the Institute of British Geographers', vol. 28, pp. 119-34.

—(1961-2), Emigration and demographic change in Ireland, 1851-1861, 'Economic History Review', vol. 14, pp. 275-88.

—(1965), The regional variations in emigration from Ireland between 1821 and 1841, 'Transactions and Papers of the Institute of British Geographers', vol. 37, pp. 15-29.

Cowie, E. (1978), Women as sign, 'm/f', no. 1, pp. 49-63.

Cox, O.C. (1970), 'Caste, Class and Race', New York, Monthly Review Press.

Curtin, P.D. (1960), 'Scientific' racism and the British theory of empire, 'Journal of the Historical Society of Nigeria', vol. 2, pp. 40-51.

—(1965), 'The Image of Africa: British Ideas and British Action, 1780-1850', London, Macmillan.

Curtis, L.P. (1968), 'Anglo-Saxons and Celts', Connecticut, University of Bridgeport Press.

—(1971), 'Apes and Angels: the Irishman in Victorian Caricature', Washington, Smithsonian Institution Press.

Dahya, B. (1972-3), Pakistanis in England, 'New Community', vol. 2, no. 1, pp. 25-33.

—(1974), The nature of Pakistani ethnicity in industrial cities in Britain, in A. Cohen (ed.), 'Urban Ethnicity', London, Tavistock.

Daniel, W.W. (1967), 'Racial Discrimination in England', Harmondsworth, Penguin.

Davis, D.B. (1966), 'The Problem of Slavery in Western Culture', Ithaca (New York), Cornell University Press.

Deakin, N. (1970), 'Colour, Citizenship and British Society', London, Panther.

Dickson, T. (ed.) (1980), 'Scottish Capitalism', London, Lawrence & Wishart.

Doeringer, P.B., and Piore, M.J. (1971), 'Internal Labour Markets and Manpower Adjustments', Lexington, D.C. Heath.

Donaldson, G. (1972), 'Scotland: Church and Nation Through Sixteen Centuries', Edinburgh, Scottish Academic Press.

Dougan, D. (1968), 'The History of North East Shipbuilding', London, George Allen & Unwin.

Driver, G. (1977), Cultural competence, social power and school achievement: West Indian pupils in the West Midlands, 'New Community', vol. 5, no. 4, pp. 353-9.

Duckham, B.F. (1970), 'A History of the Scottish Coal Industry: A Social and Industrial History', Newton Abbot, David & Charles.

Dunn, L.C. (1959), 'Heredity and Evolution in Human Populations', Cambridge, Mass., Harvard University Press.

Edwards, V. (1979), 'The West Indian Language Issue in British Schools', London, Routledge & Kegan Paul.

Eldridge, C.C. (1973), 'England's Mission: The Imperial Idea in the Age of Gladstone and Disraeli, 1868-1880', London, Macmillan.

Elkins, S.M. (1968), 'Slavery', Chicago University Press.

Endholm, F., et al. (1977-8), Conceptualising women, 'Critique of Anthropology', vol. 3, nos. 9 and 10, pp. 101-30.

Engels, F. (1969), 'The Condition of the Working Class in England', London, Panther.

Epstein, A.L. (1978), 'Ethos and Identity', London, Tavistock.

Evans, B., and Waites, B. (1981), 'IQ and Mental Testing', London, Macmillan.

Feuchtwang, S. (1980), Socialist, feminist and anti-racist struggles, 'm/f', no. 4, pp. 41-56.

Fielding, N. (1981), 'The National Front', London, Routledge & Kegan Paul.

Foot, P. (1965), 'Immigration and Race in British Politics', Harmondsworth, Penguin.

Foster, J. (1974), 'Class Struggle and the Industrial Revolution', London, Weidenfeld & Nicolson.

Freeman, M.D.A., and Spencer, S. (1979), Immigration control, black workers and the economy, 'British Journal of Law and Society', vol. 6, no. 1, pp. 53-81.

Gabriel, J., and Ben-Tovim, G. (1978), Marxism and the concept of racism, 'Economy and Society', vol. 7, no. 2, pp. 118-54.

Gallagher, J., and Robinson, R.E. (1953), 'Africa and the Victorians', London, Macmillan.

Garrard, J.A. (1971), 'The English and Immigration, 1880-1910', Oxford University Press.

Gartner, L.P. (1973), 'The Jewish Immigrant in England, 1870-1914', London, Simon Publications.

Gaskell, G., and Smith, P. (1981), Are young blacks really alienated? 'New Society', 14 May, pp. 260-1.

Genovese, E. (1969), 'The World the Slaveholders Made', New York, Pantheon Books.

—(1975), 'Roll, Jordan, Roll: the World the Slaves Made', London, André Deutsch.

Geras, N. (1972), Marx and the critique of political economy, in R. Blackburn (ed.), 'Ideology and Social Science', London, Fontana.

Giles, R. (1977), 'The West Indian Experience in British Schools', London, Heinemann.

Gilley, S. (1978), English attitudes to the Irish in England, 1789-1900, in C. Holmes (ed.), 'Immigrants and Minorities in British Society', London, George Allen & Unwin.

Gilroy, P. (1980), Managing the 'underclass': a further note on the sociology of race relations in Britain, 'Race and Class', vol. 22, no. 1, pp. 47-62.

Glazer, N., and Moynihan, D.P. (eds) (1975), 'Ethnicity: Theory and Experience', Cambridge, Mass., Harvard University Press.

Glyn, A., and Sutcliffe, B. (1972), 'British Capitalism, Workers and the Profits Squeeze', Harmondsworth, Penguin.

Godelier, M. (1972), Structure and contradiction in Capital, in R. Blackburn (ed.), 'Ideology and Social Science', London, Fontana.

Goldthorpe, J.H., et al. (1968), 'The Affluent Worker: Industrial Attitudes and Behaviour', Cambridge University Press.

Gordon, M.M. (1975), Towards a general theory of racial and ethnic group relations, in N. Glazer and D.P. Moynihan (eds), 'Ethnicity: Theory and Experience', Cambridge, Mass., Harvard University Press.

Gossett, T.F. (1965), 'Race: the History of an Idea in America', New York, Shocken Books.

Gough, I. (1979), 'The Political Economy of the Welfare State', London, Macmillan.

Gramsci, A. (1971), 'Selections from the Prison Notebooks', London, Lawrence & Wishart.

Green, E.R.R. (1944), The cotton handloom weavers in the northeast of Ulster, 'Ulster Journal of Archaeology', vol. 7, pp. 30-41.

Gutzmore, C. (1975-6), Imperialism and racialism: the crisis of the British capitalist economy and the black masses in Britain, 'The Black Liberator', vol. 2, no. 4, pp. 281-9.

Haddon, R.F. (1970), A minority in a welfare state society: location of West Indians in the London housing market, 'The New Atlantis', vol. 2, no.1.

Hall, P. (1977), The inner cities dilemma, 'New Society', 3 February.

Hall, S. (1977a), Rethinking the 'Base-and-Superstructure' metaphor, in J. Bloomfield (ed.), 'Class, Hegemony and Party', London, Lawrence & Wishart.

—(1977b), The 'Political' and the 'Economic' in Marx's theory of class, in A. Hunt (ed.), 'Class and Class Structure', London, Lawrence & Wishart.

Hall, S. (1978), Racism and reaction, in Commission for Racial Equality, 'Five Views of Multi-Racial Britain', London, CRE.
—(1980), Race, articulation and societies structured in dominance, in UNESCO, 'Sociological Theories: Race and Colonialism', Paris, UNESCO.
Hall, S., et al. (1978), 'Policing the Crisis: Mugging, the State and Law and Order', London, Macmillan.
Hall, S., Lumley, B., and McLellan, G. (1978), Politics and ideology: Gramsci, in Centre for Contemporary Cultural Studies, 'On Ideology', London, Hutchinson.
Handley, J.E. (n.d.), 'The Irish in Scotland', Glasgow, John S. Burns.
—(1970), 'The Navvy in Scotland', Cork University Press.
Hanham, H.J. (1959), 'Elections and Party Management: Politics in the Time of Disraeli and Gladstone', London, Longmans.
Harvie, C. (1977), 'Scotland and Nationalism', London, George Allen & Unwin.
Hebdige, D. (1979), 'Subculture: the meaning of style', London, Methuen.
Hechter, M. (1975), 'Internal Colonialism', London, Routledge & Kegan Paul.
Helweg, A.W. (1979), 'Sikhs in England: the Development of a Migrant Community', Delhi, Oxford University Press.
Hindess, B., and Hirst, P.Q. (1975), 'Pre-capitalist Modes of Production', London, Routledge & Kegan Paul.
Hiro, D. (1973), 'Black British, White British', Harmondsworth, Penguin.
Hobsbawm, E.J. (1969), 'Industry and Empire', Harmondsworth, Penguin.
Holloway, J., and Picciotto, S. (eds) (1978), 'State and Capital', London, Edward Arnold.
Holmes, C. (ed.) (1978), 'Immigrants and Minorities in British Society', London, Allen & Unwin.
Hooton, E.A. (1947), 'Up From the Ape', New York, Macmillan.
Howe, D. (1973), Fighting back: West Indian youth and the police in Notting Hill, 'Race Today', vol. 5, pp. 333-7.
Humphry, D., and Ward, M. (1974), 'Passports and Politics', Harmondsworth, Penguin.
Hunt, A., et al. (1977), 'Class and Class Structure', London, Lawrence & Wishart.
Husbands, C.T. (1979), The National Front: what happens to it now? 'Marxism Today', September, pp. 268-75.
Irvine, H.S. (1960), Some aspects of passenger traffic between Britain and Ireland, 1820-1850, 'Journal of Transport History', vol. 4, pp. 224-41.
Jackson, J.A. (1963), 'The Irish in Britain', London, Routledge & Kegan Paul.
Johnson, J.H. (1967), Harvest migration from nineteenth-century Ireland, 'Transactions of the Institute of British Geographers', vol. XLI, pp. 97-112.
Johnson, L.K. (1976), Jamaican rebel music, 'Race and Class', vol. 17, no. 4, pp. 397-412.
—(1980-1), Some thoughts on reggae, 'Race Today', December/January, pp. 58-65.
Jones, C. (1977), 'Immigration and Social Policy in Britain', London, Tavistock.
Jordan, W. (1968), 'White Over Black: American Attitudes Towards the Negro, 1550-1812', Chapel Hill, University of North Carolina Press.
—(1974), 'The White Man's Burden', New York, Oxford University Press.
Kamin, L.J. (1977), 'The Science and Politics of IQ', Harmondsworth, Penguin.
Kerr, B.M. (1942-3), Irish seasonal migration to Great Britain, 1800-1838, 'Irish Historical Studies', vol. 3, pp. 365-80.
Khan, V.S. (1976), Pakistanis in Britain: perceptions of a population, 'New Community', vol. 5, no. 3, pp. 222-9.
Khan, V.S. (ed.) (1979), 'Minority Families in Britain: Support and Stress', London, Macmillan.
Kiernan, V.G. (1972), 'The Lords of Human Kind', Harmondsworth, Penguin.
Kirk, N. (1980), Ethnicity, class and popular Toryism, 1850-1870, in K. Lunn (ed.), 'Hosts, Immigrants and Minorities', Folkestone, Dawson.
Langholm, S. (1971), On the concepts of center and periphery, 'Journal of

Peace Research', nos. 3-4.

Larrain, J. (1979), 'The Concept of Ideology', London, Hutchinson.

Lawrence, D. (1974), 'Black Migrants, White Natives', Cambridge University Press.

Lawton, R. (1959), Irish immigration to England and Wales in the mid-nineteenth century, 'Irish Geography', vol. 4, no. 1, pp. 35-54.

Layton-Henry, Z. (1978), Race, electoral strategy and the major parties, 'Parliamentary Affairs', vol. XXXI, no. 3, pp. 268-81.

Lea, J. (1980), The contradictions of the Sixties race relations legislation, in National Deviancy Conference, 'Permissiveness and Control', London, Macmillan.

Leach, E. (1975), Cultural components in the concept of race, in P.J. Ebling (ed.), 'Racial Variation in Man', London, Institute of Biology.

Lebow, R.N. (1976), 'White Britain and Black Ireland', Philadelphia, Institute for the Study of Human Issues.

Lee, A. (1980), Aspects of the working class response to the Jews in Britain, 1880-1914, in K. Lunn (ed.), 'Hosts, Immigrants and Minorities', Folkestone, Dawson.

Lees, L.H. (1979), 'Exiles of Erin', Manchester University Press.

Lichtheim, G. (1967), 'The Concept of Ideology and Other Essays', New York, Vintage.

Livingstone, F.B. (1964), On the nonexistence of human races, in A. Montagu (ed.), 'The Concept of Race', New York, Free Press.

Lobban, R.D. (1961), The Irish community in Greenock in the nineteenth century, 'Irish Geography', vol. 6, no. 3, pp. 270-81.

Lorimer, D.A. (1978), 'Colour, Class and the Victorians', Leicester University Press.

Lovell, J. (1977), The Irish and the London dockers, 'Society for the Study of Labour History Bulletin', no. 35, pp. 16-18.

Lowe, W.J. (1977), Social agencies among the Irish in Lancashire during the mid-nineteenth century, 'Saothar', vol. 3, pp. 15-20.

Lowenthal, D. (1972), 'West Indian Societies', Oxford University Press.

Lunn, K. (ed.) (1980), 'Hosts, Immigrants and Minorities', Folkestone, Dawson.

Lyon, M. (1972), Race and ethnicity in pluralistic societies, 'New Community', vol. 1, pp. 256-62.

—(1972-73), Ethnicity in Britain: the Gujarati tradition, 'New Community', vol. 2, no. 1, pp. 1-11.

—(1973), Ethnic minority problems: an overview of some recent research, 'New Community', vol. 2, no. 4, pp. 329-52.

McDonald, J.S., and McDonald, L.D. (1964), Chain migration, ethnic neighbourhood formation and social networks, 'Milbank Memorial Fund Quarterly', vol. 42, pp. 82-97.

MacLeod, D.J. (1974), 'Slavery, Race and the American Revolution', Cambridge University Press.

Magubane, B.M. (1979), 'The Political Economy of Race and Class in South Africa', London, Monthly Review Press.

Mandel, E. (1968), 'Marxist Economic Theory', London, Merlin Press.

Mandle, J.R. (1972), The plantation economy: an essay in definition, 'Science and Society', vol. XXXVI, no. 1, pp. 49-62.

—(1978), 'The Roots of Black Poverty: the Southern Plantation Economy after the Civil War', Durham, Duke University Press.

Marx, K. (1963), Letter to P.V. Annenkov, 28 December, 1846, in K. Marx, 'The Poverty of Philosophy', New York, International Publishers.

—(1968), Wage labour and capital, in K. Marx and F. Engels, 'Selected Works', London, Lawrence & Wishart.

—(1970), 'Capital', vol. 1, London, Lawrence & Wishart.

—(1971a), Towards a critique of Hegel's Philosophy of Right: Introduction, in D. McLellan (ed.), 'Karl Marx: Early Texts', Oxford, Blackwell.

—(1971b), 'A Contribution to the Critique of Political Economy', London, Lawrence & Wishart.

Marx, K., and Engels, F. (1965), 'The German Ideology', London, Lawrence & Wishart.

Mason, K. (1972), Irish labour in the north of England, 'Folk Life', vol. 10, pp. 131-3.

Midgett, D.K. (1975), West Indian ethnicity in Britain, in H.I. Safa and D.M. Dutoit (eds), 'Migration and Development', The Hague, Mouton.

Miles, R. (1978), 'Between Two Cultures? The Case of Rastafarianism', SSRC Working Paper on Ethnic Relations, no. 10.

—(1980), Class, race and ethnicity: a critique of Cox's theory, 'Ethnic and Racial Studies', vol. 3, no. 2, pp. 169-87.

—(1981), Scotland, capitalism and 'race relations', paper presented to BSA (Scotland) Conference on 'Capital and Class in Scotland' at the University of Aberdeen, March.

—(1982), Racism and nationalism in Britain, in C. Husbands (ed.), '"Race" in Britain: Continuity and Change', London, Hutchinson.

Miles, R., and Phizacklea, A. (1977), 'The TUC, Black Workers and New Commonwealth Immigration', SSRC Working Paper on Ethnic Relations, no. 6.

—(1978), The TUC and black workers, 1974-1976, 'British Journal of Industrial Relations', vol. XVI, no. 2, pp. 195-207.

Miles, R., and Phizacklea, A. (eds) (1979), 'Racism and Political Action in Britain', London, Routledge & Kegan Paul.

Miles, R., and Phizacklea, A. (1981), Racism and capitalist decline, in M. Harloe (ed.), 'New Perspectives in Urban Change and Conflict', London, Heinemann.

Miliband, R. (1969), 'The State in Capitalist Society', London, Weidenfeld & Nicolson.

Milner, D. (1975), 'Children and Race', Harmondsworth, Penguin.

Mintz, S.W. (1966), The Caribbean as a socio-cultural area, 'Journal of World History', vol. 9, no. 4, pp. 912-37.

Mintz, S. (1974), 'Caribbean Transformation', Chicago, Aldine.

Montagu, A. (ed.) (1964), 'The Concept of Race', New York, Free Press.

Montagu, A. (1972), 'Statement on Race', Oxford University Press.

Moore, R. (1975), 'Racism and Black Resistance', London, Pluto Press.

—(1977), Migrants and the class structure of Western Europe, in R. Scase (ed.), 'Industrial Society: Class, Cleavage and Control', London, George Allen & Unwin.

Mosse, G.L. (1978), 'Toward the Final Solution: A History of European Racism', London, J.M. Dent.

Murray, N. (1978), 'The Scottish Handloom Weavers, 1790-1850: A Social History', Edinburgh, John Donald.

Nairn, T. (1977), 'The Break-up of Britain', London, New Left Books.

Nikolinakos, M. (1973), Notes on an economic theory of racism, 'Race', vol. 14, no. 4, pp. 365-81.

—(1975), Notes towards a general theory of migration in late capitalism, 'Race and Class', vol. 17, no. 1, pp. 5-18.

Norman, E.R. (1968), 'Anti-Catholicism in Victorian England', London, George Allen & Unwin.

Nott, J.C., and Gliddon, G.R. (1854), 'The Types of Mankind', Philadelphia, Lippincott.

Nowikowski, S., and Ward, R. (1978-9), Middle class and British? - an analysis of South Asians in suburbia, 'New Community', vol. 7, no. 1, pp. 1-10.

Obregon, A.Q. (1974), The marginal pole of the economy and the marginalized labour force, 'Economy and Society', vol. 3, no. 4, pp. 391-428.

Osborne, R.H. (1971), 'The Biological and Social Meaning of Race', San Francisco, W.H. Freeman.

Paine, S. (1974), 'Exporting Workers: the Turkish Case', Cambridge University Press.

—(1977), The changing role of migrant labour in the advanced capitalist economies of Western Europe, in R.T. Griffiths (ed.), 'Government Business and Labour in European Capitalism', London, Europotentials Press.

Paine, S. (1979), Replacement of the West European migrant labour system by investment in the European periphery, in D. Seers, et al. (eds), 'Underdeveloped Europe: Studies in Core-Periphery Relations', Sussex, Harvester Press.

Palmer, R. (1977), The Italians: patterns of migration to London, in J.L. Watson (ed.), 'Between Two Cultures', Oxford, Basil Blackwell.

Paris, C. (1978), 'The parallels are striking ...' Crisis in the inner city? GB 1977, 'International Journal of Urban and Regional Research', vol. 2, no. 1, pp. 160–70.

Parkin, F. (1979), 'Marxism and Class Theory: A Bourgeois Critique', London, Tavistock.

Peach, C. (1965), West Indian migration to Britain: the economic factor, 'Race', vol. 7, no. 1, pp. 31–47.

—(1968), 'West Indian Migration to Britain', Oxford University Press.

—(1979), British unemployment cycles and West Indian immigration, 1955–1974, 'New Community', vol. 7, no. 1, pp. 40–3.

Pearson, D. (1977), West Indian communal associations in Britain: some observations, 'New Community', vol. 5, no. 4, pp. 371–80.

—(1981), 'Race, Class and Political Activism', Farnborough, Gower.

Pearson, G. (1976), 'Paki-bashing' in a north-east Lancashire cotton town: a case study and its history, in G. Mungham and G. Pearson (eds), 'Working Class Youth Culture', London, Routledge & Kegan Paul.

Peggie, A.C.W. (1979), Minority youth politics in Southall, 'New Community', vol. 7, no. 2, pp. 170–7.

Philpott, S.B. (1973), 'West Indian Migration: the Montserrat Case', London, Athlone Press.

—(1977), The Montserratians: migration, dependency and the maintenance of island ties in England, in J.L. Watson (ed.), 'Between Two Cultures', Oxford, Basil Blackwell.

Phizacklea, A., and Miles, R. (1979), Working class racist beliefs in the inner city, in R. Miles and A. Phizacklea (eds), 'Racism and Political Action in Britain', London, Routledge & Kegan Paul.

—(1980), 'Labour and Racism', London, Routledge & Kegan Paul.

Piore, M. (1979), 'Birds of Paradise', Cambridge University Press.

Poliakov, L. (1974), 'The Aryan Myth', Sussex University Press and Heinemann.

Pooley, C.G. (1977), The residential segregation of migrant communities in mid-Victorian Liverpool, 'Transactions of the Institute of British Geographers' (New Series), vol. 2, pp. 364–82.

Portes, A. (1978), Migration and underdevelopment, 'Politics and Society', vol. 8, no. 1, pp. 1–48.

Poulantzas, N. (1973), 'Political Power and Social Classes', London, New Left Books.

—(1978), 'Classes in Contemporary Capitalism', London, Verso.

Pryce, K. (1979), 'Endless Pressure', Harmondsworth, Penguin.

Radin, B. (1966), Coloured workers and British trade unions, 'Race', vol. 8, no. 2, pp. 157–73.

Redford, A. (1976), 'Labour Migration in England, 1800–1850', Manchester University Press.

Reid, J.M. (1960), 'Kirk and Nation', London, Skeffington.

Rex, J. (1970), 'Race Relations in Sociological Theory', London, Weidenfeld & Nicolson.

—(1973), 'Race, Colonialism and the City', London, Routledge & Kegan Paul.

Rex, J., and Moore, R. (1967), 'Race, Community and Conflict', Oxford University Press.

Rex, J., and Tomlinson, S. (1979), 'Colonial Immigrants in a British City', London, Routledge & Kegan Paul.

Richardson, C. (1968), Irish settlement in mid-nineteenth century Bradford, 'Yorkshire Bulletin of Economic and Social Research', vol. 20, pp. 40–57.

Richardson, K., and Spears, D. (eds) (1972), 'Race, Culture and Intelligence', Harmondsworth, Penguin.

Robinson, V. (1980), Correlates of Asian immigration, 1959–1974, 'New Community', vol. 8, nos. 1–2, pp. 115–22.

Rose, H., and Rose, S. (eds) (1976), 'The Political Economy of Science', London, Macmillan.

Rose, S. (1976), Scientific racism and ideology: the IQ racket from Galton to Jensen, in H. Rose and S. Rose (eds), 'The Political Economy of Science', London, Macmillan.

Rose, S., et al. (1974), Science, racism and ideology, in R. Miliband and J. Saville (eds), 'The Socialist Register, 1973', London, Merlin Press.

Rosenblum, G. (1973), 'Immigrant Workers: their Impact on American Labor Radicalism', New York, Basic Books.

Runnymede Trust and Radical Statistics Race Group (1980), 'Britain's Black Population', London, Heinemann.

Safa, H.I., and Dutoit, D.M. (eds) (1975), 'Migration and Development', The Hague, Mouton.

Salt, J., and Clout, H. (1976), 'Migration in Post-war Europe', Oxford University Press.

Saville, J. (1957), 'Rural Depopulation in England and Wales, 1851–1951', London, Routledge & Kegan Paul.

Sayer, D. (1979), 'Marx's Method', Sussex, Harvester Press.

Seers, D., et al. (eds) (1979), 'Underdeveloped Europe: Studies in Core-Periphery Relations', Sussex, Harvester Press.

Seliger, M. (1977), 'The Marxist Conception of Ideology', Cambridge University Press.

Senior, H. (1966), 'Orangeism in Ireland and Britain, 1795–1836', London, Routledge & Kegan Paul.

Sharpe, S. (1976), 'Just Like a Girl', Harmondsworth, Penguin.

Shaw, M. (1972), The coming crisis of radical sociology, in R. Blackburn (ed.), 'Ideology in Social Science', London, Fontana.

Sheridan, R. (1969), The plantation revolution and the industrial revolution, 1625–1775, 'Caribbean Studies', vol. 9, no. 3, pp. 5–25.

— (1974), 'Sugar and Slavery: An Economic History of the British West Indies, 1623–1775', Barbados, Caribbean Universities Press.

Sivanandan, A. (1973), Race, class and power: an outline for study, 'Race', vol. 14, no. 4, pp. 383–91.

— (1976), Race, class and the state: the black experience in Britain, 'Race and Class', vol. 17, no. 4, pp. 347–68.

Slaven, A. (1975), 'The Development of the West of Scotland', London, Routledge & Kegan Paul.

Smith, D.J. (1977), 'Racial Discrimination in Britain', Harmondsworth, Penguin.

Smout, T.C. (1972), 'A History of the Scottish People, 1560–1830', Glasgow, Fontana.

Steele, E.D. (1976), The Irish presence in the north of England, 1850–1914, 'Northern History', vol. 12, pp. 220–41.

Stone, M. (1981), 'The Education of the Black Child in Britain', London, Fontana.

Street, B.V. (1975), 'The Savage in Literature', London, Routledge & Kegan Paul.

Sutton, C.R., and Makiesky, S.R. (1975), Migration and West Indian racial and ethnic consciousness, in H.I. Safa and B.M. Dutoit (eds), 'Migration and Development', The Hague, Mouton.

Tannahill, J.A. (1968), 'European Volunteer Workers in Britain', Manchester University Press.

Taylor, J.H. (1973), Newcastle-upon-Tyne: Asian pupils do better than whites, 'British Journal of Sociology', vol. 54, no. 4, pp. 431–47.

Thurlow, R.C. (1980), Satan and sambo: the image of the immigrant in English racial populist thought since the First World War, in K. Lunn (ed.), 'Hosts, Immigrants and Minorities', Folkestone, Dawson.

Timmer, C.P. (1969), The turnip, the new husbandry and the English agricultural revolution, 'Quarterly Journal of Economics', vol. LXXXIII, no. 3, pp. 375-95.

Tomlinson, S. (1978), West Indian children and ESN schooling, 'New Community', vol. 6, no. 2, pp. 235-42.

Treble, J.H. (1972), The Navvies, 'Scottish Labour History Society Journal', 5, pp. 34-54.

—(1973), Irish navvies in the north of England, 'Transport History', vol. 6, pp. 227-47.

Troyna, B. (1979), Differential commitment to ethnic identity by black youths in Britain, 'New Community', vol. 7, no. 3, pp. 406-14.

UNESCO (1980), 'Sociological Theories: Race and Colonialism', Paris, UNESCO.

Unit for Manpower Services (1977), 'The Role of Immigrants in the Labour Market', London, Department of Employment.

Van den Berghe, P.L. (1978), 'Race and Racism', New York, Wiley.

Walker, M. (1977), 'The National Front', London, Fontana.

Walker, W.M. (1972), Irish immigrants in Scotland: their priests, politics and parochial life, 'Historical Journal', vol. 15, no. 4, pp. 649-67.

—(1979), 'Juteopolis: Dundee and its Textile Workers, 1885-1923', Edinburgh, Scottish Academic Press.

Wallman, S. (1978), The boundaries of 'race': processes of ethnicity in England, 'Man', vol. 13, pp. 200-17.

Wallman, S. (ed.) (1979), 'Ethnicity at Work', London, Macmillan.

Walvin, J. (1973), 'Black and White: the Negro and English Society, 1555-1945', London, Allen Lane.

Watson, J.L. (ed.) (1977a), 'Between Two Cultures', Oxford, Basil Blackwell.

—(1977b), The Chinese: Hong Kong villagers in the British catering trade, in J.L. Watson (ed.), 'Between Two Cultures', Oxford, Basil Blackwell.

Wellman, D. (1977), 'Portraits of White Racism', Cambridge University Press.

Werly, J.M. (1973), The Irish in Manchester, 1832-49, 'Irish Historical Studies', vol. 18, pp. 345-58.

Westergaard, J. (1970), The rediscovery of the cash nexus, in R. Miliband and J. Saville (eds), 'The Socialist Register, 1970', London, Merlin Press.

Westergaard, J., and Resler, H. (1976), 'Class in a Capitalist Society', Harmondsworth, Penguin.

Williams, B. (1980), The beginnings of Jewish trade unionism in Manchester, 1889-1891, in K. Lunn (ed.), 'Hosts, Immigrants and Minorities', Folkestone, Dawson.

Williams, E. (1964), 'Capitalism and Slavery', London, André Deutsch.

—(1970), 'From Columbus to Castro: The History of the Caribbean, 1492-1969', London, André Deutsch.

Williams, R. (1965), 'The Long Revolution', Harmondsworth, Penguin.

—(1973), Base and superstructure in Marxist cultural theory, 'New Left Review', no. 82, pp. 3-16.

—(1977), 'Marxism and Literature', Oxford University Press.

Wilson, A. (1978), 'Finding a Voice: Asian Women in Britain', London, Virago.

Wolpe, H. (1972), Capitalism and cheap labour power in South Africa: from segregation to apartheid, 'Economy and Society', vol. 1, no. 4, pp. 425-56.

—(1975), The theory of internal colonialism: the South African case, in I. Oxaal et al. (eds), 'Beyond the Sociology of Development', London, Routledge & Kegan Paul.

—(1976), The 'white working class' in South Africa, 'Economy and Society', vol. 5, no. 2, pp. 197-240.

Wright, P.L. (1968), 'The Coloured Worker in British Industry', Oxford University Press.

INDEX

199